THE SPIRITUAL HISTORY OF ICE

ROMANTICISM, SCIENCE, AND THE IMAGINATION

ERIC G. WILSON

palgrave
macmillan

THE SPIRITUAL HISTORY OF ICE
Copyright © Eric G. Wilson, 2003.
All rights reserved.

First published in hardcover in 2003 by PALGRAVE
MACMILLAN® in the United States–a division of St. Martin's
Press LLC, 175 Fifth Avenue, New York, NY 10010.

Where this book is distributed in the UK, Europe and the rest of
the world, this is by Palgrave Macmillan, a division of Macmillan
Publishers Limited, registered in England, company number
785998, of Houndmills, Basingstoke, Hampshire RG21 6XS.

Palgrave Macmillan is the global academic imprint of the above
companies and has companies and representatives throughout the
world.

Palgrave® and Macmillan® are registered trademarks in the
United States, the United Kingdom, Europe and other countries.

ISBN: 978-0-230-61971-5

Library of Congress Cataloging-in-Publication Data is available
from the Library of Congress.

A catalogue record of the book is available from the British
Library.

Design by Letra Libre, Inc.

First PALGRAVE MACMILLAN paperback edition:
October 2009

Transferred to digital printing in 2009.

CONTENTS

In an age whose dominant philosophy is some one or another of the several current forms of materialism, the arts cease to perform their normal function. In ignorance of the language of cosmic analogy (and what else is true poetry but such a language?) some form of humanism or naturalistic "realism" usurps every field of thought. Works of the past are misread in the light of this novel opinion, with a consequent distortion of judgment that necessarily leads to the deposing of what has been thought high and an exaltation of what was formerly thought low.

—*Kathleen Raine*, Blake and Tradition

The cosmos or world soul, according to Plato's Timaeus, *is a perfect living animal, feeding on its own waste, with no need of eyes or ears since there is nothing outside to see or hear, that also happens to possess the perfect form: "a sphere, without organs or limbs, rotating on its axis."* The Republic *presents the cosmos as eight hollow or concentric spheres set inside one another like "nested bowls" with Earth at the center. The celestial axis holds the Earth still while the three Fates at the North Pole—apex of the Earth and its interface with the celestial axis and heaven—wheel the spheres and their attached fixed stars around it.*

—*Victoria Nelson*, The Secret Life of Puppets

I had begun to think that there, at only one of two motionless places on this gyrating world, I might have peace to solve Vheissu's riddle. Do you understand? I wanted to stand in the dead center of the carousel, if only for a moment; try to catch my bearings. And sure enough, waiting for me was my answer. I'd begun to dig a cache nearby, after planting the flag. The barrenness of that place howled around me, like a country the demiurge had forgotten. There could have been no more entirely lifeless and empty place anywhere on earth. Two or three feet down I struck clear ice. A strange light, which seemed to move inside it, caught my attention. I cleared a space away. Staring up at me through the ice, perfectly preserved, its fur still rainbow-colored, was the corpse of one of their spider monkeys.

—*Thomas Pynchon*, V.

ACKNOWLEDGMENTS

Certain works that I have read obsessively over the years have inspired this book far beyond footnotes: Angus Fletcher's *Allegory*, Barbara L. Packer's *Emerson's Fall*, John T. Irwin's *American Hieroglyphics*, Edward Kessler's *Coleridge's Metaphors of Being*, Stephen J. Pyne's *The Ice*, Philip Kuberski's *The Persistence of Memory*, Joscelyn Godwin's *Arktos*, and Victoria Nelson's "Symmes Hole, Or the South Polar Romance."

Friends and colleagues have also encouraged this book in innumerable ways. I am extremely indebted to Philip Kuberski—not only for his profound book on memory but also for his spiritual and intellectual guidance, which informed this study from beginning to end. Once again, Marilyn Gaull generously offered her encouragement and expertise at all stages—my book would not exist without her. I am also very thankful for the support of James Hans, Robert Richardson, Joseph Wittreich, Allen Mandelbaum, Laura Dassow Walls, Mark Lussier, and Joan Richardson. I have benefited as well from spirited conversations with Dennis Sampson, Jane Mead, Granville Ganter, Pranab Das, and Phil Arnold.

Kristi Long, my editor at Palgrave, has once again been very patient with my worries as well as an astute critic of my writing. I can't imagine working with anyone else. I'm also very thankful for the expert help of Roee Raz, also at Palgrave. I would like to thank Gale Sigal, the chair of my department during the years I wrote this book. She has consistently bolstered my work. Wake Forest

University helped me to complete this book by granting me a research leave and summer travel money. The staffs at the Wake Forest University Library, the New York Public Library, and the British Library were extremely helpful. I am also very appreciative of the efforts of William Weber, who expertly and promptly checked quotations and proofread the text.

Parts of Chapter 1 were published in *Nineteenth-Century Prose.* I would like to thank this journal for permission to reprint these materials. I would also like to thank Harper Perennial for permission to quote from Thomas Pynchon's *V.* in the series of epigraphs to this book.

I am deeply indebted to Glenn and Linda Wilson and Bill and Helen Hamilton, who have buoyed me in countless ways. Sandi Hamilton has endured and nurtured my compulsive researches from the beginning. She remains the pole star around which my being turns. Finally, I dedicate these pages to Una, the daughter whose glorious birth coincided with the completion of the book.

ABBREVIATIONS

AM   *The Rime of the Ancient Mariner, The Collected Works of Samuel Taylor Coleridge*, vol. 16 (part 1), ed. J.C.C. Mays (Princeton, NJ: Bollingen Press of Princeton Univ. Press, 2001), 365–419.

CC   *The Collected Works of Samuel Taylor Coleridge*, gen. ed. Kathleen Coburn, 14 vols. (Princeton, NJ: Bollingen Press of Princeton Univ. Press, 1969-).

EJ   *The Journals and Miscellaneous Notebooks of Ralph Waldo Emerson*, ed. William H. Gilman, Ralph H. Orth, et al., 16 vols. (Cambridge, MA, and London: Belknap Press of Harvard Univ. Press, 1982).

EL   *The Early Lectures of Ralph Waldo Emerson*, ed. Stephen Whicher and Robert E. Spiller, 3 vols. (Cambridge, MA, and London: Harvard Univ. Press, 1959–72).

EW   *The Collected Works of Ralph Waldo Emerson*, ed. Robert E. Spiller, Joseph Slater, et al., 5 vols. (Cambridge, MA, and London: Belknap Press of Harvard Univ. Press, 1971-).

F   *Frankenstein, or The Modern Prometheus*, ed. Maurice Hindle (New York: Penguin, 1985).

M   *Manfred, The Complete Poetical Works of Lord Byron*, ed. Jerome J. McGann, vol. 4 (Oxford: Clarendon, 1986).

MB   "Mont Blanc," *Shelley's Prose and Poetry*, 2nd ed., eds. Donald H. Reiman and Neil Fraistat (New York and London: Norton, 2002).

N   *Nature: A Facsimile of the First Edition*, intro. Jaroslav Pelikan (Boston: Beacon, 1985).

NH   "A Natural History of Massachusetts," *The Portable Thoreau*, ed. Carl Bode (New York: Penguin, 1947).

NP   *The Narrative of Arthur Gordon Pym, The Collected Writings of Edgar Allan Poe: Volume One: The Imaginary Voyages*, ed. Burton R. Pollin, 2 vols. (Boston: Twayne, 1981), 53–210.

PS   *Shelley's Prose, or The Trumpet of Prophecy*, ed. David Lee Clark (Albuquerque: Univ. of New Mexico Press, 1954).

PU   *Prometheus Unbound, Shelley's Poetry and Prose: A Norton Critical Edition*, sel. and ed. Donald H. Reiman and Sharon B. Powers (New York: Norton, 1977), 130–209.

SL   *The Letters of Percy Bysshe Shelley*, ed. Frederick L. Jones, 2 vols. (Oxford and London: Oxford Univ. Press, 1964).

SP   *The Complete Poetical Works of Percy Bysshe Shelley*, ed. Neville Rogers, 2 vols. to date (Oxford and London: Oxford Univ. Press, 1972-).

TJ   *The Journal of Henry David Thoreau*, ed. John C. Broderick (vols. 1–3) and Robert Sattelmeyer (vols. 4-), *The Writings of Henry David Thoreau* (Princeton, NJ: Princeton Univ. Press, 1981-).

W   *Walden*, ed. J. Lyndon Shanley, *The Writings of Henry David Thoreau* (Princeton, NJ: Princeton Univ. Press, 1971).

WC   *A Week on the Concord and Merrimack Rivers*, ed. Carl F. Hovde, *The Writings of Henry David Thoreau* (Princeton, NJ: Princeton Univ. Press, 1980).

For Una

PREFACE

When this book went to press back in 2001, I was committed to "deep ecology," a vision of nature devoted to the idea that humans are only one small part of the web of life and no better nor worse than any another strand. In my mind, this stance necessitated this rather startling conclusion: if the earth as a whole would be better without a destructive human presence, if its owls and peonies and oaks would breathe more cleanly in the absence of civilization, then so be it—men and women should die off as quickly as possible. I reveled in the shock effect of this logic while I finished this book. With perverse glee, I propounded it to those who dreamed of forever dominating the beasts of the field, of playing Adam endlessly. I wanted the blind forces of nature to take revenge on human selfishness, to rise up in impossibly potent waves and smite the arrogance. This desire inspired me to conclude my study with a gesture toward the anti-humanism of deep ecology; on the final page I imagined what it would be like if humans indeed destroyed themselves through their narcissistic disregard for their fellow species. After the death of this vast population of wastrels, I intimated, new life would emerge, maybe a new and truer Eden devoid of God and man alike.

There are always existential motivations behind our grand and abstract theories, and I wonder what compelled me to envision, even to urge, such an apocalyptic disaster. Certainly there is merit in the deep ecological view—not only as a non-biased vision of global health, regardless of human suffering, but also as a vivid warning of the deadly days to come if we don't learn to live more harmoniously with our planet. But there is also an irreducible flaw in this view, at least in my mind: it ignores the fact that it's virtually impossible for most men and women to place aside their purely human commitments in favor of the plight nonhuman creatures. Perhaps we are wired to look after our own, and any thought to the contrary could well go against our evolutionary heritage. But our propensity to emphasize the human over the nonhuman need not be seen as simple selfishness. On the contrary, anthropocentrism has produced the far-reaching and clear-eyed generosity of the humanistic tradition and also the profound ameliorations of the conservation movement, grounded firmly on the Christian idea of stewardship, the earth is God's temple, and we should carefully attend to its fragile beauties.

Such is the conflict between deep ecology and humanism, between nature and human nature. Both visions have their merits, and both their limits. When one is childless and rightly disgusted by human hubris and also feeling, because of this disgust, rather melancholy, as I was when I finished this book almost ten years ago, one is perhaps more prone to embrace the non-sentimental rigors of deep ecology. When one is a new parent and more hopeful and more indulgent toward human weakness, as I am now, one is likely to value the implicit humanism of the conservation movement—let's be kind to nature so it will be kind to us.

I now realize this tension, probably inevitable in all serious thinking about the environment, is the organizing principle of this book. Even though I was writing with deep ecology at the forefront of my consciousness, in the back of my mind was a commitment to humanism that I could not shake. It makes sense, of course, that this polarity is implicit in these pages, for this opposition between wilderness's indifference and human desire is at the heart of the primary aesthetic of the Romantic age—the sublime.

In fact, it is precisely this torque that gives the sublime its seductive powers. During a sublime experience, which might occur, say, when I'm beholding the icy heights of Mont Blanc, I am dwarfed before terrifyingly boundless forces coldly calloused to all human concerns. Try as I might to capture and thus to familiarize this spectacle in an appropriate concept or image, I am unable to do so. My mind utterly fails to function, and I am frustrated and fearful under the peaks, a failed humanist. But this pain is balanced by pleasure. Just at the moment that my conceptual and imagining faculties falter, another part of my mind, call it the intuitive, thrives. Though I can't reduce the abysmal potencies to a manageable mental form, I nonetheless grasp ideas that are formless and that also actually transcend the crushing energies resounding in the clouds. For instance, I intuit notions like infinity and eternity, and thus elevate my mind beyond the spatiotemporal occurrence that engages me, no matter how immense and incomprehensible this occurrence might be. In this way, I feel superior to nature, as though I am in touch with realms of being not constrained by horizons, no matter how capacious, or by durations, no matter how constant. I am a humanist fully realized, a man whose mind has freed itself from the dark materials surrounding it and can roam freely among ravishing ideas that will never die.

Of all the landscapes in nature, those that are frozen are perhaps the most sublime. The reason: the blankness of ice. When we gaze into the semi-transparent crystal of frost or scan the unending paleness of the polar floe or stare at the blanched undulations of the glacier, we undergo the vertiginous tension between meaningless void and significant plenitude. On the one hand, the whiteness is pure emptiness, a bland, monotone space featuring no distinctions at all, no break in the engulfing sameness. To brood over such a region, be it big or small, is to lose any sense of separate identity, to become nothing, only an indistinct cipher of the vacuum. Such is the horror of ice—it reduces difference to the same, beings to blanks, life to death. On the other hand, the whiteness is utter fullness, a realm of fecund potential where nothing has yet become anything, a reservoir of pure possibility. One can project any image one likes onto this invitingly unsullied plane and can transform the tabula rasa into a canvas of rainbows. This is the exhilaration of ice—it is the birthplace of beautiful distinctions, of noble and essential truths, of our heart's delight.

In brooding over the duplicity of ice, one meditates on the contradictory structure of the sublime, and in considering sublime doubleness, one studies the irreducible tension at the heart of all theories of nature, the pull between things that don't care and humans that do. And these interconnected contemplations inevitably lead to the overwhelming and immensely important question: can these various oppositions ever be reconciled? Is there a miraculous third term that can marry the indifference of nature and the affections of the human heart? Can quietly self-contained things be synthesized with the raucously overflowing desires of men and women?

It is exactly these questions that *The Spiritual History of Ice* seeks to answer. Even if I wasn't fully aware of these questions when drafting the book, I now realize that they are at the core of my analyses. And I'm glad they are, for these questions are now more pressing than ever before. With global warming rapidly melting our earth's ices—much more rapidly, it appears, than during the days I finished this book—we are daily coming closer to the ecological apocalypse we have feared for so long. While our ice is still around and our coastal cities are still standing, we should think diligently and rigorously about our complex, vexed attitudes toward nature. We must try to find a vision of earth, frozen or otherwise, that does not set asunder our loves for our daughters or our raptures over snow.

Winston-Salem, April 28, 2009

INTRODUCTION

FROZEN APOCALYPSE

Dazzling ice stars bombarded the earth with rays, which
splintered and penetrated the earth, filling earth's core with
their deadly coolness, reinforcing the cold of the advancing
ice. And always, on the surface, the indestructible ice-mass
was moving forward, implacably destroying life.

—*Anna Kavan*, Ice

If a collective or cultural unconscious exists, then it was at work
during the dawn of the third millennium. Millions quaked in ex-
pectation of apocalypse. Some feared that a vast computer crash
might reduce the world to waste. Others nervously fantasized over
the quick and the dead discovering a godly doom. Still more sunk
into deeper dreams—luridly uncanny, ambiguous as Leviathan. In
the midst of these prophetic reveries, from April 1997 to July
2001, the *New York Times* noticed at least twenty-two books on
polar phenomena. During an earlier period, from April 1990 to
June 1996, the *Times* reviewed only four polar texts.[1] What secret
link exists between ice and apocalypse? What ghostly bergs cruise
in the millennial undertow?

Perhaps on the surface of the apocalyptic unconscious floated terrifying visions of frozen deserts or melted icecaps smothering the post-Y2K world.[2] Lower, under the dystopias of modern technology, there possibly lingered horrors of Dante's icy hell or hopes of St. John's crystal heaven. In more profound regions of this millennial abyss, in half-remembered dreams, stranger polar specimens likely lurked. Possibly there gleamed Madame Blavatsky's northern polar paradise shining at the beginning of time, an "Imperishable Sacred Land" inhabited by immortal Hyperboreans.[3] Near this fading image—ostensibly a harmless portrait of a first utopia—were perhaps Nazi nightmares of a eugenically engineered breed bent on reclaiming pristine Hyperborean origins.[4] Beneath this perniciously political Arctic, did there hover a more redemptive polar apparition: the *axis mundi*, still point of the turbid world, gathering enemies into secret concord?[5]

These potential connections between millennial disquiet and polar meditation suggest that ice, in its striking, extreme forms—deathly bergs and crushing floes, crevasses and calving glaciers—shares the same paradoxes as Western visions of apocalypse. Occidental Armageddons tend to picture both violent dissolutions of time and blissful revelations of eternal realms—annihilation and restoration, horror and joy. Likewise, polar *terrae incognitae* and other frozen shapes kill and cure. They blanch the earth into a corpse. They translucently reveal life's vital core. The whiteness of ice is the whiteness of the whale.

These significations of ice—paradoxical, revelatory, perhaps unexpected—inspire this threefold book: a spiritual history of Western representations of frozen shapes from ancient times to the early nineteenth century; an anatomy of these representations of ice;

and an apology for a Romantic mode of seeing that ecologically inflects the spiritual history and anatomy of ice.

In tracking the spiritual history of ice, I focus on the *exoteric* and the *esoteric*.[6] The exoteric way of seeing is interested in external surfaces, understandable visibilities, and social orders. This mode of cognition—shared by orthodox forms of Christianity, political systems, and conventional sciences—often views ice as a deathly coldness to be transcended, raw material to be converted into commodity, or static matter to be reduced to law. The esoteric perspective considers internal depths, invisible mysteries, and individual experiences. This mode of vision—instanced by hermetic dreamers, alchemical adepts, and Romantic visionaries—frequently sees icescapes as revelations of an abysmal origin, marriages of opposites, mergings of microcosm and macrocosm. Hence, while exoteric institutions tend to interpret ice from negative or neutral points of view, esoteric visionaries are disposed to read ice in positive lights. A medieval Christian degrades ice to waste. An eighteenth-century scientist studies frost as a manifestation of mechanical law. A Romantic poet finds in the frozen plane the universal no-color behind all particular hues.

This diachronic study of ice discloses an anatomy, a synchronic structure. Although representations of ice historically change, frozen phenomena in the West have been persistently figured in three forms: crystals, glaciers, and the poles. Each of these categories subsumes factual qualities and symbolic possibilities. The crystal class contains microscopic frozen shapes. These include the miniscule geometries and transparent prisms studied by physicists interested in the structures of matter and the laws of light; the transient hoar frosts and more enduring icicles read by exoteric Christians as signs of time's insubstantiality or harbingers of New Jerusalem's gems; the rime floating on the pond, celebrated by a Romantic seer—a Thoreau, for instance—as a clarification of vital energy into elegant form. The glacier category encompasses ice as mesocosm: the Alpine glaciers observed by geologists bent on understanding geomorphic agencies; the frozen peaks demonized or glorified by exoteric Christians as blights on God's harmony or reminders of heaven's heights; the roofs of sublime snow sought by Romantic climbers such as Shelley. The polar classification entails macrocosm: the immense Arctic and Antarctic regions explored by adventurers and scientists; the vast *terrae incognitae* cursed by exoteric Christians until they can transform them into holy cities; and the esoteric poles sought by Coleridge, hungry for the harmony salving the hurt world.

Until the Romantic age, most Western representations of these types of ice were exoteric and thus largely neutral or negative. With few notable exceptions, writers from Herodotus to Pope tended either to ignore the special qualities of ice or, worse, to demean frozen shapes to signs for aloofness, numbness, stasis, transience, monstrosity, or death.[7] However, at the turn of the nineteenth century, scientists for the first time were beginning to understand that ice is not evil matter to be transcended or bland material to be commodified but is instead a vehicle and revelation of vital energy. In the early years of the century, Humphry Davy drew from the science of crystallography to find in the crystal a window to the laws of electromagnetism, and thus perhaps to the earth's vitality. At the end of the eighteenth century, James Hutton gleaned a theory of glaciation from Horace Bénédict de Saussure's observations of Mont Blanc and guessed that glaciers are agents of terrestrial transformation. Earlier, James Cook first crossed the Antarctic Circle. Though endless fields of ice horrified him, he nonetheless excited in his contemporaries dreams of the magnetic pole.

Aware of these emerging sciences of ice, Romantics on both sides of the Atlantic translated the data of the scientists into literary dreams. Poe's Pym, informed in polar explorations, is drawn to the unmapped ice at the South Pole, where his boat likely slides through a milky cataract into the interiors of the earth and, deeper, to the core of the cosmos. Coleridge, also versed in polar journeys, sends his Mariner into an Antarctic freeze that changes the sailor forever, teaching him that life thrives in birds and snakes as much as in men. Mary Shelley, well aware of the factual and symbolical densities of the Arctic, begins and ends her *Frankenstein* near the North Pole. But the creator of the "Modern Prometheus" was also schooled in glaciology, realizing that Alpine glaciers shape the globe. Ironically, Shelley stages the first meeting between her failed creator and his botched creation in the midst of Mont Blanc's demiurgic glaciers. Mary's husband Percy draws from the science of glaciers in "Mont Blanc," in which he likens the creative ice to the imagination, universal and individual. Byron places his magical protagonist in *Manfred* among the Swiss glaciers, where the conjurer discovers wondrous energies unknown below. If cosmic poles and massive glaciers reveal the life coursing within miniscule man, the tiny ice crystal opens into forces pervading the solar system. Aware of crystallography, Thoreau studies morning frosts and frozen ponds, finding in Concord ice analogues to reticulated leaves, feathered wings, the harmonies of the spheres. Likewise versed in crystals, Emerson in "The Snowstorm" and *Nature* casts ice crystals as transparent revelations of the currents of universal being.

These writers are among the first poets, essayists, and novelists to embrace ice as a *positive*—not neutral or negative—fact and symbol: as a unique manifestation of the principle of *life*. Transforming scientific ice into literary subjects, these Romantic figures thus not only point to a neglected hermeneutic context for reading their works; they also redeem ice from its exoteric past and establish it as a site of esoteric redemption. Hence, in interpreting Emerson and Thoreau in light of crystallography, the Shelleys and Byron in the contexts of glaciology, and Coleridge and Poe against the backgrounds of polar exploration, I offer new literary analyses as well as ponder the ecological possibilities of ice—the ways in which frozen forms pattern and reveal invisible, imponderable, holistic, causal, vital powers, ranging from electromagnetic waves that can be measured to psychological energies, vague yet discernible, to cosmological principles beyond fact and image. A transparent window to lines of invigorating force; a mirror in which men and women behold interior hums; an indifferent blank, no color and all colors, void and plenitude: Ice, curiously, thrives in the living as much as the dead, in the gorgeous as well as the horrible—in winds, in spirits, salubrious and disturbing, that blow where they list.[8]

ONE

CRYSTALS

In many dreams the nuclear center, the Self, also appears as a crystal. The mathematically precise arrangement of a crystal evokes in us the intuitive feeling that even in so-called "dead" matter, there is a spiritual ordering principle. Thus the crystal often symbolically stands for the union of extreme opposites—of matter and spirit.

—*M. L. von Franz,* Man and His Symbols

THE FROZEN HEAVEN

In *Pseudodoxia Epidemica* (1646), Sir Thomas Browne, an essayist close to the heart of Thoreau, reports that authorities as venerable as Pliny, Seneca, Saint Augustine, and Gregory the Great believed that crystals were "nothing else, but Ice or Snow concreted, and by duration of time, congealed beyond liquation."[1] Participating in this tradition—and affirming the etymology of crystal, from the Greek verb *krustaimein*, to freeze, and its cognate noun, *krustallos*, ice—Saint Jerome in his commentary on Ezekiel translates the Hebrew *qerah* ("ice, frost") into the Latin *crystallus*. The prophet, beholding four strange beings wheel about the Babylonian sky, envisions as a field of ice (*qerah, krustallos, crystallus*) the "likeness of the firmament upon the heads of the living creatures." Established in Genesis when God divided the lower waters from the upper, this frozen network, this threshold of jewels (translated in the King James Bible as "terrible crystal"), shines between these whirling forms and the "likeness" of a throne above. Separating and joining the heavens and the earth, this icy boundary is a transparent conduit conjoining Ezekiel and his mysterious God.[2] Inheriting the mantle of Ezekiel, John in his Revelation likewise experiences the heavenly freeze. Early in his vision, he sees before the throne of heaven a "sea of glass" like unto *krustallos*. Later, having passed through this starry window into the New Jerusalem, John compares the city's splendor to a "jasper stone" glistening like ice crystals.[3]

In these prophetic books, the meaning of crystal—frozen or lapidary—is optical. Gazing through the glistening prism, the prophet, like a scryer, perceives esoteric destinies and divine mysteries. Not surprisingly, Emanuel Swedenborg, the Swedish seer of angels and hero of Romantic visionaries, began his career as a crystallographer interested in how crystals of ice reveal the inner laws of the universe. Before hells and heavens haunted his waking sight, Swedenborg composed in 1721 a treatise on crystals, *The Principles of Chemistry*. In this work, Swedenborg posits a hypothesis that occupied scientists throughout the eighteenth and early nineteenth centuries: The minute geometries of crystals are portals to the essential monads of the cosmos and the modes by which these monads combine. Taking seriously this notion—scientifically explored by René-Just Haüy, Eilhardt Mitscherlich, Humphry Davy, John Herschel, and Michael Faraday—Thoreau throughout his Concord days concludes that crystals, despite their cool geometry, are *alive*, growths of a vital principle.

Scientist and prophet, Thoreau embraces the ice crystal as a microcosmic revelation of both reassuring law and unsettling mystery. Gazing on the frozen prism's reticulated surfaces, he beholds comfortable regularity—world as geometrical organ. Yet, staring deeper into the stone's interiors, into its flitting reflections and refractions, he sees blurred colors and images that startle—the weird universe of holy vision. He explores connections between the bright lattices and the obscure auguries below. He realizes: The cosmos is double—lawful and enigmatic, organized yet abysmal. Split himself, he tries to reconcile—in deed and word—the minute pyramids, seemingly simple, and the kaleidoscopes, complex, flickering in the core.

Embracing the frozen prism as a special muse of such explorations, Thoreau, like Paul Valéry after him, sees the crystal as a "privileged object"—a form (like a flower or nautilus) that stands out "from the common disorder of perceptible things" because it is "more intelligible to the view, although more mysterious upon reflection." A duplicitous site of "order and fantasy, invention and necessity, law and exception,"[4] the crystal to Thoreau is a numinous disclosure of matters that deeply occupied his soul: the mysteries of transparency, the curious laws of organic formation, the irreducible extravagance of the world. Hence, Thoreau's crystallography goes far beyond the morning frost. It opens into the theory of scrying and the history of optics, electromagnetic affinity and botanical archetypes, the poetics of nature as well as a natural poetics.

THE SHEW-STONE

In his *History of Magic* (1948), Kurt Seligmann observes that the divinatory arts of the ancient Chaldeans emerged at about the same time that astronomers first noticed planets moving predictably through the fixed stars. This moment, occurring around the middle of the fourth millennium B.C., elevated humans from a fear of a random universe to a desire to live in accord with a regular cosmos. A caste of priests presided over these quests for sidereal concord. They attempted to understand how the laws of the heavens affect the destiny of humans. Their mode of inquiry was divination, seeing the future in the signs of nature. Eternal laws shined in the livers of animals, smoky shapes, the babblings of brooks, the surfaces of stones.[5]

As Thoreau knew—"divining" as he did in time's streams (*W* 98)—the astronomical fates might also appear in transparent substances. Theodore Bestermann in *Crystal Gazing* (1924) reports that priests in ancient Babylonia and Assyria sometimes discerned cosmic intentions in standing water and translucent stones.[6] This latter method of divination is "scrying," a practice that requires the seer (the priest, the augur, the sorcerer) to stare into a pellucid or reflective object, a *speculum*, until he observes the future.[7] From the many ancient forms of scrying—catoptromancy (scrying in a mirror), gastromancy (scrying water in a belly-shaped glass), onychomancy (scrying finger-nails), and hydromancy (river scrying)—one method, though not originally popular, has survived through the Middle Ages, Renaissance, and Enlightenment into our age, even becoming synonymous with scrying itself. This mode is "crystallomancy"—divining the stars in earthly prisms.[8]

According to Armand Delatte in *La catoptromancie grecque et ses dérivés* (1932), crystal gazing did not become a common mode of scrying until the age of the Byzantine Empire.[9] However, by the time of the Middle Ages and Renaissance, crystallomancy had become a primary method of divination. Rupert Gleadow suggests that one reason for the ascendancy of the crystal in medieval magic is the provocative virtues of the crystalline shape. If "the essence of magic is the achievement of an effect by exciting the powers of the imagination," then the crystal lattice, with its labyrinthine interiors and glowing surfaces, is more likely to stoke the mind than "tea-cups or the hand." The crystal distorts vision. It blurs clear lines of sight into strange refractions and fragmented reflections. Staring long enough into such a cauldron of flickering images, the scryer imagines that he sees things beyond his normal sight, especially, as Gleadow jokes, if he is astigmatic.[10]

Astigmatic or not, medieval magicians gazed into the crystal to glimpse holy secrets. As Lynn Thorndike reports in *History of Magic and Experimental Science* (1929), magicologists of the Middle Ages offered various theories of scrying. In about 1240, William of Auvergne in *De universo*, a compendium of magical lore, described scrying in stones and mirrors as key medieval modes of divination. William admits that this practice can be diabolical, an effort to pull God to earth. However, he also maintains that scrying can constitute meditative art, a mirroring of the mysteries of the soul.[11] Other medieval commentators were less optimistic about the apocalyptic possibilities of crystal gazing. Some simply saw scrying as an astrological practice, an attempt to understand how the moon, the planet in accord with crystal, influences humans.[12] Others viewed the crystal as a necromantic stone for conjuring angels and dead kings.[13]

To many medieval commentators, crystal gazing was synonymous with magic itself. The case of Roger Bacon reveals this connection. A devout, learned friar of the thirteenth century, Bacon, master of many branches of natural philosophy, was especially skilled in optics, the science of images and mirrors. He spent his life establishing a scientific method and thus was dubious of magic. However, regardless of his practices and statements, his contemporaries viewed him as a magician, a scryer. Legends grew, the most famous of which involved a magical glass in which Bacon allegedly saw all things, past, present, and future. This apocryphal tradition had it that this magical crystal not only revealed the outcomes of events but also even *caused* these consequences.[14]

By the early sixteenth century, scrying had become a prime marker of magical practice. The art was associated with Cornelius Agrippa (1486–1535) and Nostradamus (1503–1556), even though neither magician actually gazed into the crystal. Likewise, the Faust legend, which emerged at this time, is connected with scrying—recall Goethe in his *Faust* featuring a magic mirror in the

Witches' Kitchen.[15] The logic went: If you were involved in magic, you were a scryer.

There is truth in this logic. Events occur in the crystal that do not happen elsewhere. Images and colors appear from nowhere in the stone's intricate corridors. What was before invisible finds shape. Distributed spirit—air, wind, light—coheres and shines in a frame of diaphanous matter. Well-versed in the medieval lore of scrying,[16] Paracelsus, an early sixteenth-century magician, valued the crystal for these virtues. He found in it a wedding of unseen and seen, soul and body. Writing in his *Coelum Philosophorum* (ca. 1540) on how "to Conjure the Crystal so that all things may be seen in it," Paracelsus claims that "[t]o conjure is nothing else than to observe anything rightly, to know and to understand what it is. The crystal is a figure of the air. Whatever appears in the air, moveable or immovable, the same appears also in the speculum or crystal as a wave. For the air, the water, and the crystal, so far as vision is concerned, are one, like a mirror in which an inverted copy of an object is seen."[17] The crystal is not a portal to hallucinations or demons but an optical technology capable of revealing invisible powers. Like a sheet of water reveals in ripples the viewless wind, so the conjurer's glass discloses currents—wispy lights and quavering shades—unavailable to the naked eye.

Drawing from Paracelsus and his theurgical contemporaries—like Ficino and Pico—Frances A. Yates in *Giordano Bruno and the Hermetic Tradition* (1964) has shown that the humanistic dignity of the Renaissance emerged from theories of magic. Philosophers like Paracelsus, Ficino, and Pico established magic not as a demonic craft but as a worthy science capable of channeling the salubrious currents of the cosmos into sick souls. Renaissance magic, inspired by Ficino's translation of the *Corpus Hermeticum* (ca. 200–300 A.D.), consisted in "guiding or controlling the influx of *spiritus* into *materia*."[18] Although talismans and symbols associated with planets and stars provided technologies for this craft, the crystal held a special place in the magician's repertoire. As Jean Servier has observed in *L'homme et l'invisible* (1964), the crystal has traditionally represented "a level intermediate between the visible and the invisible" and thus has typically been the "symbol of divination, wisdom, and of the hidden powers granted to mankind."[19] The crystal comprises a marriage between matter and spirit. Made of matter, it is nonetheless transparent. Translucent, it still refracts and reflects visible forms.[20]

Aware of these powers of the crystal, John Dee, the Elizabethan scryer, bought in 1582 a crystal "as big as an egg: most bryght, clere, and glorious." He proceeded, with the help of Edward Kelley, to conjure spirits of things unseen: angels, ghosts, past and future happenings. Cloistered in his laboratory in Mortlake, Dee recorded what Kelley's alleged keener sight saw in the *speculum*—variously called a "shew-stone," "great Christaline Globe," "diaphanous globe," or "Angelicall stone."[21] On one occasion, later described in Meric Casaubon's *A True and Faithful Relation of What Passed for Many Years between Dr. John Dee and Some Spirits* (1659), Kelley saw standing in the "middest of the Stone" a "little round thing like a spark of fire" that increased in size until it seemed to be "as Big as a Globe of 20 inches in Diameter." Kelley's vision of internal glowing signaled the presence of spirits, which, Dee concluded, required a material medium for their transmissions.[22] As Dee once said to an angel flaming in the stone's core, "I do think you have no organs or Instruments apt for voyce, but are meere spirituall and nothing corporall, but have power and property from God to insinuate your message or meaning to ear or eye [so that] man's imagination shall be that they hear and see you sensibly."[23] Without the crystal echoing and reflecting disembodied sounds and gestures, the angel remains invisible, inaudible. Like a poet's symbol giving to airy spirits a "local habitation and a name," like a rainbow refracting white light, this magus's stone is indeed an *angelus*, a messenger, transmitting between unknown and known.

Meditating on the essence of scrying, Reginald Scot in his study of Renaissance magic, entitled *Discoverie of Witchcraft* (1584), provides a remarkable description of this relationship between the crystal and the scryer's imagination. He suggests that the complex perspectives of the latticed glass image the colors of the magician's mind: "But the woondrous devises, and miraculous sights and conceipts made and conteined in glasse, doo farre exceed all other; whereto the art perspective is verie necessarie. For it sheweth the illusion of them, whose experiments be seen in diverse sorts of glasses; as in the hallowe, the plaine, the embossed, the columnarie, the pryamidate, or piked, the turbinall, the bounched, the round, the cornered, the inversed, the eversed, the massie, the regular, the irregular, the coloured and cleare glasses: for you may have glasses so made, as what image or favour soever you print in your imagination, you shall thinke you see the same therein."[24] On one hand, this passage debunks as illusion the sightings of Paracelsus and Dee, who actually believe that their glasses reveal spiritual energies.[25] On the other hand, these words propose an integral relationship between crystal and mind, a theory of correspondence between imagination and fact. Unlike a simple mirror, which only reflects the magician's own subjective image (and thus proves a site of narcissistic vision), and unlike an ordinary window, which merely reveals the magician's objective surroundings (and thus frames physical events stripped of subjective imbuings), the crystal is a manifold of mirrors and windows. It gathers and blends subjective projections and objective events. In the kaleidoscopic flickerings of illuminated crystal, the magician pictures his internal imaginings manifested externally. However, his interiors are not merely mimicked but blurred into external data, distorted and transformed by the palpable world. Hence, the magician's mental images do not seem illusory but somehow real, existing within the fabric of the empirical world. The crystal places the angels generated by his metaphysical desire right beside the table, the inkstand, and the yellowed parchments glowing in the moon. The invisible mind gains flesh and blood while the papers in the corner become quivering wings. Angels become substantial while the table turns ghostly.[26]

From this brief survey of the scryer's crystal, we understand three of its virtues, all of which point to Thoreau's conclusion in *Walden* (1854): The crystalline pond is a "Lake of Light" that "betrays the spirit that is in the wind" (*W* 188, 199). First of all, the crystal, because of its prismatic angles, distorts normal, everyday perception. Hence, it breaks optical habits with striking visions and refreshes one's relationship to the universe. Second, the crystal, through its prismatic reflections, visualizes—brings to image—unseen agencies. It thus comprises a threshold between visible and invisible, matter and spirit. Third, because it blends reflections of interior desires and refractions of external objects, the crystal merges subject and object, self and other. It therefore reveals a secret conjunction between beholder and beheld, an esoteric marriage of opposites.

PRISMATIC OPTICS

When the crystal, a mode of vision as much as a stone, first came into scientific prominence, it did not entirely shed its occult traditions. Used as a vehicle for studying polarizations of light—extraordinary optical events (rainbows and double visions) that suggest that there is more to seeing than meets the eye—the laboratory crystal remained something of an angel frame: a medium in which otherwise viewless laws make themselves known.

Around 1669, Erasmus Bartholinus, a Danish mathematician, held to the sunlight a shard of Iceland spar. Turning this transparent crystal in different angles toward the light, Bartholinus noticed that in some positions the stone split the images that shined through it. This phenomenon, later called "double refraction," prompted the Danish scientist to write the first description of a polarization effect in *Experimenta crystalli islandici disdiaclastici* (1669), in which he concluded that the divided and duplicated images polarize in a perpendicular relationship to one another.[27]

Almost thirty years later, Christiaan Huygens, a Dutch natural philosopher, proposed an ingenious theory for explaining this polarization effect. Espousing a wave theory of light—as opposed to Newton's corpuscular one—Huygens in *Traité de la lumière* (1690) proposed that light traveling through Iceland spar moves more slowly than when propagating through air. Drawing from geometrical analyses, he speculated that densities inside the crystal divide a light wave in two and cause one half to travel more slowly than the other. The result of such splitting is two identical refractions.[28]

In 1704 Newton in his *Opticks* likewise considered the luminous divisions of the Iceland spar. Maintaining that light propagates in particles, he concluded that the crystal acts as a sieve allowing corpuscles of a certain shape to pass through while screening others. When the crystal splits its refractions, it offers passage to rays of light that possess "sides" and therefore project two images.[29]

For a century after Newton's explanation, few studied light polarization. However, as the nineteenth century dawned, scientists returned to the problem. Around the time he was deciphering the hieroglyphs on the Rosetta Stone (Champollion would in the end receive credit for unraveling this mystery), Thomas Young construed light. Inspired by Huygens's optics, Young in 1801 proved that light travels not in particles but waves. In a famous experiment, he shined a beam of light through two adjacent pinholes onto a screen. In certain places on the screen, the beams overlapped, forming in their blendings alternating bands of brightness and darkness. Young concluded that these rays behave like water: Crests of light combine to form bigger waves (brighter bands) while troughs meet only to cancel each other out (creating darker lines).[30] By 1817, Young had refined his "interference" theory of light to account for double refraction. Most light waves are transverse, comprised of several waves moving in various directions; however, when vibrations flow in one direction, the rays are polarized. Hence, Iceland spar splits mutidirectional waves into two constant currents.[31]

In 1808, when Young was still pondering luminous waves, Étienne-Louis Malus (recently returned from a fact-finding tour of Egypt) discovered crystals in air. One evening, Malus looked through a shard of Iceland spar at the crepuscular sun reflected in a window of the Luxemburg Palace. As he rotated the crystal, the doubly refracted solar images variously disappeared—first one, then the other, sometimes both together. He concluded that the reflection from the palace window had split the light, and that the polarization of light, far from being an isolated phenomenon, is always present, in varying degrees, in all refractions and reflections. He discovered that the degree of polarization is contingent upon the angle of incidence—the site where the ray meets the medium— and that certain angles, called polarized angles, almost always polarize reflected or refracted light, even if these polarizations are not visible to the naked eye.[32]

By 1815, Sir David Brewster confirmed Malus's findings. He revealed a direct relationship between the angle of incidence and the refractive qualities of a medium. Brewster also demonstrated that the blue sky and the rainbow exhibit the properties of crystals. The water droplets in the atmosphere bend and bounce light into gorgeous shades and contortions.[33]

The air itself is a faint crystal. The crystal is a shape of air. The strange appearances in the Iceland spar are no different in kind from all optical phenomena. The crystalline images are distinct, however, in degree: They reveal through their reflections and refractions what is latent in almost everything seen. For the scryer and scientist alike, the crystal is a "shew-stone," an illumination of omnipresent laws invisible outside the glass—as Thoreau intones in an early essay, the crystal makes more "obvious" the one law of life, ubiquitous though hidden (NH 53).

Aware of these crystal virtues, the Viking explorers of the eighth through the twelfth centuries used crystals, "sun-stones," to navigate seas of low visibility without the aid of a magnetic compass. Holding an Iceland spar toward the foggy horizon, these seafarers could catch in its lens a yellow gleam otherwise invisible. There was the sun, the east. A mental map appeared. The Vikings sailed through the fog.[34] In the midst of much safer pursuits, the same scientists who used the Iceland spar to study polarization employed the prism, yet another crystal form, to understand colors. Newton found that white light, when passed through a first prism, separates into the colors of the spectrum, only to return to whiteness after moving through a second prism. These divisions and meldings led him to conclude that white light contains *in potentia* all the colors of the rainbow.[35] After years of studying Newton, Brewster found yet another crystalline instrument that could reveal the laws of light and color: the kaleidoscope. In 1816, interested in how the polarization of light manifests itself in rainbows, Brewster concocted his own spectrum, a whirling revelation of unseen beams, as manifold and bizarre as the four creatures of Ezekiel.[36]

CORPUSCULAR CRYSTALS

The crystal has served as a "shew-stone" not only for the optical sciences, occult and legitimate. It has also functioned as an angel frame to the physicist studying the laws by which matter moves; the chemist observing how elements combine; and the biologist focused on life—its origin and its functions. The crystal—a rock that grows, ice that creeps—offered this possibility: The physicist, the chemist, and the biologist study the same subject: *organizations* of a holistic principle coursing through atoms and molecules as well as cells and anatomies. This organic virtue of the crystal, frozen or otherwise, ultimately drew Thoreau to lose himself in the pellucid lattices, fascinated to find "ghost leaves" in the frost, and in the green palms of the elm, "crystalline botany" (*NH* 52).

In 1669, the year Bartholinus held a crystal to the Danish sky, Nicolaus Steno, under the same horizon, studied prismatic symmetries. After slicing geometrical faces from different pieces of quartz and tracing these faces onto paper, he found that the angles of these similar surfaces were constant, regardless of shape or size. Later, in *De solido intra solidum naturaliter contento dissertationis prodromus* (1669), he concluded that crystal structures are regularly geometrical and that all angles in similar crystal shapes are the same. The latter claim became the basis for Steno's law of the constancy of inter-facial angles, the first crystallographic law, conclusively established in 1772, when Jean-Baptiste Romé de l'Isle in *Essai de cristallographie* demonstrated the constancy of dihedral angles among crystal faces of the same species of mineral.[37]

While Steno was analyzing the geometry of crystals, other natural philosophers were sounding relationships between the crystal and material monads. According to John G. Burke in *The Origins of the Science of Crystals* (1966), the primary theories of crystal and matter in the seventeenth and eighteenth centuries were "molecular": visions of crystals as aggregates of indivisible atoms moving and combining in a void.[38] In *The Origine of Formes and Qualities* (1666), Robert Boyle supposed that matter is comprised of "prima naturalia," extremely small particles set in motion at the creation of the world and capable of clustering into larger bodies.[39] For Boyle, the crystalline shapes of gems offer special exemplifications of this theory, for—as he explains in *An Essay About the Origine and Virtues of Gems* (1672)—the regular structures of these specimens suggest that matter is an aggregation of basic, possibly uniform, corpuscles.[40] Refining Boyle's theory by hypothesizing that gravity—not interlocking shape—is the cohesive force between atoms, Newton in his *Opticks* also turned to the crystal to exemplify his theory of matter. For him, the crystal shows how atoms cohere into larger shapes through attraction and repulsion and suggests that the corpuscles possess regular geometries.[41] Assuming that crystal geometries are comprised of spherical atoms, Johann Kepler, René Descartes, and Robert Hooke had already proposed this latter notion.[42] In the same way, Huygens, though no strict atomist, contended that crystals reveal monads as rotating ellipsoids.[43]

This atomic theory of crystals had become entrenched by the middle of the eighteenth century because its atomic basis supported the mechanical theories of motion issuing from Newton.[44] A proponent of the molecular theory, Haüy, the ostensible father of modern crystallography, in 1784 allegedly dropped a calc spar and watched it break into uniformly shaped components. He later concluded in *Essai d'une théorie sur la structure des crystaux* (1784) that crystals are comprised of "molécules intégrantes" that aggregate into larger crystalline shapes according to mathematical rules.[45] By 1801 he had worked this theory into a system of classification, arguing in *Traité de minéralogie* that there are six crystal forms, each dependent upon a particular integral molecule.[46]

However, as Eilhardt Mitscherlich soon demonstrated, Haüy's theory, despite its mathematical elegance, ignored the chemistry of crystals. Mitscherlich in 1819 announced his law of isomorphism, which claimed that substances that crystallize in the same form share similar *chemical* compositions. This law, based upon the assumption that crystals (like everything else) are comprised of spherical, electromagnetic atoms and not integral, corpuscular ones, helped Jöns Jacob Berzelius consolidate his own atomic theory: The basics of matter are points of positive and negative energy.[47] Still, although Mitscherlich and Berzelius overturned Haüy's clumsy theory of geometrically shaped chunks, these two sophisticated chemists nonetheless assumed that matter is comprised of spheres, and thus remained in the molecular school, albeit with an eye toward a more dynamic, electromagnetic current.

SWEDENBORG'S CRUSTALS OF FORCE

The molecular school more or less informed crystallography from the late 1600s to the early 1800s. However, a counter tradition was also present, exemplified, according to Lancelot Law Whyte, by Vico, Leibniz, Swedenborg, Boscovich, and Kant.[48] Each of these figures, to use Burke's words, "rejected the concept of hard finite atoms extended in space and, instead, viewed matter as arising from the combination of centers of action or force which pervaded space."[49] This latter view, which Whyte calls "point atomism," as opposed to "naïve atomism," hearkens back to Stoic thought (as well as to Pythagorean and Neoplatonic ideas) in assuming that space is an infinite plenum of energy that coheres into discrete, polarized whirls, nonidentical centers of the whole. Swedenborg's scientific work provides a rich example of this "polar" theory of crystal. His opus not only describes the crystal as a revelatory pattern of infinite energy but also predicts Thoreau's American Romanticism.

Before becoming a prophet in 1745, Swedenborg was a respected metallurgist, chemist, and mining engineer. Indeed, the nineteenth-century French chemist Jean-Baptiste André Dumas claimed that Swedenborg, not Steno or Haüy, originated crystallography.[50] Skilled in interpreting the physical world as much as the spiritual, Swedenborg is one of the few figures in intellectual history to contribute to science and theology. Remarkable for marrying hard facts to invisible worlds, Swedenborg informed Blake and Emerson, and also Thoreau, who praised him in *A Week on the Concord and Merrimack Rivers* (1849) for his ability to experience *palpably* spiritual powers (*WC* 386). What Emerson and Thoreau most admired in Swedenborg were his visions of relationships between microcosm and macrocosm. As Emerson remarks in his 1850 essay on Swedenborg, this Swedish seer found that "[e]ach law of nature has the like universality; eating, sleep or hybernation, rotation, generation, metamorphosis, vortical motion, which is seen in eggs as in planets. These grand rhymes . . . delighted the prophetic eye of Swedenborg" (*EW* 4:62).

Swedenborg's crystallography is at the core of his analogical vision. In his *Principles of Chemistry*, he notes that the hexagonal shapes of ice combine and spread in the same way that vegetables bud and branch. Botanical seeds under the influence of heat and water press outward into leafy encrustations. Aqueous globules in freezing temperatures solidify into transparent stars. Swedenborg discovers a similar process when he studies how water produces crystals of salt. Both modes of crystallization illustrate the transformation of amorphous spheres into cubes.[51]

In the context of Swedenborg's theory of creation, the crystal is a window to and mirror of the infinite energy that originates and sustains the cosmos. According to Swedenborg in his 1734 *Philosophical and Mineralogical Works*, the process by which infinite spirit originates and sustains the finite universe is essentially crystallization, the transformation of shapeless energy into regular structures, "crustals." The universe began when infinite spirit condensed its force into a single, transparent, spiraling point. (Think of a single eddy in an immense ocean.) Overwhelmed by the boundless energy it contained, this point—a portal between infinity and the finite— whirled eventually into the first "crustal": a vortex comprised of inner motion and a highly tenuous, transparent crust. (Now picture a tornado; call its outer shape a crust.) The force of this motion eventually exploded the outer crust into fragments that likewise formed into translucent spherules of energy, or crustallized eddies. These spheres became primary "particles." They in turn combined to form "elements"—gravity, magnetism, ether, and air—which organized the particles into a vast solar vortex. Eventually, this solar rotation, like the first point of infinity, flew apart at its edges. The resulting fragments formed the chaos described at the beginning of the biblical Genesis. This abyss—yet another huge vortex—at some point divided into planets, among which is the earth, a more stable and opaque crustillization that frequently freezes into crystals—nebulous spheres transformed into cubes and hexagons.[52]

There are five salient points of this cosmology. One, Swedenborg rejects Newton's atoms moving mechanically in a void and instead believes that the universe is comprised of motion organized in geometrical forms. Two, particles and elements, though organized by crusts of varying degrees of plasticity, are transparent in their pristine forms. They become opaque only when combined into irregular patterns. Three, events are polarized—distributed motion and discrete pattern, centripetal and centrifugal forces. Four, the universe is analogical. The original infinity cohering into a primal point is homologous to the solar vortex condensing into a sun, the primal chaos organizing into planets, mushy seeds pressing into leaves, and globes of water stiffening into crystals. Five, each part, properly seen, is a window to and a mirror of infinity: As geometrical patterns of spirit, beholder and beheld refract and reflect the first light.

The crystal is no different in kind from other creatures in Swedenborg's universe. Everything is a geometrical form of infinite motion. The crystal is, however, distinct in degree. It reveals the cosmic processes that remain hidden in more opaque, lubricious events. Observing crystals of ice—as Thoreau does on cold Concord mornings—one sees geometrical patterns and wonders if such patterns exist in more complex, less apparent modes in clouds or eagles. Staring through the translucent symmetries, one further suspects that things are essentially transparent, that primal monads are windows. One moreover speculates—still looking at the ice—on how these crystals combine to form a uniform surface. He guesses that there is a central power that unifies while differentiating, which is attractive and repulsive. He looks up at the frost-covered leaves. He finds in their green reticulations patterns similar to those in the ice. He marvels: Maybe in the stars are further homologies to these earthly analogues. He returns to the ice. He sees through it to the bottom of the pond. He sees in it his own face. He is in the ice; he is above and below the freeze. It dawns on him. He, too, is similar in kind to the ice, different only in degree. He also is a window to and reflection of the whole.

Swedenborg's later doctrine of correspondence—based on the assumption that the visible corresponds to the invisible—is incipient in his early work on physics and chemistry. In these scientific treatises, Swedenborg laid foundations for his effort, to use Emerson's words, "to put science and the soul, long estranged from one another, at one again" (*EW* 4:63). As Emerson further remarked, Swedenborg was the rare man who could discern the rhythms of the concrete as well as the wonders of heaven. His early scientific studies were remarkable for their cosmic sweep. His later visions, like *Heaven and Hell* (1758), are notable for their particularity. His earthly crystals open to the far heavens while his angels have a familiar face and a name.

GALVANIZED STONES

Swedenborg's crystallography suggests that crystallization is not a secondary phenomenon but the primary pattern of all matter—as Thoreau would later note, the "type of all growth" (*NH* 53–4). Other dynamically minded thinkers of the late eighteenth and early nineteenth centuries developed this theory. On the one hand, the science of electromagnetism, led by H. C. Oersted, Humphry Davy, and Michael Faraday, refined and substantiated Swedenborg's speculations on holistic force and polarized pattern. On the other, German *Naturphilosophie*, inaugurated by Goethe and practiced by Schelling, inflected Swedenborg's theories as well as those of the electromagnetists through organic grids, assuming that the crystal, like the leaf, is *alive*. Studied in these trends, Emerson spent his days, as did Thoreau, searching for the world in the nearest frost.

In 1799, Oersted completed a doctoral thesis on Kant's *Metaphysical Foundations of Natural Science* (1786). From this text, as well as from *Critique of Pure Reason* (1781), Oersted learned of

Kant's theory of matter, remarkably similar to Swedenborg's. Kant claimed that space and time are categories of the mind. Thus, the mind cannot perceive the empty Newtonian space required for the atomic theory. If the mind cannot perceive void space, then it must apprehend a plenum of force. Kant's conclusion: Space is comprised of attractive and repulsive forces; matter itself is a dynamic force.[53] Galvanized by these conjectures, Oersted tried to discover the force underlying light, heat, magnetism, and electricity. After years of theorizing and experimentation, in 1820 he accidentally placed a wire charged with an electrical current beside a magnetized needle; noticed that the needle was deflected; and concluded that electricity and magnetism behave in the same manner and are possibly manifestations of the same holistic energy.[54]

Meanwhile, Davy was likewise supplementing his scientific training by studying Kant's theory of force. After reading Kant in 1799 and spending the next years in philosophical conversation with Coleridge, Davy set out to discover the force generating electricity, magnetism, light, and heat. By 1807, he had found that chemical relations and the elements that comprise them are electrical.[55] Five years later, he wondered in *Elements of Chemical Philosophy*—which Emerson read in the 1830s[56]—if matter might be constituted not by atoms but by "physical points endowed with attraction and repulsion."[57] Like Swedenborg before him, Davy embraced the crystal as a rich revelation of these polarized powers. Drawing from Haüy's work on integral molecules yet refining it with his own electromagnetic speculations, he wondered if the "laws of crystallization" and the "electrical polarities of bodies" are "intimately related."[58] The crystal offered to him—as it did to Swedenborg before—a bright window to the interiors of matter. In the translucent crystal, he saw how nature's charged geometries bond through electrical affinity to form larger aggregates.

Davy's prized protégé Faraday likewise turned to the crystal to substantiate his theories of electromagnetism. Schooled in Kant's theory of holistic force and Coleridge's notion of a unifying consciousness, Faraday by 1831 reached an understanding of the abysmal energy generating all forms. In discovering electromagnetic induction, he demonstrated that space itself—and the matter that pervades it—is an immaterial field of electromagnetic waves.[59] He thus opened the world's eyes, as Emerson later wrote, to the "secret mechanism of life & sensation" (*EJ* 4:94).[60] Throughout the rest of his days, Faraday labored in his *Experimental Researches in Electricity* (1831–1852) to understand the implications of this finding. In the course of these efforts, he frequently turned to the crystal, for he found in its transparent lattices "beautiful" manifestations of the "electrical condition."[61]

One year before Faraday discovered electromagnetic induction, John Herschel in *Preliminary Discourse on the Study of Natural Philosophy* (1830)—a book that Emerson compared favorably to *Paradise Lost*[62]—highlighted the emerging science of crystallography as a method for ascertaining the nature of matter itself. As Herschel reports, recent studies of crystals by Haüy and Mitscherlich have established the laws by which primitive crystalline forms combine into more complex patterns. For Herschel, these theories of Haüy and Mitscherlich, different as they are, are important for understanding not only crystals but also the "mutual attractions and repulsions of particles of matter," the ways that "polarity" functions in the combination of atoms. As the scientist observes tiny crystals accrue into diamonds, he is watching, in Herschel's words, "little machines" working out the most basic principle of the universe: electrical affinity and repellency.[63]

LATTICES AND LEAVES

Herschel, Davy, and Faraday were intrigued by properties that eventually made the crystal a primary conductor of radio waves and the centerpiece of solid-state physics. The crystal moved other more bio-

logically minded thinkers—Goethe, Schelling, and Christian Samuel
Weiss (as well as Emerson and Thoreau)—because it could *grow*.

For Goethe crystallization is similar in kind to the development of leaves and muscles. Goethe's primary scientific idea was
this: Nature develops through the agency of archetypal forms that
metamorphose into diverse phenomena. As he claimed in his 1790
work, *The Metamorphosis of Plants*, the primal plant form is the
leaf.[64] Four years earlier, he proposed that the archetypal zoologi-
cal phenomenon is the vertebra.[65] Even earlier, Goethe concluded
that the primal rock form is granite, a first crystallization of an
original liquid fire.[66] One leaf develops into all plants; a single
bone emanates into every animal; a granite crystal is the seed of
the earth's rocks. Hence, though nature appears to have no "system"—to develop "from an unknown center toward an unknowable periphery"—the cosmos is in fact structured by centripetal
powers, cohesions of formlessness, *Urbilden*.[67] In Goethe's cosmos—as Emerson well knew[68]—unbounded life organizes itself
into polarized eddies, variously accelerated: round bone, eye of
leaf, and quartz spheroid. Everything *crystallizes* the whole.

Although Goethe through scientific rigor sought to separate
himself from the speculative excesses of Schelling's *Naturphilosophie*, Goethe's natural philosophy nonetheless influenced and cor-
responded to Schelling's thought.[69] In *Ideas for a Philosophy of
Nature* (1797)—a book Emerson studied in the 1830s (*EJ* 5:30)[70]—
Schelling claims that an abysmal Absolute explores its own mysteries by emanating outward into dialectical processes, such as
interactions between ideal and real, infinite and finite, subject and
object, irritation and satisfaction, attraction and repulsion. Hence,
each form of the cosmos is not only a polarized pattern of this invisible principle; it is also a marker of this principle's developing
consciousness of itself. Stones are not inanimate but manifestations
of spirit at a low level of consciousness. Plants reveal spirit at a
higher grade of awareness. Animals show spirit thinking. Humans

perfect the spirit, self-consciously reflecting it back to itself.[71] Describing a cosmos in which a distributed vitality manifests itself in discrete forms, Schelling places special emphasis on crystallization. In *On the World Soul* (1798), he maintains that *all* nature is a vast crystal. Rock or ice crystals are primitive organizations of life that will one day evolve into more conscious geometries—plants, animals, and humans. Crystallization is a primary phenomenon. It is the archetypal organization of the absolute. Crystals are early humans. Humans are advanced crystals.[72]

In the year he published his book on the soul, a synthesis of electromagnetic polarity and biological panpsychism, Schelling met and influenced Weiss, a young medical student. After receiving his doctorate in medicine, Weiss spent the next years studying the *Naturphilosophie* of minerals. In 1804, he translated Haüy's *Traité de minéralogie*, to which he appended an essay, "Dynamische Ansicht der Kristallisation." In this piece, Weiss draws from the polar theory—found in Swedenborg and Kant—as well as from biological holism—developed by Goethe and Schelling—to argue that crystallization is a primary manifestation of cosmic attraction and repulsion. Crystallization occurs when repulsive forces in a fluid dominate the attractive ones and thus disrupt the liquid state. The remaining positive forces direct these negative powers into various angles, which solidify into crystal faces. Weiss' conclusions not only transform Schelling's ideas into more scientifically rigorous theories; they also indicate "the vectorial nature of crystallization" and thus show that "direction"—not the geometrical atom—is the primary characteristic of crystal types. The crystal is a snapshot of motion, a static translucence of holistic dynamism, similar in kind to leaves, feathers, and stars, different only in mobility and consciousness.[73]

Before turning to Emerson's and Thoreau's inflections of these theories of crystal, I should note that these "panpsychical" ideas of living crystals are not merely Romantic notions discredited in the twentieth century. D'Arcy Wentworth Thompson, one of the earliest proponents of self-organization (and a student of Goethe's morphology), claims in *On Growth and Form* (1942) that a natural form is a "diagram of forces," a self-interfering pattern of holistic energy. Indeed, the snow crystal "illustrates to perfection how Nature rings the changes on every possible variation and permutation and combination of form."[74] Likewise, Erwin Schrödinger in *What Is Life?* (1944) suggests that all forms in nature are crystals, cogent structures of amorphous energy. The physicist studies "periodic," or regular crystals; the biologist attends to "aperiodic," or irregular crystals.[75] More recently (and perhaps with less scientific legitimacy), Rupert Sheldrake, in *A New Science of Life* (1981), argues that nature's present forms are "memories" of previous forms that organized themselves in similar contexts. These repeated patterns of nature, organizations of the larger whole of life, are not simply sentient beings but also "crystals, molecules, atoms, and subatomic particles." Nothing is mechanical. Everything is alive. "Biology," Whitehead wrote, "is the study of larger organisms, whereas physics is the study of smaller organisms."[76]

EMERSON'S SNOWSTORM

In late December of 1834, Emerson beheld a snow-storm cover in ice his Concord environs (*EJ* 4:129). Witnessing the flakes transform his native mud to fiery white, he was likewise transmuted. Aware of the virtues of crystal—frozen or otherwise—from his studies of Swedenborg, Goethe, Schelling, Davy, and Faraday, Emerson saw in the ice not death in winter's nadir but the vigor of summer—the artist's sap. Inflecting his fascination over the snow through his researches into crystal, he recorded his impressions in "The Snow-Storm," a poem he would publish in 1841. This poem, as well as Emerson's other frozen revelation—the transparent eyeball sequence in *Nature*—introduce the poetics of crystal: a theory of seeing and saying that informs Thoreau's practices of observation and description.[77]

"The Snow-Storm" reveals the vitality of ostensibly static ice. After detailing the "tumultuous" storm—a driving snow that veils the land and halts commerce—Emerson turns to the result of the turmoil: a wildly altered environment.

> Come see the north wind's masonry.
> Out of an unseen quarry evermore
> Furnished with tile, the fierce artificer
> Curves his white bastions with projected roof
> Round every windward stake, or tree, or door.
> Speeding, the myriad-handed, his wild work
> So fanciful, so savage, nought cares he
> For number or proportion.[78]

The ice crystals demonstrate the presence of an intense demiurge, the north wind impetuously concocting extravagant works. However, what emerges from this energy—which originates from a bottomless quarry and ignores "number or proportion"—is not simple anarchy but graceful shape: an elegant "wreath" hangs on "coop or kennel"; a "swan-like form" "invests the hidden thorn"; a "tapering turret" rises from the gate. Emerson's speaker marvels at these felicitous convolutions of turbulence and repose. Astonished by this "frolic architecture of the snow," he complains that his own "Art" can only "mimic in slow structures, stone by stone" what the "mad wind" conjures in a night.

Staring into the frozen shapes, Emerson's speaker experiences a fourfold revelation. First, he understands that ice is alive, a vigorous manifestation of an abyss of being, transcendent (beyond the limitations of space and time) and immanent (flowing through wild geometries). Second, he realizes that the snow crystals are polar—chaotic and calm. Third, the speaker recognizes a natural poetics. The world's forms are coincidences of opposites, marriages of centripetal and centrifugal energies. Fourth, the ice—as paradoxical image of boundless energy—is sublime, a disclosure of mysterious powers that mock egotistical desire while inviting the unselfish artist to merge with their frosts.

These four aspects of Emerson's snowy gnosis recall the "vital" crystallography of Davy and Faraday and the "organic" crystals of Goethe and Schelling. The "unseen quarry evermore / Furnished with tile" is analogous to Davy's galvanic forces sustaining the cosmos and Goethe's invisible font of life. Likewise, the "wild work" that originates from this quarry corresponds to Davy's crystal diagrams of unbounded energy and Goethe's centripetal coagulations of centrifugal exuberance.

These correspondences are not coincidental. In several early passages, Emerson invokes crystallography to illustrate relationships between mysterious energy and pellucid form. In "Humanity of Science" (1836), he wonders if the fact that the "phenomena of crystallization resemble electric laws" might reveal the "common law that pervades nature from the deep centre to the unknown circumference" (*EL* 2:29). Likewise, in "The Uses of Natural History" (1833), Emerson marvels at the "formation of snow." The "texture of that self weaving blanket"—comprised of "little hexagon[s]," each featuring "invariable angles" in the "radii" of its "star[s]"—is a "philosophical experiment performed in a larger laboratory and on a more magnificant scale than our chemists can command" (1:15). Emerson further wonders at snow crystals in "Water" (1834), amazed that the "invisible water" in the ubiquitous air can so felicitously organize itself into "stars of six rays," "primitive crystal[s]" (1:64). The hidden core of these public contemplations on how amorphous force turns into shining jewels is perhaps an 1832 journal entry in which Emerson forges a striking analogy between the mental and the physical.

> There is a process in the mind very analogous to crystallization in the mineral kingdom. I think of a particular fact of singular beauty & interest. In thinking of it I am led to many more thoughts which show themselves . . . first partially and afterwards more fully. But in the multitude I see no order. When I would present them to others they have no beginning. There is no method. Leave them now, & return to them again. Domesticate them in your mind, do not force them into arrangement too hastily & presently you shall find they will take their own order. And the order they assume is divine. It is God's architecture. (*EJ* 3:316)

Random thoughts suddenly leap into gorgeous arrangements in the same way that chaotic powers quickly crystallize into ordered structures.

Instancing these ideas, "The Snow-Storm" not only reflects Emerson's reading in the sciences of crystal. It also exemplifies a primary idea of *Nature* (1836): The world, properly seen, is always crystalline, a transparent organization of unfathomable energy.[79] While the "Understanding," or empirical faculty, perceives objects as discrete, opaque phenomena, the "eye of Reason," the intuitive power, transforms these "outlines and surfaces" into "transparent" windows through which invisible "causes and spirits" can be apprehended (*N* 62). Yet, as Emerson suggests elsewhere in his book, the "transparent" world, like the snow crystal, is not simple lucidity—not limpid revelation of heavenly harmonies or pristine laws. Emersonian "transparency" reveals mystery as much as clarity, turbulence as well as pattern. When the "universe becomes transparent, and the light of higher laws than its own, shines through it," it does not turn pellucid and tranquil but resembles a "summer's cloud." Escaping intellectual category, this ephemeral wisp of light inspires "special wonder." Beyond conclusion, it riddles like a Sphinx (43). Likewise, when the stars make the atmosphere seem "transparent with design," they do not intimate order but "the perpetual presence of the sublime," the inaccessible (1–2).

These Emersonian meditations on transparency suggest that the spirits and causes circulating through the translucent patterns are powers as much as laws, obscurities as much as solutions. Though these causes and spirits add "grace and expression" to "outline and surface," they also intimate unfathomable energies beyond elegant gesture and significant representation. Throughout *Nature* transmuting the world to glass, Emerson the scryer realizes—as he did as the poet of "The Snow-Storm"—that the cosmos is indeed as agitated as it is calm, as confusing as it is intelligible: Powerful "floods of life stream around and through" the universe; ostensibly tranquil things are "fluid" and "volatile"; things are polarized symbols of the living flows; events, both deeds and words, cannot fully reveal the enigmatic fluxes that animate them (*N* 5, 93, 41–5, 56–7).

Emerson in *Nature* crystallizes these curious currents in his "transparent eye-ball" passage. In the midst of a crepuscular, cloud-covered trek across an icy common (covered in "snow puddles"), he intuits, again, the "fierce artificer" of "The Snow-Storm," the abysmal power coalescing into turbid orders: "Standing on the bare ground,—my head bathed by the blithe air, and uplifted into infinite space,—all mean egotism vanishes. I become a transparent eye-ball; I am nothing; I see all; the currents of the Universal Being circulate through me; I am part or particle of God" (*N* 12–13). Walking over slush—water spangled with frozen prisms—Emerson, aptly, experiences himself as a crystal, a transpicuous lens through which infinite forces oscillate. His eye of Reason opens, revealing that he is not distinct and separate but a discrete pattern of distributed energy—a polarized point, an agitated orb, of infinity. Hence, his autonomous "ego" is "nothing," an illusion. Yet, his sight, viewing the ungraspable whole hum through his parts, is everything. Equating his transparency with optical revelation, Emerson recalls the prism's power to disclose light and color. As prism, he refracts and reflects: He turns (tropes) the invisible currents of Universal Being into multicolored pattern, his distinct image of himself as an eye-ball; at the same time, he mirrors the world, losing his individuality in the all.[80]

Different and indifferent, transpicuous and dense, uncircumscribed and spherical, Emerson as glassy ball, as shew-stone, is not pellucid. Duplicitous, conflicted, he clusters cosmic poles. Yet, in turning into a surreal *coincidentia oppositorum*, he is not aberrant but a convoluted part of a torqued whole. In his landscape, numerous contraries coincide. The common is slushy, liquid and solid. The time is twilight, day and night. The sky, obscure and clear, is cloudy yet opens to infinite space. The blithe air, spirit, bathes, as matter. Emerson turned crystal simply finds his place in a crystalline cosmos.

Later in *Nature*, Emerson admits that this crystalline vision is difficult to achieve, for the human orb is as likely to flatten to granite as it is to explode into quartz: "The ruin or the blank, that we see when we look at nature, is in our own eye. The axis of vision is not coincident with the axis of things, and so they appear not transparent but opake. The reason why the world lacks unity, and lies broken and in heaps, is, because man is disunited with himself" (91). As B. L. Packer has shown in *Emerson's Fall* (1982), Emerson here draws from Brewster's optical meditations in his 1831 biography of Newton. Brewster proposes that a thick transparent medium—a crystal or prism—reflects or refracts light based on the alignments between the electrical charges of the light particles and the electrical charges of the medium. Organized by "two attractive and two repulsive poles at the extremities of two axes at right angles to each other," a revolving light particle can approach a medium with either its attractive or repulsive axis directed toward the angle of entry. If the attractive axis first touches the medium, the particle is drawn by attractive forces, and thus refracted. If the repulsive axis initially meets the medium, the particle is repulsed by negative forces, and therefore reflected.[81] Translating physical to spiritual, Emerson supposes that proper seeing requires a "coincidence" of inner and outer. If the observer is at odds (egotistically resisting the distributed energies sustaining him), then he is "negatively" directed and repulsed by opaque walls. However, if the beholder agrees with his being (charitably consenting to his unique patterning of universal currents), then he is "positively" disposed. Penetrating transparent surfaces, he himself becomes translucent—shape of air, pervious crystal.

But a man of flesh and blood cannot become a permeable prism. For this conceit to make sense, one must experience double vision, double refraction. On the one hand, all material beings are opaque solids, impervious densities. Yet, on the other, each form of matter is a transparent current, pattern of an invisible whole. Most times, fraught with egotistical fears and desires (fears of the world outside the skin, desire to subdue such threatening terrain), one identifies entirely with one's material being. One is an impenetrable subject against thick objects. However, in rare moments, during walks across icy fields in twilight, one's worries and wants fall away. He feels part of immeasurable energies coursing through the grass, his heart, the stars. He realizes that he is a transpicuous form of distributed flow. His "I" and the All mutually interpenetrate. He is something (a cogent structure) and nothing (an infinite abyss). Not simply a translucent window, not merely an impervious mirror, he, crystalline, is both. Somewhat opaque, he reflects his world, merges with it, and relinquishes his ego. Mostly transparent, he refracts the universe, stands separate from it, turns it to suit his discrete disposition.

This crystal vision, duplicitous, quickly slips away. As Emerson writes in "Experience" (1844), "The consciousness in each man is a sliding scale, which identifies him now with the First Cause, and now with the flesh of his body" (*EW* 3:42). Most, conscious almost only of flesh, need reminding of the scale, of the abysmal cause. For Emerson, the poet, studied in occult relationships between First Cause and lubricious flesh (whole and part, mystery and solution), produces shocking memorials. He recalls men and women to the sublime core that they, raging for order, soon forget. He fulfills this office, as Emerson intones in "The Poet" (1844), by transmuting cosmos to crystal. Dissolving things to spirit, the poet "turns the world to glass" and thus sees that "within the form of every creature is a force impelling it to ascend into a higher form." "Following with his eyes the life," this scrying writer "uses the forms which express that life. Thus, "his speech flows with the flowing of nature" (*EW* 3:12).

Aspiring to become such a scrying poet, Emerson in *Nature* creates arresting linguistic crystals—intricate, complex, polarized structures poised to jolt complacent readers with disturbing currents. Notice the first sentence of the "transparent eye-ball" passage, quoted above: "Standing on the bare ground,—my head bathed by the blithe air, and uplifted into infinite space,—all mean egotism vanishes" (*N* 12–13). Enacting in language the transformation of ego into "nothing," Emerson employs a dangling modifier. He does not provide the subject, "I," that the phrase "[s]tanding on bare ground" clearly modifies. The "I" falls away. Yet, it immediately reappears in another form: "I become a transparent eye-ball; I am nothing; I see all; the currents of the Universal Being circulate through me; I am part or particle of God" (13). How can Emerson's visionary be both nothing and something, formless and formed? Moreover, if he is a purely transparent lens, and thus unable to reflect light (and thus blind[82]), how can he see anything, much less everything? Either he is totally transparent and therefore both blind and clear-sighted, or he is simultaneously transparent and opaque and hence actually capable of sight. We further ask: As a "current" of the "Universal Being," is this visionary a physical flow, an electromagnetic current, or a divine power, a spiritual draft? Finally, why is the visionary "part or particle" of God? If a part, is he then a synecdoche of God, a cogent pattern revealing and containing the whole? If a particle, is he a speck or fragment broken from a whole, and thus separate from God?

Nothing and something, vague and cogent, blind and all-seeing, translucent and obscure, physical and spiritual, distributed and discrete, Emerson, like crystal, is a *paralogical* figure—beyond the law of noncontradiction. On the one hand, these linguistic polarities support the polarities of the convoluted cosmos Emerson inhabits. Hence, they are not contradictions but paradoxes— seeming opposites that secretly reconcile. Yet, on the other hand, these rifts in logic are contradictory, for a man cannot literally be present and absent, blind and perceptive, limpid and dense. These linguistic oppositions themselves thus form a more general polarity. The passage is a paradox and a contradiction, a marriage and a divorce of opposites.[83]

Emerson's language here is a snowstorm, an uncommonly crystalline disclosure of nature's turbid harmonies. Like the crystal itself, the passage reveals what is always already true of everything else—all other things and words—though hidden, lurking under dense, seemingly stable surfaces. As I have argued in *Emerson's Sublime Science*, Emerson's especially intricate sequences function like sublime eruptions—storms or tornadoes or numinous symbols or flashes of lightning or loves at first sight. Such explosions move beholders to consider the possibility that *all* matter patterns immense energy, that all material forms are polarized. If so, then even clear days, ordinary twigs, lazy clouds, and casual acquaintances are likewise, properly seen, tumultuous involutes, oscillating forms of darkly bright energy. In the same way, Emerson's linguistic prisms alter readers' senses of the ostensibly discursive sequences coming before and after. Once one has read closely the "transparent eye-ball" sequence or the "Orphic poet" passage (or the stunning opening or the description of clouds floating like "fishes in the sea of crimson light"), one suspects that other, more static parts are not what they seem, that even abstract definitions of "nature" or "end" or "spirit" dissolve into curious paradoxes and obscure flickerings. Returning to such discursive *topoi*, one's

suspicions prove true. Even Emerson's "ordinary" passages, intensely perused, prove to be agitated, fields of strange semantic
force, crystals, though somewhat subdued in their brightness. I
have said before that the essay, inspired by Emerson's studies of
electromagnetism, is a field of force in varying degrees of inten-
sity.[84] I can now say that the book, informed by crystallography, is
also a crystal cabinet alternating between striking light and more
soothing shade.

To read Emerson's *Nature* is to tour a crystalline asylum. For
some of the tour, one moves with relatively little strain or surprise,
studying familiar, ordinary planes of glass, either reflective or
transparent. (One reads "philosophical" or "discursive" sequences.) Yet, in certain places, the tourist happens upon "privileged objects"—extremely intricate gems, opaque and limpid,
luridly bright. (He experiences complex, densely figured styles
that defy logic and resist denotation.) Staring into the eerie lattices, he sees strange distortions, dreamy interpenetrations between part and whole, hallucinatory blurrings of self and other.
Still moving, he returns to unremarkable sheets—flat mirrors and
windows. (He comes back to the philosophical discourse.) Yet, all
is now different. The calm surfaces now themselves strangely
flicker, inducing feverish reveries. They are now duplicitous
prisms, somewhat less gloomy and luminous.

Recalling scryers like Dee, optical theorists such as Brewer,
physicists like Swedenborg, chemists like Davy, and biologists
such as Goethe, Emerson's "transparency"—inspired by visions in
snow, exemplified by stylistic kaleidoscopes—requires an inversion. What were formerly thought to be transparent, univocal, intelligible experiences—ordinary, understandable events (worn
paths) and logical, lucid words (plain styles)—become opaque:
coverings of complexity with simplicity, polarity with singularity.
What were earlier considered to be opaque, equivocal, mysterious
occurrences—extraordinary, confusing occasions (snow storms)

and illogical, convoluted language (baroque explosions)—turn transparent: numinous revelations of a polarized cosmos.

Emersonian transparency, resembling crystal, revises traditional transparency.[85] Traditional transparency, *pure* transparency, is pristine clarity, unadulterated spirit, unsullied invisibility. To apprehend such transparency, one must transcend matter, rise to unseen worlds of unhindered lucidity. This elevation, if intuitive, might result in a vision of Plotinus's ideal intelligence, described in the *Enneads* (ca. 270 A.D.): "There . . . all is transparent, nothing dark, nothing resistant; every being is lucid to every other, in breadth and depth; light runs through light."[86] Likewise, this levitation, if an act of abstraction, could end in a comprehension of Newton's numbers, the quantifiable essentials of matter described in *Principia Mathematica* (1713, 2nd ed.)—bloodless masses and motions, extensions and hardnesses.[87] Revising these rarefied transparencies, Emerson's *crystal* transparency—"opaque" transparency, "transparent" opacity—merges lucidity and obscurity, abstraction and concretion: matter and spirit. Pure transparency, total light, is blinding. It ignores the kaleidoscopic wonders of the world. Crystal transparency, luminous gloom, inspires attentive gazes on sparks and shades. It focuses on open secrets, boundaries where colors dissolve into enigmatic white.

Holding darkness in the midst of its light, Emersonian transparency (crystal transparency) is, like Goethe's archetype or Schelling's primitive organization, a middle way between thinking and thingness. Hence, in theory, it heals the rift between Emerson the "transcendentalist" and Emerson the "pragmatist." In the crystal cosmos, the idealist must be pragmatically devoted to the power of matter, for he turns the world to glass only through detailed empirical observation (becomes a hyaline eye only through closely registering snow puddles at twilight). Likewise, the pragmatist must be intuitively attuned to spirit, for he grasps the potency of events only through knowledge of the whole (turns reforming poet only through envisioning universal currents). Idealistically pragmatic, pragmatically idealistic, Emerson the scryer attempts to embrace parts without forsaking wholes, to sense wholes without ignoring parts.[88]

Emerson often struggles to locate this middle path. Though he desires to marry spirit and matter, abstract and concrete, his essays *lack* particular details (keen descriptions of lubricious events, peculiar confessions of intense compulsions) and are replete with general concepts (theoretical contemplations on nature, intellect, fate; impersonal conclusions on self and society). He opens his 1836 edition of *Nature* with an epigraph from Plotinus that demeans nature to a mere image of wisdom. Early in the essay, he proclaims, "the most abstract truth is the most practical" (*N* 7). Though Emerson is a brilliant philosopher of the golden mean, his constitution, it appears, disposed him toward Being over beings, Man over men. Differently natured, Thoreau, however, toes the line. He presses close to things, mucky and moribund. His nose to the ground, he nonetheless discerns, rising from the subterranean channels, stars that shine like ice.

THOREAU'S SCRYING

If Emerson through his reading became aware of various *theories* of crystallography, Thoreau through his own observations closely connected to cold crystal *facts*. This is not to say that Thoreau was not versed in theories of the crystal. In the 1840s, he was studying Goethe's archetypal forms in the *Italian Journey* (1786) and Schelling's *Naturphilosophie* in J. B. Stallo's *General Principles of the Philosophy of Nature* (1848).[89] Likewise, he was familiar with Swedenborg, favorably alluding to the Swedish seer in *A Week on the Concord and Merrimack Rivers* (*WC* 386).[90] Moreover, he probably learned about Davy's and Faraday's electromagnetic crystals from his conversations with Emerson. But Thoreau was not only in-

formed in the sciences of ice. He was also a student of the shew-
stone—of disquisitions on divine optics in the *Corpus Hermeticum*, of
Emerson's sequences on transparency.[91] Still, Thoreau valued experience over authority.[92] Unlike Emerson, content to glean his crystallography from treatises, Thoreau went regularly to the ice,
where, fascinated by reticulated hexagrams, he gathered facts and
ideas. Analyzing these lattices during the Concord winters, Thoreau
in the end found them much more interesting and important than
did Emerson. He not only crafted numerous descriptions of their
forms and functions. He also meditated on their lessons concerning
his persistent interests: transparency, formation, and extravagance.

Embracing the ice as a privileged revelation of life, Thoreau
combines heterogeneous offices. He is a scryer, studying crystals to
find the destiny of the cosmos, the rhythm by which everything—
pond, loon, human—moves. He is an optical theorist, searching in
the frozen lens for laws by which light bends into colors, by which
his own eyes curve thoughts and feelings into images. He is a physicist and chemist, looking in the crystalline shape for the principles by
which matter functions. A biologist as well, Thoreau sounds the ice
for the laws of life—the processes by which living things function—
and life itself—the original abyss beyond its concrete forms. Merging
these offices, Thoreau is above all a poet—a scribbling magus, a scientist armed with tropes—transforming seeings into sayings, cosmos
into *logos*, ice crystals into crystalline symbols.

Thoreau began his studies of crystals on December 24, 1837,
only months out of Harvard and a few pages into his journal
(begun at Emerson's suggestion). He notices some "curious crystallizations" in the "side of the high bank by the leaning hemlock."

> Wherever the water, or other causes, had formed a hole in the
> bank—its throat and outer edge . . . bristled with a glistening ice
> armor. In one place you might see minute ostrich feathers,
> which seemed the waving plumes of the warrior . . . in another

the glancing fan-shaped banners of the Liliputian host—and in another the needle-shaped particles collected into bundles resembling the plumes of the pine, might pass for a phalanx of spears.

The whole hill was like an immense quartz rock—with minute crystals sparkling from innumerable crannies.

I tried to fancy that there was a disposition in these crystallizations to take the forms of the contiguous foliage. (*TJ* 1:22)

Picturing these curious prisms, Thoreau mixes war implements and organic forms. The crystals appear as plates of shining armor, ostrich feathers waving like plumes, fans turned miniature banners, and pine needles become spears. While the crystals *seem* to be static, Thoreau sees activity—growth and flight, the energy of soldiers before the attack. In the midst of this tension, the ice explodes. The bank turns fiery quartz. Warmed, Thoreau imagines the crystals as closely linked leaves.

These crystals attract Thoreau for several reasons. First, like Emerson in "The Snow-Storm," he is fascinated by their bristling shapes, their "frolic architecture." Second, these interesting frozen shapes inspire him to create his own forms—a series of tropes in which he likens crystals to feathers, banners, and spears. Three, as Thoreau fashions his tropes, he senses a flaming energy lurking in the calm crystals. Four, he realizes that these coruscating crystals, not dead, might hold the key to foliage.

In addition to these salient features—which recall Goethe and Schelling as well as Emerson—we observe Thoreau's mode of observation. We first note that his sense of the ice is extremely concrete. He is attuned to its particular geometries, textures, and colors, finding in these shapes analogies to other finely rendered images, like feathers and leaves. This specific vision, however, is not an end in itself: Thoreau's attention serves as a seed from which richer visions grow; or, to change the metaphor, as a pebble

splashing a pond into concentric circles. From his initial descriptions of the ice, he rises to a more general metaphor—ice as plane
of quartz shimmering with pervasive fire—and then to an even
more general trope—the crystals as revelations and vehicles of life
itself. The ice *activates* Thoreau's mind. It stimulates in him imaginative acts of perception that open into intuitions of holistic energies coursing not only through crystals but also stones and leaves.
The frozen bank shines into a shew-stone.

Thoreau's agents of visual transformation in this process require further explanation. Instead of leaping from part to whole,
Thoreau *works* his way from particular to general through the
power of tropes. He focuses his attention on the minute forms of
the crystal. He *feels* a relationship between this prism and a ubiquitous energy, but he cannot *think* exactly what this relationship is. Inspired by the crystalline shape and his desire to grasp a whole
beyond the parts, he forges correspondences. The transparent reticulations suggest the networks in the leaf, which in turn point to imbrications of the feather, and the feather opens into more complex
human productions: not only elegant armor and instruments of war
but also, as we shall see, musical chords and poetic rhymes. Each
successive trope serves as a *lens*, a crystal in its own right, an angeli-
cal glass, through which Thoreau sees his way to the next level.

Thoreau's mode of observing crystals—a blend of objective
recording and subjective imagining—recalls Goethe's ideal method
of seeing, *Anschauung*, "intuitive perception." Described in *Color
Theory* (1810), this perceptual activity begins in an intense, sensitive
gaze on the particular—on the prism of frost not as separate object
but a form of life with which the perceiver, as a living being, feels
sympathy. Yet, sensual apprehension of the event, no matter how
sympathetic, is not sufficient for understanding the function and
form of the phenomenon—the growth and structure of the crystal.
The naturalist additionally activates his imagination to forge analogies between his present empirical occasion and similar events from

the past. He creates metaphors that lead to increasingly expansive generalizations—the crystal appears to grow and cohere like the leaf, perhaps like a feather. Ascending from part to whole, the seer does not, however, desire only to generate tropes. He aspires through his intuition to break through the images to the archetypal form, the invisible yet palpable pattern generating and organizing particular organs. Intuiting this primal form, the naturalist does not rest, though, in unseen absolutes. He returns to tangible processes—melting or freezing frost—to measure the whole against the parts. This renewed attention to parts modifies his intuition of the whole, which in turn alters again his vision of parts.[93]

Resembling Goethe's "dialectical" mode of vision, Thoreau's way of seeing is, like the crystal itself, a middle way between object and subject, fact and imagination, visible and invisible. This precarious balance requires that the perceiving mind itself be crystalline, a passive mirror and active lamp.[94] Turning his mind into prism, Thoreau reflects the fascinating frost, absorbs its curious forms; at the same time, he irradiates his own light, transforming the frozen shapes into leaves, feathers, and soldiers. These vistas become increasingly general, finally dissolving before the invisible power of life itself—the white light sparkling through the quartz crannies, the ideal form structuring crystals, feathers, and leaves. Yet, Thoreau never relinquishes his attachment to concrete shapes. Fancying the ideal disposition organizing both crystals and leaves, he nonetheless keeps his eyes firmly on the ice. He measures part against whole, whole against part; subject against object, exterior against interior; fact against fantasy, reverie against stark noon.

Thoreau's intuitive perceptions of crystals bend new light on his most enduring idea, pithily expressed in *A Week on the Concord and Merrimack Rivers* at the beginning of a discussion, fittingly, of Goethe: "A true account of the actual is the rarest poetry" (*WC* 325). Not satisfied with positivism (reduction of the world to empirical object) or idealism (reduction of the universe as shadow of mind), Thoreau in his crystal gazing combines both modes: accurate description of unique concreteness and creative imagining of general power. Such a merger informs Thoreau's later musings on the limits of positivism and the virtues of "poetic" seeing. For instance, in 1851, Thoreau in his journal suggests that static facts alone are dead while events connected to the whole appear to thrive: "Even the facts of science may dust the mind by their dryness—unless they are in a sense effaced each morning or rather rendered fertile by the dews of fresh & living truth" (*TJ* 3: 291). A year earlier, Thoreau explores this "poetic" science in more detail: "The scientific startling & successful as it is, is always some thing less than the vague poetic . . . it is the sun shorn of its beams a mere disk—the sun indeed—but—no longer phospher—light bringer or giver. . . . Science applies a finite rule to the infinite.—& is what you can weigh and measure and bring away. Its sun no longer dazzles us and fills the universe with light" (3:44).

Watching the frost dazzle the world with light, the young Thoreau enjoys an experiential basis for these mature meditations. In his early study of crystals, he intimates that noble seeing is a kind of crystallographic epistemology: the transformation of the mind into crystal, an accurate mirror and an irradiating lamp, capable of reflecting and forging relationships between finite geometries and infinite energies. Thoreau the scryer, practicing this way of seeing, looks, like Blake, not "with" the eye but "thro it." He beholds not simply the lowest common denominator of "corporeal" sight—ice as static pyramid, sun as "round Disk of fire somewhat like a Guinea"—but also the striking revelation of intuitive vision—ice as leaves of light, sun as "Innumerable company of the Heavenly host crying Holy Holy Holy is the Lord God Almighty."[95]

PRISMS AND RHYMES

Thoreau enriches and expands these connections in his 1842 "A Natural History of Massachusetts," in which he recalls a walk on an icy morning of 1837 that was favorable for "crystalline botany."

When the first rays of the sun slanted over the scene, the grasses seemed hung with innumerable jewels, which jingled merrily as they were brushed by the foot of the traveler, and reflected all the hues of the rainbow, as he moved from side to side. It struck me that these ghost leaves, and the green ones whose forms they assume, were the creatures of but one law; that in obedience to the same law the vegetable juices swell gradually into the perfect leaf, on the one hand, and the crystalline particles troop to their standard in the same order, on the other. As if the material were indifferent, but the law one and invariable, and every plant in the spring but pushed up into and filled a permanent and eternal mould, which, summer and winter forever, is waiting to be filled.

This foliate structure is common to the coral and the plumage of birds, and to how large a part of animate and inanimate nature. The same independence of law on matter is observable in many other instances, as in the natural rhymes, when some animal form, color, or odor has its counterpart in some vegetable. As, indeed, all rhymes imply an eternal melody, independent of any particular sense. . . .

Vegetation has been made the type of all growth; but as in crystals the law is more obvious, their material being more simple, and for the most part more transient and fleeting, would it not be as philosophical as convenient to consider all growth . . . but a crystallization more or less rapid? (*NH* 52–4)

Thoreau is drawn to the frost-covered blades. They shimmer like "innumerable jewels" and reflect the "hues of the rainbow." Inspired by this image of kaleidoscopic gems, he elevates to a new trope: the blades as phantom adumbrations of leaves. He generalizes further. He conjectures that these frosty revelations and the more sappy ones in summer pattern one law. Widening his circle, he wonders if *all* material forms are manifestations of this law. If so, the favored form of this principle is the crystal, an archetypal structure, the "rhyme" scheme of all nature. Gathering into poetic harmony not only vegetable forms (leaves) and animal shapes (feathers) but also colors and odors, these crystal assonances and alliterations point to an "eternal melody," the music of the spheres humming beyond fleshy ears. Crystals, not leaves, should be "the type of all growth," for in crystals being is more brightly revealed.

Crystal shapes again captivate Thoreau. Their anatomies once more inspire him to create increasingly general tropes. These tropes empower him to intuit the primal form of life. In sum, his mind again turns crystal: reflective mirror and irradiating lamp, subjective power and objective recording.

Yet, Thoreau here recognizes new potencies. In likening the illuminated frost to jewels reflecting the rainbow, Thoreau notices that ice is a prism refracting white light into the diverse colors of the spectrum. The morning ice is a mediator between undifferentiated brightness and the different hues of the world, and thus a threshold between the one and the many (Ishmael's "colorless all color" and Hopkins' pied beauty). The crystal as prism bends, or turns, white light into diverse colors that hide and reveal the transparent brightness immanent in their opaque hues. This troping of colorless beams into kaleidoscopic fulgurations is "characterized by a translucence. . . . of the Eternal in and through the Temporal. It always partakes of the Reality which it renders intelligible; and while it annunciates the whole, abides itself as a living part in that Unity of which it is representative" (*CC* 6:30). These last words come from Coleridge's definition of the symbol in *Statesman's Manual* (1816) and suggest that the ice crystal as prism is a symbol of the symbol, an organic exemplification of what literary symbols sometimes achieve—"a living momentary revelation of the Inscrutable"[96]—to use Goethe's words in *Maxims and Reflections* (1829). Smitten by the poetics of nature (gazing at the crystal turn unsullied light into dazzling spectrums), Thoreau aptly creates his own tropes, turns of transparent feelings into words.

The crystal's colors point to a ubiquitous brightness. Its "foliate structure" suggests a form repeated throughout the universe. "Rhyming" with other structures—leaves and feathers—the crystal opens into a cosmic poem or symphony that expresses the eternal law through which vital energy becomes cogent form. Though this law is beyond observation and description ("independent of any particular sense"), it nonetheless partially reveals its virtues in a recurring foliated form common to frost (stable crystals), leaves (crystals that flutter), feathers (jewels that fly), and even humans (with minds like diamonds). Like Goethe's archetypes and Schelling's primary polarities, this crystalline form organizes—differentiates—the infinite, undifferentiated energy of life. Precipitations of holistic power, Thoreau's crystals are prototypical patterns of all growth—mergings of centrifugal vitality and centripetal cohesion, unity and diversity, mystery and solution.

As strangely attractive portals to holistic powers—pervasive light, reiterated form—Thoreau's crystals are not only extraordinary shapes that reveal mergings of form and energy. Weird windows, they are also strange mirrors. Disclosing both the universal white light and the pied forms into which this light coheres, crystals reflect to the beholder the energy and structure of his own being. They mirror to him his deepest self. They show him that beneath his discrete ego, he is a ubiquitous current: His "I" is really "nothing"—not this or that—but also "all"—a power gathering all thises, all thats. In pointing to the conclusions of Emerson's "transparent eye-ball" sequence, Thoreau suggests that each person, like every prismatic event, is a unique turn of ubiquitous light as well as a form common to all beings. Hence, people, properly seen, are simultaneously identical to and different from the whole, distributed and discrete.

To apprehend such an insight while gazing at the crystal is to experience what Emerson's visionary undergoes soon after metamorphosing into a "transparent eye-ball." After watching the world turn prism, Emerson's speaker concludes that "[t]he greatest delight which the fields and woods minister is the suggestion of an occult relation between man and the vegetable. I am not alone and unacknowledged. They nod to me, and I to them. The waving of the boughs in the storm is new to me and old. It takes me by surprise, and yet is not unknown" (*N* 13–14). The stormy scene, like Emerson's snows and Thoreau's frosts, is old and new, strange and common, because it reveals holistic powers both unfamiliar and familiar: unfamiliar because they are generally repressed by the discrete ego, familiar because they are the primordial currents distributed through all beings. The billowing storm, the snow puddles on the common, the hoar frost in the dawn are "uncanny": events that inspire the return of the repressed, alien because long hidden and intimate because always secretly present. Whether the repressed material is psychic and arises from the unconscious, as Freud maintains, or whether it is ontological and upsets reductive theories of Being, as Heidegger suggests, the uncanny is disturbing—akin to the gothic—but also transforming—associated with the sublime.[97] Experiencing an uncanny image—an illuminated crystal, or perhaps a nautilus, sea-torqued, or a storm-blown crocus—one is both disoriented and comfortable, bewildered by curious flickers and soothed by secure forms. Habitual ways of seeing are shattered by queer forces. These odd reverberations are inmost existence.

Thoreau's two uncanny sequences on frost—from 1837 and 1842—are not exceptional but reveal virtues of ice that persistently fascinated Thoreau. For instance, in February of 1851, Thoreau fixates on "fleets of ice flakes" that reflect the sun like "mirrors" and embody nature's "art" (*TJ* 3:190). Likewise, in January of 1852, Thoreau likens ice to "foliage" as well as "the characters of some oriental language" (4:238–9). Later that month, the snow inspires him to conclude that there is "a vegetable life as well as a spiritual and animal life in us" (279). In January of 1853, Thoreau marvels over a frozen waterfall spangled with "egg shaped diamonds" and "branch fungus icicle[s]" (5:456). Snow crystals in January of 1856 motivate this insight: "[T]he same law that shapes the earth-star shapes the snow star . . . [E]ach of these countless snow-stars comes whirling to earth, pronouncing . . . Order, *kosmos.*"[98]

TRANSPARENCY, ORGANICITY, EXTRAVAGANCE

Thoreau's early and abiding studies of crystals yield to him insights on vision, nature, and language. Scrying the morning frost, he sees *through* the shimmering lattices to the primal crystalline form organizing the amorphous force of life. He realizes: The crystal is not only in the ice but also in trees, birds, and men. Hence, everything—well perceived by a mind that becomes itself a crystalline mirror and lamp—is a crystal: a transparent portal through which one might discern invisible powers criss-crossing the cosmos. Viewing the world through a crystal lens, Thoreau penetrates the hidden law by which the one becomes the many, energy turns to form. He understands that holistic life functions in polarized patterns, gatherings of centrifugal power and centripetal stability, turbulence and geometry. Organic forms, Thoreau further realizes, resemble poetic forms. Crystal structures—whether they thrive in ice, leaves, wings, or brains—are tropes, turning invisible energy (white light) into visible images (pied spectrums). Specifically, they are synecdoches, parts partaking of and revealing the whole, opaquely transparent windows and uncanny mirrors partially disclosing the mysterious power of which they—and everything else—are made.

Thoreau's crystallography, then, not only offers an intrinsically interesting interpretation of frozen shapes. It also provides potent hermeneutical tools for analyzing three of Thoreau's most persistent concerns in *Walden:* "transparency," "formation," "extravagance," registers, respectively, for "optics," "organicism," and "poetics."[99]

One of Thoreau's main endeavors at Walden Pond is to turn the world to a glass through which he can study nature's deepest secrets. He highlights this optical quest in the first chapter, "Economy," in which he indirectly compares his poor sight at the beginning of his sojourn to the clouded vision of a "groping" goose. Only days into his season, he has not yet learned to penetrate his opaque environment. Like the goose, he is lost in fog (*W* 42). As he announces in the next chapter, "Where I Lived, What I Lived For," one reason that he leaves Concord is to escape such opacity: "We inhabitants of New England live this mean life that we do because our vision does not penetrate the surface of things" (96). To avoid such a base existence, firmly linked to the inability to scry, Thoreau retires to the pond, where he hopes to turn the moving shapes of time into a transparent stream through which he can "detect" the "bottom"—the basics of life pervading muck and stars, ephemerality and eternity (98). Aptly, he begins his next chapter, "Reading," by suggesting that noble books, properly construed, can unveil "the statue of divinity" and thus vouchsafe a vision of eternity (99). Likewise, in his fourth chapter, "Sounds," he conjectures that the more universal grammar of nature might, if a "seer" could peer into its forms, reveal "fate," a path to "futurity" (111). In the next chapter, "Solitude," Thoreau supposes that all events—textual, natural, and otherwise—might disclose to the "awakened" man that "power which fashions . . . being" (134).

These passages account for Thoreau's fixation on the Pond: The water is perfectly transparent, constituting a "great crystal on the surface of the earth" (*W* 199), and thus features a quality that he desires to discover in *everything*: "crystalline purity." "The water," he observes, "is so transparent that the bottom can be easily discerned at the depth of twenty-five or thirty feet." Sailing over the pond, he can "see many feet beneath the surface the schools of perch and shiners, perhaps only an inch long." From the pond's frozen surface, he can find and retrieve a lost ax, even though it rests some twenty-five feet below (177–8). Likewise, he finds that "such transparent and seemingly bottomless water" not only reveals its depths below but also reflects the clouds above. Hence, to float on this translucent surface is also to fly in the air, and to watch fish become birds (189–90). This "sky water" is in addition a "mirror which no stone can crack," "in which all impurity presented to it sinks, swept and dusted by the sun's hazy brush" (188). To stare into such a clear mirror is to perceive one's own best self merged with the fish below and the clouds above as well as to sense subtle spirits otherwise unseen, for a "field of water betrays the spirit that is in the air" (188). Disclosing the deeps and marrying opposites, the pond moreover comprises a standard of beauty. It—along with White Pond—is "much more beautiful than our lives," "much more transparent than our characters" (199). Hyaline like "precious stones," these liquid surfaces are better able to reflect and thus to intensify light than are more opaque bodies. They are "Lakes of Light," fiery concentrations of the ubiquitous luminosity often unnoticed in the loose atmosphere. Frozen, Walden water features similar virtues. As Thoreau claims in "House-Warming," the pond's first ice—"being hard, dark, and transparent—"affords the best opportunity that ever offers for examining the bottom where it is shallow" (246). In "Pond in Winter," the transparency of the blue ice inspires him to consider "ice" as "an interesting subject for contemplation," for frozen water seems to remain "sweet forever" while thawed liquid "soon becomes putrid (297).

Like the morning ice Thoreau earlier observed in his journal (*TJ* 1:22) and in "Natural History of Massachusetts," the crystalline water—frozen or thawed—constitutes a special means of vision. The transparent surface—which Thoreau actually calls "earth's eye" (*W* 186)—allows Thoreau to view depths, interpenetrations, brightnesses, and durations that he would not normally perceive. Looking into the sheet of thawed water (using it for his eyes), he apprehends the pond's "bottomless water"; notices marriages between muck and clouds, form and space, spirit and matter, subject and object; discerns the air's currents and the sun's beams more intensely revealed; and apprehends mergings of time (blue ice) and eternity (eternal sweetness). Sounding from the frozen surface, he recovers things otherwise lost, such as his axe and the pond's deepest bottom—which, though measurable, inspires thoughts of abysmal depths.

In each of these cases, Thoreau meshes his organs of vision, his physical eye and his perceptive mind, with the optical powers of the crystalline pond. He reflects (records the physical configurations of the pond) as well as irradiates (creates tropes that transform the water to lens, mirror, jewel, air). He gathers lucid images (clouds on the surface, fish underneath) and murky blurrings (the muddy bottom that seems bottomless). He melds visible rhythms (the blue-green ripples) and invisible currents (the spirits of air). Scrying thus—metamorphosing into and thus mimicking the angel frame—he consents to his place in the crystal cosmos. He is a form of ubiquitous light. He is a particular refraction of the brightness.

If the pond's transparency facilitates the means of seeing, it also symbolizes the ideal end of vision. In "Pond in Winter," soon after he has measured the distance between the pond's surface and its bottom, Thoreau admits that he is "thankful that this pond was made deep and pure for a symbol" (*W* 287). Though he does not say exactly what the pond symbolizes, he suggests that it points to crystalline qualities that all beings, including himself, secretly possess. Properly seen—viewed through a crystal lens—each being is not merely a unit of opaque matter but also a transparent pattern of holistic energies. As we have seen, Thoreau desires to spend his Walden days engaged in such acts of proper seeing. He wishes to turn his activities—ranging from building to reading to listening to digging to bathing to fishing to planting—as well as the phenomena he studies—such as books

and loons and owls and woodchoppers and leaves that blow—
into windows through which he can see constant laws and mirrors in which he can view his own essential nature. In essaying to
discover covert crystals in opaque elements, Thoreau tries to
find in *everything* what he perceives in the Pond, what he enacts
in his own seeing.

Thoreau's mode of scrying—his crystallographic epistemology—
is richly instanced in the thawing-bank sequence in the "Spring"
chapter, a revelation of the process by which vital energy crystallizes
into discrete formations. Standing before the melting mud, Thoreau
fixates, again, on foliated shapes, leaf crystals.

> Innumerable little streams overlap and interlace one with an-
> other, exhibiting a sort of hybrid product, which obeys half way
> the law of currents, and half way that of vegetation. As it flows it
> takes the forms of sappy leaves or vines, making heaps of pulpy
> sprays a foot or more in depth, and resembling . . . the lacini-
> ated, lobed, and imbricated thalluses of some lichens; or you are
> reminded of coral, of leopards' paws or birds' feet, of brains or
> lungs or bowels, and excrements. . . .
>
> When I see . . . this luxuriant foliage, the creation of an
> hour, I am affected as if in a peculiar sense I stood in the labora-
> tory of the Artist who made the world and me,—had come to
> where he was still at work, sporting on this bank, and with ex-
> cess of energy strewing his fresh designs about. I feel as if I were
> nearer to the vitals of the globe, for this sandy overflow is some-
> thing such a foliaceous mass as the vitals of the animal body. You
> find thus in the very sands an anticipation of the vegetable
> leaf. . . . The feathers and wings of birds are still drier and thin-
> ner leaves. . . . The very globe continually transcends and trans-
> lates itself, and becomes winged in its orbit. Even the ice begins
> with delicate crystal leaves, as if it had flowed into moulds which
> the fronds of water plants have impressed on the watery mirror.
> (*W* 305–6)

Thoreau studies the mud through his "crystal" eye, discerning in it depths, interpenetrations, brightnesses, and durations that he might not normally discern. Under this gaze, the sliding muck becomes more than mere dirt. It opens into the "vitals of the globe," the chthonic surge of being. It reveals interdependencies between bounded (earthy globes) and unbounded (birds unfettered); flux ("sandy overflow") and structure ("vegetable leaf"); chance (the Ur-Artist "sporting") and law (nature's recurring forms). Formerly opaque, this muck now shimmers with invisible laws. Creeping in time, finite, it discloses organic processes transcending temporality, infinite—not confined to this or that but present in everything.

Thoreau in this passage senses in the flowing mud what he earlier perceived in the crystal dawn: the law of natural formation. Amid the burgeoning blooms of spring, he aptly apprehends in the leaf, not the crystal, the primal cosmic form. However, the leaves now coalescing the mud are strikingly analogous to the crystals that before organized the water. In both cases—walking on a winter morning or standing, stunned, before the spring thaw—Thoreau witnesses what Goethe saw in plants, bones, and rocks, what Schelling intuited in the universe's polarized rhythms: not simple order, cosmos, nor mere disorder, chaos, but rather a mutual arising of abyss and pattern—*chaosmos*.[100] Envisioning the Artist of the universe metamorphosing muck into lobes and globes, Thoreau realizes that this creator is no Jehovah separating chaos and order and no Platonic maker mimicking the static forms of eternity. This demiurge is playful. He sports in the ooze. He strews fresh designs. Yet, disciplined, he persistently concocts the same basic form: the leaf. In the mire, is the incipient leaf. The hawk's flick: leaf rarified. The brain is bulbous lichen. The heart photosynthesizes blood. Everything is sap cohered into a frond. But what is a leaf but a foliate structure, a verdurous crystal?

Watching chaos turn into form, Thoreau thinks of tropes—of how each reticulated pattern is a symbol of the whole, a word of the abyss. Leaf crystal is *logos*, word frond, water made flesh. Internally, this archetypal pattern is liquid potential (the unformed abyss, a centrifugal energy). It is a "lobe," a word embodying in sound its properties. "[L]*obe*" is "especially applicable to the liver and lungs and the *leaves* of fat, (λειβω, *labor, lapsus*, to flow or slip downward, a lapsing; λοβοζ, *globus*, lobe, globe; also lap, flap, and many other words)." This sap presses into a more stable material form (a balance of centrifugal and centripetal forces), rendered linguistically by the liquid "B" stiffening into the more solid "F" or "V." Externally, the lobe forms "a dry thin *leaf*, even as the *f* and *v* are a pressed and dried *b* . . . with a liquid *l* behind it pressing it forward" (*W* 306).

The natural process by which water takes the shape of the crystalline leaf is enacted by the word "leaf." The word "leaf," like a biological leaf, is nature's "constant cypher." It bears the sense and sound of universe. Fluid, figured by "l" pushing into "b," and form, "f" and "v," "leaf" reveals the cosmic polarity between turbulence and pattern. Liquid "l," alveolar sonorant, flowing into bilabial voiced stop "b," and forming eventually into labiodental voiceless spirant "f," the word sounds the rhythm by which the world hums. All events, ceaselessly metamorphosing imbrications of liquid energy and solid organization, are thus "translations" of lobes into crystals or crystal into lobes.

Moved by nature's uncanny tropes—leafy crystals and crystalline fronds—Thoreau attempts to mirror organic process by creating his own transparent leaves: the pages of *Walden*. For Thoreau, studied in winter's convoluted crystals and spring's intricate leaves, linguistic transparency is not discursive pellucidity, not Bacon's plain style or Locke's clear communication. On the contrary, for Thoreau, as for Emerson, a transparent style should reveal the manifold paradoxes and powers coursing through the gracefully turbid universe. Hence, Thoreau's *crystal* transparency—as opposed to the *pure* transparency of a mystical Plotinian or an abstracting Newtonian—requires inversion: Untroubled clarity is opacity, a reduction of dynamic polarity to stable harmony; agitated convolution is transparency, a revelation of tense imbrications between obscure energy and geometric form.

To understand this crystal transparency—duplicitous, perplexed, *paralogical*—is to feel the force of a seeming contradiction troubling the pages of *Walden:* the book's persistent call for simplicity in a bewilderingly complex style. Though Thoreau spends most of the "Where I Lived, What I Lived For" chapter urging "Simplicity, simplicity, simplicity," he concludes his book by fearing "chiefly lest [his] expression may not be *extra-vagant* enough, may not wander far enough beyond the narrows limits of [his] daily experience" (*W* 91, 324). Yet, this ostensible clash is in fact perfectly logical. The "simplicity" of nature is not its accessibility or clarity but rather its strangeness, its sublimity. Recall: "simple" emerges from the Indo-European root *sm-*, which means "samefold," and from the Latin *simplus*, signifying "single." To be simple is literally to be undifferentiated and thus beyond diversity— abysmal, ungraspable. The simplicity of nature, then, is not only its elegant laws—its harmonious geometries—but also its "mysterious," "unexplorable" powers—its infinite wildness (317–8).

Ice crystals and spring leaves alike reveal nature's simplicity, nature's extravagance. Mimicking the playful maker of this luridly transparent cosmos, Thoreau creates his own simple crystals, his own extravagant leaves. For instance, in the melting-bank passage quoted above (*W* 305–6), his diction yields a series of disorientating polarities. The "Artist who made the world" inhabits a "laboratory"—a site of disciplined labor—but spends his "work" time by "sporting"—frolicking with random glee. Yet, this "excess of energy"—overflowing the tubes of his lab—is nonetheless ruled by "law," a principle that admits no superfluity. How can this artist be both scientist and jester? How can his creations be orderly and chaotic? Moreover, we wonder how the "atoms" produced by this artist "learn" his laws. How can an unconscious element consciously accrue knowledge? Certain individual words likewise disconcert. When Thoreau stares at the melting bank, he is "affected as if in a *peculiar* sense" he stood before the primal artist. "Peculiar" here clearly means "unique" or "special" but also suggests "odd" or "eccentric" as well as "possessive" ("peculiar" derives from French and Latin roots concerned with the ownership of private property). Hence, standing before the mud, Thoreau is both "proper"—at home, as it were, on his property, self-possessed on his possession—and "strange"—displaced from the norm, not at home in the familiar world. Double, he watches the "Artist who made the world" "*still* at work." As in Keats's "Ode on a Grecian Urn," "still" as adverb connotes both "without movement" and "up until this time"—tranquility and perpetual motion. Agitated yet calm, this artist strews about fresh "*designs.*" A "design" is of course a composed pattern, a planned artifice, but also, etymologically, a movement from meaning—a motion from (*de*) the stable sign (*signum*).

On the one hand, these various tensions are paradoxes, surface contradictions that are nonetheless true—Thoreau's extravagantly simple cosmos plays between chance and law, spontaneity and structure, identity and difference, perpetual motion and unmoving calm, meaning and meaninglessness. Yet, on the other hand, these semantic gaps remain unclosed, irreducible contradictions. Laws cannot be random, atoms are not able to study, comfortable men are not strange to themselves, an artist cannot be still and still moving, and designs are not both present and absent at the same time. As in the case of Emerson's *Nature*, these tensions, reconcilable and irreconcilable, form a yet larger rift that pervades the entire book, a synthesis of and division between opposites. *Walden* is Keats's Grecian urn and James's golden bowl.

Thoreau's passage instances the linguistic extravagance strewn throughout *Walden*. For example, the final paragraph of "Where I

Lived, What I Lived For" is a disorienting mixture of puns and paradoxes, odd images and surreal conceits:

> Time is but the stream I go a-fishing in. I drink at it; but while I drink I see the sandy bottom and detect how shallow it is. Its thin current slides away, but eternity remains. I would drink deeper; fish in the sky, whose bottom is pebbly with stars. I cannot count one. I know not the first letter of the alphabet. I have always been regretting that I was not as wise as the day I was born. The intellect is a cleaver; it discerns and rifts its way into the secret of things. I do not wish to be any more busy with my hands than is necessary. My head is hands and feet. I feel all my best faculties concentrated in it. My instinct tells me that my head is an organ for burrowing, as some creatures use their snout and fore-paws, and with it I would mine and burrow my way through these hills. I think that the richest vein is somewhere hereabouts; so by the divining rod and thin rising vapors I judge; and here I will begin to mine. (*W* 98)

Likewise, the final sentences of the book feature startling disjunctions, curious torquings: "The light which puts out our eyes is darkness to us. Only that day dawns to which we are awake. There is more day to dawn. The sun is but a morning star" (333). In the same way, several strangely arresting sentences introduce the reader into crystal chambers, gloomy and flaming: "A man is rich in porportion to the number of things which he can afford to leave alone" (82); "I long ago lost a hound, a bay horse, and a turtle-dove, and am still on their trail" (17); "Olympus is but the outside of earth everywhere" (85); "The value of a man is not in his skin, that we should touch him" (136); "The life in us is like the water in a river" (332).

After undergoing the dreamy convolutions of these passages—ironically transparent in their power to reveal complex simplicity—the one wonders if the ostensibly denotative moments in the book—unexpectedly opaque by comparison—are likewise, when scried, portals to the core. One begins to track Thoreau's uses of seemingly common words, like "account," "labor," or "economy." He realizes that these words in the end oppose themselves, and thus paralogically violate the principle of noncontradiction. "Account" becomes pragmatic mathematics and fantastic confession; "labor" is deadening work for pay and miraculous act of birth; "economy" transforms into the greed of monetary exchange and the care for one's ownmost ecology. Likewise, this same reader, still altered by shocking transparencies, rethinks the significance of Thoreau's seemingly mundane descriptions of building, fishing, hoeing, fire building, measuring, eating. He understands that each of these tasks is not merely a daily job but also a synecdoche of the whole—a merging of wild instinct and civilized discipline, vital heat and cool form.

If reading Emerson's *Nature* is like touring a crystal asylum, a mostly colorless abode flickering between shade and light, then persuing Thoreau's *Walden* feels like peregrinating over a wild forest, pied and alive, fecund with heterogeneous forms—ants, ferns, loons, woodchoppers, a dead horse. Yet, in both cases, the reader oscillates between relatively untroubled movements and disturbing arrests, between accessibly "opaque" discourse and cryptically "transparent" prose poems. For periods, he treads on somewhat familiar ground without much strain or surprise. Yet, at certain turns, he unexpectedly encounters coruscating quartz, a leaf on fire. In the weird window, the uncanny mirror, he sees unreal shapes, mergings of light and color, here and beyond, self and other. He returns to the common terrain, to the relatively untroubled prose. Nothing is the same. What seemed habit is now hypnagogic.

POETICS OF SELF-ORGANIZATION

Picture the flat, smoothly flowing surface of a calm river. Each part of this uniform plane resembles every other part—indifferent green or self-same brown. This tranquil flux, this monotonous course in which nothing is distinct from anything, constitutes a heterogeneous symbol. It suggests the stream of time, blandly creeping forward, one moment just like the last. It intimates habit, which reduces difference to the same. It evokes entropy, the pure equilibrium of extreme disorder, in which everything blurs into indifference. Curiously, it gestures toward the undifferentiated energy of being, life *in potentia*, not yet torqued into actual organs.

The flow, on a December day, suddenly freezes into floating crystals of ice, soon to cohere into a plane of shining fire. The distributed flow organizes itself into discrete patterns. Out of nowhere, the formless leaps into form—silence to word, mud to jewel. Time as bland succession becomes temporality as rhythm—movement and stasis, force and geometry. The habitual shatters into interesting gems, fresh experiences. Entropy jumps into negentropy, flat disorder into cubic textures. Being becomes beings.

The crystal, coalesced from a featureless sheet of water, suggests a poetics of self-organization[101]—poetic forms that mimic the processes by which holistic powers metamorphose (turn, trope) into individual organs. This is Thoreau's cosmos (as it is Emerson's, and Goethe's and Schelling's): an organic system in which distinct beings organize an indifferent energy of life. Organs arise from this abyss as crystals from the pond, but also as eddies from the stream, waves from the sea, knots from the oak, rainbows from light. Everything—as form and energy, pattern and turbulence—is a crystal in various states of solidity. All things—differences of indifference, vortices of the void—are eddies in different states of liquidity.

This cosmos is the revelation of crystal. A crystalline poetics discloses the crystalline universe. To read in a certain mood Thoreau's *Walden*—an oscillation between stable argument and agitated lyricism, steady flow and quick crystallization—is to be shocked into a new awareness of the world: a new sense of nouns as verb, verbs as nouns, stones as storms, and tornadoes as calm cones. Though all natural and linguistic patterns always embody and exhibit these interfaces, we in our desire to keep disorder in one category and order in another, forget that cosmos floats on chaos. We need sacred symbols to remind us of this fact. We need ice shining from the flood, and from logic, the *logos* rising.

FROZEN NETWORKS

Thoreau's transparency, like Emerson's, is not *pure* transparency but a crystalline coincidence of limpidity and obscurity. Achieving this merger is difficult. Most, unable to sustain the balance, grasp for pure transcendency, total clarity, or fall into mere opacity, impervious density. Problems exist at either extreme. To desire pure transparency is to ignore the forms of nature, to turn organs to ghostly frames of unseen principles. To fixate on opacity is to neglect invisible laws, to see events as hunks of matter. In the former case, one is overly attentive to the abstract. In the latter, one is too concerned with the concrete. The abstractor severs himself from particulars—every cow is white in his eternal day. The concretizer divorces himself from universals—he fixates on *this* cow only, piebald. Each sees with only one eye.

Transforming the world to crystal is as dangerous as it is exhilarating. If the crystal can vouchsafe holy visions, then it can also seduce its beholder into forests of error. Its opaque reflections, dazzling and bewildering, can pull him to the part and sever him from the whole. Its transparent windows, clear as water, can lead him to ignore the concrete and relate only to concepts. If the crystal is a luminous eye through which infinity appears, it is also a network, a labyrinth of angles capable of constraining its observer in a tangle of confusing opacities or a ghostworld of bloodless transparencies.

Thoreau is aware of these seductions. Essaying to balance thinking and thingness, he meditates on unbalanced men entrapped by the pond's nets. Those constrained by crystal fall into two classes: those who desire pristine clarity and thus reduce matter to mind, and those who sink to mere density and hence flatten mind to matter.

Men of the former class assume that they are superior to and different from the natural qualities that they abstract into priced commodities fit only for human consumption. This desire to transform nature into number, thing to nothing, is exemplified by the Walden ice cutters. These cutters—"a hundred Irishmen, with Yankee overseers"—slice the crystalline surface into equally sized cakes and stack these cakes "as so many barrels of flour," "evenly side by side, and row upon row." Valuing the ice only for the price it will bring, the cutters ignore the fascinating qualities of the be-jeweled surface. They carve its fragile diamonds into a mess of "deep ruts" and "cradle holes." However, in spite of these efforts to turn the crystals into marketable units, much of the ice defies commodification. It melts, returns to Walden Pond (*W* 294–6).

Ostensibly an example of the free enterprise, this business of cutting is an instance of slavery. The Irish workers are "slaves" to their Yankee overseers. The bosses are dependent upon the workers' labor. But Irish subordinate and Yankee foreman alike are further constrained by a more subtle form of slavery—the double bind of the desire for pure transparency. On the one hand, these cutters are imprisoned by their own abstractions. Transmuting quality to quantity, they reduce different events—ice aqua in the sun, and in the shade, bluish—to the same idea: profitability. They flatten radiance to ratio. They see the same abstractions wherever they look. They blind themselves with the brightness of their own concepts. They are trapped in what Blake calls the "dull round."[102] On the other hand, these same cutters are slaves to the concrete events that they try to master. The ice, seeping back into the pond, resists the cutters' commodification. It secretly dictates their activities and agitates their speculations.

Transforming Thoreau's description of the cutters into a parable, we understand that their activities are dangerous reductions of organs to machines. Blind to spontaneous events that do not conform to their anthropocentric grids, these cutters perceive only their own dreams of order. They flatten the world to Blake's Ulro: a Newtonian universe in which inanimate atoms are mechanically moved by blind force into predictable configurations. Yet, this perfectly arranged world is waste, for organization without fluctuation is moribund.[103] To degrade the numinous to number, crystal to commodity, is to conceive the cosmos as a motionless plane, a surface of *dead* ice. Onto this unmoving sheet, the Concord entrepreneur, the Newtonian physicist, imposes his graphs and charts. He thinks that he is nobly translating the intractable world into thriving human institutions. He believes that he is exercising his freedom to transmute his environment into a double of human order. However, unbeknownst to him, he creates a colossal motor in which he is but a cog.

Crystal nets also enweb a second class of men. Unlike the cutters, these men assume from the start that they, though human, are material hunks determined by other material hunks. For Thoreau, these more passive inmates of matter fall into two classes: the dissatisfied and the satisfied. In the former category is John Field, an impoverished Irishman living with his family in a shack near Fair Haven Pond. He sees the nearby pond and neighboring meadow not as abstract grids of numbers or sites of entrepreneurial speculation but as vats of immediate sustenance: fish to be eaten, peat-bog to be burned. Stupid, lethargic, unhappy, Field is confined by a limited horizon, beset by "boggy ways," moored by "bog-trotting feet." The crystalline pond tells him only this: He is simply a bit of existence, pushed and pulled about like so much flotsam (*W* 204–9). Countering Field, yet still unconsciously moored to matter, is the Canadian woodchopper, Alex Therien, a happy, "simple and natural man." A noble savage, this woodsman overflows with animal spirits, attracting Thoreau with his honesty, spontaneity, and energy. He is more "at home" in his world than many learned or rich men. However, though Thoreau admires this man, he finds that Therien is as limited as Field. Though in him the "animal man" is developed to a high and engaging degree, "the intellectual and what is called spiritual man in him [are] slumbering as in an infant." Like Field, he believes that opaque matter is all there is—immediate shapes, dark, dictate his behavior (144–50). He and Field, despite their differences, are confined by a single bind. Possessing no desire to transcend or skill to abstract, they are no freer than fish or cow.

Though Field and Therien avoid the mechanistic leveling of the cutters, they nonetheless envision and inhabit a severely limited universe. If the cutters move in Ulro, Field and Therien struggle in Blake's realm of Generation: a Darwinian environment in which everything lives only to survive.[104] Generation reduces a man to his lowest instincts: desire to eat, fear of being eaten. Constrained thus, the man of Generation—either the noble savage or the ignoble vulgarian—cannot free himself into distinctively *human* activities: artistic creation, philosophical speculation.

SKATING ON THE SURFACES

Avoiding these extremes, Thoreau, informed by crystal, takes a middle path. He views the cosmos as an exuberant substance and insubstantial spirit, wild instinct and pristine form. He explores the difficulties of achieving this balance between primitive energy (the desire for the concrete) and civilized elegance (the yen for the abstract) in his discussion of "chastity." As Thoreau suggests in his "Higher Laws" chapter in *Walden*, chastity is not sexual abstinence but a mode of negotiating between animal attachment to mere opacity and civilized fixation on pure transparency.

Thoreau believes that we can probably never escape the "animal in us." Enjoying a "health of its own," this "reptile and sensual" energy is likely an essential part of us. However, unchecked animal instinct results in crass "sensualism." To avoid vulgarity without denying animal energy, one must open to "spirit," which can "pervade and control every member and function of [the] body" and "transmute what in form is grossest sensuality into purity and devotion" (*W* 219). Inspired and invigorated by this "generative energy," the "chaste" man "flows at once to God." He "flowers" into a creative being and produces fruits: "Genius, Heroism, and Holiness" (220).[105]

Chastity frees one from animal needs and thus opens him to invisible energies that inspire graceful turns. Yet, chastity is not merely liberation from fixation on the concrete. It is also an emancipation from compulsion for the abstract. As "the flowering of man" that produces the "fruits" of civilization, chastity requires a palpable feeling for organic energy, the hum of life. Refusing to reduce this current to concept, the chaste man gives over to its flow. Nourished, he channels the stream into brilliant poems, heroic leaps, saintly postures. He is a photosynthesizing plant, passively inhaling ubiquitous air and light, only to exhale these powers, actively, in new forms that inspire the environment. He is ice. He transmutes pervasive white into gorgeous hues.

Chastity is not for the prude but the *parthenos*. Associated with Diana and Artemis, *parthenos* suggests a woman who is not sexually abstinent but simply unattached, not married to this man or that, everyone's lover and no one's. Maiden and strumpet, the *parthenos* enjoys the virtues of asceticism and sensuality without being limited by either. Free to draw from the virtues of the animal without sliding into vulgarity, free to enjoy civilized forms without becoming stiff, the *parthenos*, like Thoreau's chaste poet, hero, or saint, *plays* at life.[106]

Thoreau's chastity resembles what Friedrich Schiller in his *Letters on the Aesthetic Education of Man* (1795) calls the play drive (*Spieltrieb*). This impulse liberates one from attachments to the sense drive (*Stofftrieb*) or the form drive (*Formtrieb*) and thus releases him to merge these opposing principles into aesthetic syntheses. Schiller, like Thoreau, maintains that most people are obsessed by sensuality or rationality. The man overcome by the sense drive is concerned only with his "physical existence" or "sensuous nature." He is set "within the bounds of time" and therefore little different from matter. He is John Field or Alex Therien, fixated on mere opacity. On the other hand, if one is bent on his form drive, he associates himself with an absolute, rational principle above the vicissitudes of time. He believes that his reasonable ego is an eternal substance untouched by the accidents of matter. He falls into the same class with Thoreau's ice cutters, men blinded by pure transparency.[107] Both the overly formal theorist and the excessively sensual practitioner are very limited, attaching themselves only to one half of existence and ignoring the other. The sensuous man is confined to matter at its lowest level, mere physical necessity. The formal man is moored to his concepts. Wherever he looks, he sees only his own mind outwardly projected.

A way to escape these binds is through the play drive, the energy behind the contemplation, embodiment, or creation of beauty. Engaging in aesthetic activities, one finds himself in "a happy midway point between law [domain of the form drive] and exigency [realm of the sense drive]." The playing man draws from the powers of the sensual and formal "since the former relates in its cognition to the actuality" and the "latter to the necessity of things." Yet, he is bound to neither. He realizes that the sensual, when measured against formal ideas, becomes "*small*," and that the reason, when related to immediate perceptions, grows "*light*." The playing man is able to place the formal and the sensual into a perpetual, creative dialogue in which one side constantly delimits and

ennobles the other.[108] Thus, the aesthetically educated man takes
the sensual and the formal *somewhat* seriously. He knows that each
impulse is required for beauty but that neither alone can provide
aesthetic education. Oscillating between law and chance, he is
Thoreau's sporting artist. Simple and extravagant, he is Thoreau.

Through aesthetic chastity, playful and serious, Thoreau rises
above Ulro and Generation to Blake's Beulah, nature humanized
into a beautiful garden.[109] Apprehending in nature not mere order
or simple turbulence, Thoreau senses the coincidence of both.
The world, properly seen, is always Beulah, crystalline wildness.
Indeed, as Blake intimates in "The Crystal Cabinet" (ca. 1807),
Beulah is a crystalline geometry of mirrors and windows. Though
its labyrinthine reflections can seduce its denizens to narcissistic
gazing, and thus to Ulro, it can also inspire its inhabitants to see
through its glass portals to Eden, realm of eternal energy devoid
of temporal forms.[110]

Thoreau, like Blake, knows that "Eternity is in love with the
productions of time."[111] Though both poets seem at times to want
to transcend the painful divisions of time to the blissful harmonies
of eternity, Blake and Thoreau in the end realize that the physical
world, intuitively perceived, is not different from eternity, not a
botched imitation of some timeless perfection. Visible nature is
the aesthetic expression of an eternal artist—a cosmic artificer, un-
constrained by clock or map, playfully creating forms that delight
his imagination. The temporal realm is the proper precipitation of
untimed energy. To grasp unbounded power, one must embrace
bounded forms. The fact is fantastic—a circumference between
Here and There. The symbol is synecdoche—a part partaking of
and containing the whole. To become obsessed by either the part
or the whole, by either there or here, is to split into a half-life. To
live "amid surfaces"—frozen ponds and icy leaves—while
"skat[ing] well on them" is, as Emerson theorizes and as Thoreau
teaches, "the true art of life" (*EW* 3: 35).

In his eulogy of Thoreau, Emerson reported that his difficult friend "returned Kane's Arctic Voyage to a friend of whom he borrowed it, with the remark, that most of the phenomena noted might be observed in Concord."[112] Thoreau concludes *Walden* by questioning the wanderlust of John Franklin, the polar explorer who disappeared in the Arctic Circle, and of John Symmes, the St. Louis captain who dreamed of a hole at the South Pole through which he could access the earth's core (*W* 322). Travels to these Arctic climes, Thoreau believes, are escapes from the most pressing and important regions: local interiors, earth household, ecology. In the morning frost, one can see the cosmos, and then he will never see anything the same way again.

The crystal is ice in its most microcosmic, accessible form. Not all admire such *minima*. Others require larger forms of ice, vaster glimmerings of white and light, more extreme motions. These embracers of the glacier go for the mesocosm, ice not as atom but as organ, not as bright diagram but as dynamic force. Traveling to Alpine peaks, the poet of glaciers leaves his homestead, the rime on his window. He goes where the overt wonders are, the strange groanings of ice. There, overwhelmed by crushing heights, he perceives what the burghers below can never experience: the snowy demiurge that transforms planet to globe. He can see what Shelley, stunned, saw below Mont Blanc, what Byron's Manfred, bewildered, beheld in the Alps.

Two

GLACIERS

Snow mountains, more than sea or sky, serve as a mirror to one's own true being, utterly still, a void, an Emptiness without life or sound that carries in Itself all life, all sound. Yet as long as I remain an "I" who is conscious of the void and stands apart from it, there will remain a snow mist on the mirror.

—*Peter Matthiessen,* The Snow Leopard

THE COLD DEMIURGE

In *Suspiria de Profundis* (1845), his reverie on how the "dreaming organ" "throws dark reflections from eternities below all life," Thomas De Quincey directs his hallucinatory gaze toward the phantom of Brocken. Appearing from time to time on this peak in the Harz Mountains, this misty specter mimics the gestures of climbers robust enough to ascend to its cloudy lair. Though this phantom is actually a haze whose water drops reflect images, scientific explanation does not reduce the spirit to comfortable fact. On the contrary, to learn that this mountain wisp is "but a reflex of yourself" is to understand that "in uttering your secret feelings to him, you make this phantom the dark symbolic mirror for reflecting

to the daylight what else must be forever hidden." This "Dark In-
terpreter" mirrors and thus reveals desires repressed during the
day.[1] He is an uncanny double. He discloses the shadows of the unconscious as the springs of familiar light.

De Quincey's conflation of mountains, magic, science, and the
uncanny—a merging that also occurs in Shelley's "Mont Blanc"
(1816)—is not a unique concatenation. The history of Alpine glaciers is replete with sorcery in the crags, positivistic studies of
moving ice, and curious revelations of primal energies men
nonetheless forget.

Appropriately, Goethe, a magus of Brocken,[2] first imagined
miraculous glacial powers almost a decade before Louis Agassiz
offered empirical evidence for the shaping actions of "God's great
plough[s]."[3] In *Wilhelm Meister's Journeyman Years* (1828), the second installment of his *Bildungsroman*, Goethe places his hero at a
mining festival. A debate ensues on the geological "creation and
origin of the earth"—the globe's own *Bildungsroman*. Some of the
debaters maintain the Neptunist theory: The present surface of
the globe is a product of a "gradual recession" of waters once covering the world. Countering this notion, made famous by
Abraham Gottlob Werner, are Vulcanists. Following James Hutton, they argue that an "all-pervading" fire, now raging in the
bowels of volcanoes, once heated and melted the earth into its
present shape. Another school proposes that mountains now ascending from the plains once lurked in subterranean realms before
"irresistible forces" drove them through the crust. This violent
convulsion randomly scattered chunks of rock throughout lower
elevations. Yet another party claims that these stones fell from
above. "Two or three quiet guests" return the conversation to a
more empirical level. They claim that there was once a "period of
fierce cold" when glaciers spread from the highest mountain
ranges far into the flatlands. These creeping freezes formed immense slides over which rocks skated free of their cloudy origins

down into the plains. During a later thaw, these rocks sank deep into the ground, "forever locked in alien territory."[4]

This theory of an ice age, during which glaciers like cold demiurges fashioned the structure of the globe, meets with violent criticism. The other scientists prefer to believe that the world was "created with colossal crashes and upheavals, wild raging and fiery catapulting."[5] Still, Goethe himself speculated in 1829 that "there was an epoch of great cold, at a time when waters covered the continent up to 1,000 feet in height [and] . . . the glaciers of the Savoy mountains went farther down, all the way to the sea."[6]

Goethe likely deserves scientific credit for imagining the Pleistocene Ice Age before Agassiz. Yet, while Goethe's possible contribution to the history of science is important, the historian of spiritual ice, perhaps preoccupied by De Quincey, is most interested in how Goethe's thoughts on glaciers relate to his theories of animated nature. Goethe conjectures that the glacial ice is a manifestation of immense durations and unbounded forces—of the timeless laws of global morphology and the crushing powers that execute these laws. He also believes that nature is analogous to art. Like art, nature is a lawful, outward pattern of inner, unruly energy; it is disciplined and extravagant; it is purposeful and purposeless.[7] A conclusion: The creeping Alpine ice is earth poet, the globe-maker of the past, present, and future, troping (turning) the raw earth to fit its cold ideas of form and function.

These Goethean connections fall within and without the domain of the history of science. On the one hand, they are informed by a science of glaciers that begins with Horace Bénédict de Saussure, develops with Hutton, and reaches its nineteenth-century fruition with Agassiz. On the other, Goethe's remarks, viewed in the context of his theory of an artistic nature, suggest a tradition of magic in which ice lives, speaks, and creates. This nonscientific vision is also shaped by a tradition—a history of glaciers as bearers of occult powers. Saxo Grammaticus viewed the glaciers of medieval

Iceland as "marvels" that magically rotate.[8] Later, a seventeenth-century bishop actually exorcised the demonic glaciers creeping into Chamonix.[9] As late as 1723, a scholar assumed that wingless dragons inhabit the ices of Mont Blanc.[10] Glaciers at the turn of the nineteenth century are daemonic revelations as much as universal laws, magicians of the word as much as geomorphic agents.

Hungry for a science of ghosts as well as a spiritual empiricism, Shelley embraces this double nature of glaciers. Testing de Saussure's glaciology in Chamonix during the summer of 1816, Shelley concludes that glaciers are agents of scientific necessity and bearers of strange magic. The glaciers, he finds, create and destroy. They carve riverbeds. They uproot entire forests. In transforming the earth from dead to living, from living to dead, they most resemble poets and magicians. Like poets, these freezes shatter old forms to fashion new ones. As magicians, they miraculously conjure fresh valleys while making large groves vanish. Facing the strange language of the ice, Shelley tries himself to rise to poetry, to magic. He wonders if he is the creator of the Alpine scene as much as a perceiver of it, if his imagination transmutes glacial forces into humane forms (SL 2:495–501; MB 84–126).[11]

Shelley, in much of his verse, hated ice. He found it distant, cold, aloof, deadly.[12] Yet, glaciers, sublime and alive, strangely attracted him. He knew: glaciers, numinous, are more than geology. They are ambiguous immensities of rectitude and weirdness, necessity and violation. They flicker with the illuminated darkness of blasphemy and the obscure light of genius. They are demons, inhuman and destructive. They are *daimons*—familiar spirits connecting poets to life.

DEMONS ABOVE THE SNOWLINE

The Alpine ice during the classical and medieval periods of European history was as eerie as the moon and dangerous as the sea.

Largely unexplored until the sixteenth and seventeenth centuries, the cloudy glaciers evoked mostly terror. As a Roman chronicler of the first century reported, the peaks were eternally frozen, monstrous aberrations. Facing this unmelting ice, St. Ambrose, a bishop of Milan during the fourth century, feared that the freeze might one day spread over all civilization. By the Middle Ages, monastic orders established Alpine hospices to aid pilgrims foundering in the ice. The St. Bernard monks even trained large hounds to rescue stranded travelers. In 1690, the villagers of Chamonix, afraid that the ice would soon overrun them, hired the Bishop of Annecy to exorcise the glaciers. Apparently, the ice retreated one-eighth of a mile.[13]

Early climbers brave enough to negotiate the glacier did not assuage these horrors. Livy's description of Hannibal's Alpine crossing in 218 B.C., translated into English in the early sixteenth century, told of the invader's fear of "people with long shagd hair" dwelling amidst the treacherous "bare yce" and "slabberie snow-broth."[14] Likewise, in 1188, John de Bremble, a monk from Canterbury, crossed the ranges to find only icy misery: "I found my ink-bottle," he reports," filled with a dry mass of ice; my fingers too refused to write; my beard was stiff with frost, and my breath congealed into a long icicle." His conclusion: The frozen crags are places of "torment."[15] Even though a knight named Rotario climbed Roche Melon in 1358 and the chamberlain of Charles VII ascended Mont Aiguille in 1492, the majority of medieval and early Renaissance Europeans entered the Alps only when necessary and then with extreme trepidation. Many travelers choose to be carried through the icy peaks blindfolded.[16]

By the middle of the sixteenth century, the frozen peaks—often called the "Accursed," the "Unapproachable," or the "Inaccessible"—had produced specific superstitions.[17] Many plain-dwellers maintained that the upper glaciers were the habitat of monsters, malformed humans, witches, and demons. According to other legends, wizards lurked in the crags, eager to hurl men into the icy abysses. One legend claimed that the Devil's Bridge, which runs across the Reuss near Andermatt, marked a site where the Devil once crash-landed after an airborne battle with St. Theodule.[18]

Dragons also slithered among the Alpine caves, ready to singe those who trekked above the snowline. Occasionally these beasts bore "dragon stones," crystals embedded in their foreheads. If a brave traveler could steal one of these stones while a dragon slept, then he would possesses the stone's powers, which included the ability to cure diarrhea, poisoning, and plague.[19]

The ghost of Pontius Pilate haunted Pilatus, a mountain near Geneva. Pilate, soon after committing suicide, was thrown into the Tiber. Immediately, foul weather overwhelmed nearby areas. Believing that Pilate's corpse was the cause, authorities threw the body into the Rhône, where it also generated storms. Frustrated, those concerned then disposed of the body in a lake on a mountain above Geneva, where again it created bad weather. To end to these destructions, the local bishop exorcised the lake. The ghost of Pilate arose. He promised to cease his weathers if he could annually ascend from the lake on a judge's throne and kill anyone who looked at him. The bishop agreed. After this pact, Mount Pilatus was deemed forbidden territory. This restriction lasted until the sixteenth century, when Joachim von Watt, Conrad Gesner, and Johann Müller at different times climbed the peak without disaster.[20]

Glaciers spawned their own legends. Many believed that supernatural beings deployed these icy monsters to swallow sinful villages. For instance, some thought that a magical being froze over a village near Kanderstag because the inhabitants were lax in their church offerings. The Alpine dwellers also maintained that glaciers sometimes swallowed unwary walkers and buried unlucky nappers. Yet, though glaciers were generally seen as evil—Alpine dreams of golden ages featured glacierless landscapes—the water from their melt nonetheless was thought to cure illness.[21]

Even the sixteenth-century demystifications of Watt, Gesner, and Müller—who comprised the first "school" of Alpine explorers—did not dispel these Alpine terrors. Johann Scheuchzer, a professor of physics at Zurich University, interspersed his scientific study of the Alpine flora and fauna, *Itinera per Helvetiae Alpinas Regiones* (1723), with lengthy descriptions of the dragons bedeviling the peaks. He described one dragon with the head of a cat and a snake's body; another with a coxcomb and four stumpy legs; and a third with the head of a tomcat, a forked tongue, scaly legs, and a hairy tail.[22]

These dragons were not necessarily evil or even very big. Still, they echoed, however faintly, the tradition of destructive, "black" (or "egocentric"[23]) magic surrounding the glacial peaks, a magic characterized by demons, witches, ghosts, monsters selfishly violating God's laws in hopes of harming others.

SUBLIME DAIMONS

While Scheuchzer was hunting for dragons, a brighter tradition of mountain description was beginning to flourish: a new sense of the Alpine glaciers as sites of a "white" (or "cosmological"[24]) magic based on the holistic powers generating the cosmos. The aforementioned Conrad Gesner inaugurated this tradition in the sixteenth century. He ascended the Alps not to kill dragons but to vitalize his vision. As he wrote in 1541, the frozen peaks are not demonic scowls but symbols of the soul: "The consciousness is in some vague way impressed by the stupendous heights and is drawn to the contemplation of the Great Architect. Men of dull mind admire nothing, sleep at home, never go out into the Theatre of the World, hide in corners like dormice, through the winter, never recognise that the human race was sent out into the world in order that through its marvels it should learn to recognise some higher Power, the Supreme Being himself."[25] This exquisite passage—which might have been written by Shelley or Byron—celebrates the Alpine heights as paths to God and as markers of heightened wakefulness, awareness, and courage. He restated this vision in 1557, two years after he ascended Pilatus. The crags are "the The- atre of the Lord, displaying monuments of past ages, such as precipices, rocks, peaks, chasms, and never-melting glaciers."[26]

Gesner's enthusiasm for the Alps as ennobling powers was dupli- cated at the beginning of the eighteenth century, when the "Moun- tain Gloom" of previous centuries gave way to "Mountain Glory."[27] Scientists and poets during this time began to see the Alpine ice not as a lair of harmful magic but as a luminous revelation of healthy cur- rents. In 1732, Albrecht von Haller, a Swiss naturalist and philoso- pher, published *Die Alpen,* a poem extolling the virtues of the frozen peaks. Inspired by an Alpine journey of 1728, this work—widely printed and translated throughout Europe—argues that the moun- tains instill profound goodness that recalls the Golden Age. The Alps are unique revelations of cosmic benevolence and thus embody laws that humans should mimic. Resembling Mount Sinai more than an "Unapproachable" abode of devils, Haller's "Wordsworthian" Alps constitute moral lessons in stone and crag.[28]

Probably versed in Haller's poetry, Rousseau likewise found moral measures in wild nature, specifically in the rugged Alps loom- ing over his native Geneva. Believing civilized society to be artificial and stifling, Rousseau contended that those living close to natural rhythms were nobler than city dwellers. Although Rousseau never climbed in the Alps or even described them firsthand, he nonethe- less expressed a deep appreciation for the transformative powers of mountains. As he writes in *Julie; or, La Nouvelle Héloïse* (1761), "There is something magical and supernatural in hill landscapes which entrances the mind and the senses; one forgets everything, one forgets one's own being; one ceases to know where one stands."[29] This bewildering hill magic is terrifying. It annihilates one's sense of personal identity. Yet, it is also exhilarating, for it car- ries one outside of oneself into an ecstatic ride on distributed currents. This experience of the occult mountain is, to use the word that would soon give Alpine vistas a habitation and a name, *sublime:* pain at the mind's inability to *image* vast energies, pleasure over the same mind's powers to *intuit* the virtues of these same energies.

Rousseau most likely garnered this Alpine sensibility from conversations with the brothers Deluc. Jean-André and Guillaume-Antoine spent their lives climbing and studying the Alps near their Geneva home. Aside from sailing around Lake Geneva in 1754 with Rousseau, they spent much of their time ascending the peaks of Buet, where they measured air pressure and the temperature at which water boils. After mastering these pinnacles, they essayed others, such as the Col de la Seigne and the Velan. Their impressions of these ascents are close to those of Rousseau.[30] Once caught in a storm on the face of the Col de la Seigne, Guillaume-Antoine saw in a moment of clearing "[t]he high summits . . . all white with fresh snow . . . giants of enormous size, as old as the world, who were at their windows looking down upon us, poor little creeping creatures."[31] The sublime mountains dwarf a climber while expanding him with mighty forms and unknown powers.

Another early initiate into the mysteries of the Alps was a priest of the old St. Bernard Hospice, Abbé Murith. Like the Delucs, he was an amateur scientist interested in the empirical qualities of the mountains. However, his scientific projects were overwhelmed by the occult grandeurs of the heights, which reduced him to a speck at the foot of a frozen giant. In 1779, after reaching the peak of the Velan, he wrote to de Saussure: "[Had you been with me] you would have enjoyed the most splendid spectacle of mountains and glaciers you can imagine; you would have been able to gaze on a wide circle of peaks from different heights. . . . But I cannot promise I will help you to enjoy so ravishing a view. In spite of my own intrepidity, I had too much trouble in gaining the summit of this wintry giant."[32] Revealing immense presences, disturbing and alive, such mountain vistas—as Murith later claimed in a letter to Marc-Theodore Bourrit, a fellow Alpinist—magically transform "the points and needles of the highest hills" into "a tumultuous sea."[33] Murith's scientific interest in the Alps cannot account for his avid climbing.[34] He is most fascinated by the unearthly beauty of the peaks, their unfamiliar familiarity—their uncanniness, their power to reveal, through pleasing terror and horrifying homeliness, that his true dwelling is in the strange storms of the summits while his village house is but a dream.

Bourrit understood Murith's sentiment. He was also obsessed by the mountains for reasons irreducible to science. A mediocre painter, an uninspired engraver, and amateur scientist, he spent his life tenaciously exploring the Alps and shamelessly publicizing his rather modest achievements. Still, he is an important figure in the history of glacier climbing, for his constant advertising of the sublimities of the Alps helped to erase the evils associated with the mountains.[35] Like Gesner, Haller, Rousseau, the Delucs, and Murith, he realized that the true motive behind mountaineering is a yearning to experience the strange powers of the universe, the sublime magic that makes the world. On the top of the Glacier de Valsorey, Bourrit describes such an experience:

> A new universe came into view; what words can I use to describe a spectacle which struck us dumb? . . . This view burst in a single moment on our surprised and astonished sight. These prodigious mounds of ice, these mountains which seemed to touch the sky were serrated in innumerable ways. The richness and variety of colour added to the beauty of the shapes. Gold, silver, crimson, and azure were shining everywhere, and what impressed me with a sense of even greater strangeness were the arches supporting the snow-bridges over the crevasses, the apparent strength of which encouraged us to walk across. We were even courageous enough to stop in the middle and gaze down into the abyss.[36]

Like Columbus smitten with the energizing vertigo of a new land, Bourrit finds himself suspended between a bottomless ground and an infinite sky, a part or particle of the unbounded plenum that enlivens ice to plough the globe.

MOUNTAIN THEOLOGY

These accounts of amateur Alpine explorers suggest that the glaciers of the eighteenth century were just as haunted as those of the earlier times. Yet, while the groaning ice of the Middle Ages and Renaissance was possessed by devils, the sublime ice of the eighteenth century was haunted by *daimons*, spirits connecting human souls with cosmic powers.[37] I have been calling these visions of glaciers "magical," claiming that the demonic interpretation of glaciers invokes a tradition of negative magic while the more angelic reading is grounded on a positive magic. Let me be clear about this vocabulary.

In *Giordano Bruno and the Hermetic Tradition*, Frances A. Yates distinguishes between the "old ignorant, evil, or black magic" of the Middle Ages, characterized by inelegant invocations of devils and stinking concoctions, and the "reformed and learned" magic of the Renaissance, marked by elegant hymns to astral currents and the tasteful use of bright jewels.[38] Richard Cavendish in *The Black Arts* (1967) defines this former magic, the "black" form, as a craving to "conquer the universe" by mastering "everything within it—evil as well as good, cruelty as well as mercy, pain as well as pleasure."[39] The "black" magician is a supreme egoist. He is bent on transforming the world into a double of his wishes, on controlling the forces that threaten the persistence and power of his ego.[40] Thus, though full of *hubris*, he is consumed by fear and desire—terrified by forces that compromise his ego and desirous of destroying these forces. Goethe's Faust recalls this form of magic. He sacrifices Gretchen simply to fulfill his will to power. Likewise,

Melville's Ahab transmutes his world—men, ocean, and whales—into his monomaniacal projects and ends by killing his crew, save one. Alpine dwellers fearing the glaciers as lairs of demons, witches, or dragons assumed that the glaciers manifest a "black" magician, perhaps Satan himself. These superstitious villagers viewed the glaciers as violations of God's laws, aberrations generated by the selfish will of an evil force. This dualism is significant, for those who believe in "black" magic necessarily maintain that two mutually exclusive forces of light and darkness are forever at violent odds.

In contrast, the devotee of "white" magic leans toward monism. He believes, as Paul Christian claimed in his still persuasive *History and Practice of Magic* (1870), that the visible universe is a pattern of a spiritual energy whose center is everywhere and circumference nowhere.[41] This magician does not bend these cosmic flows to his selfish will. He opens to the salubrious powers, reveals their hidden virtues, and directs them toward ameliorative ends.[42] To find his proper place in the current, he transcends fear and desire—the ego that wants control and fears being controlled. Shedding this divisive self, this magus sees himself and the things of the universe not as self-contained units at constant war but as waves on an unbounded ocean. Literary followers of this tradition are Goethe's Wilhelm Meister, who desires through art to participate in the rhythms of nature, and Melville's Ishmael, who transmutes the Pequod into a spiritual vessel, a soul floating on eternal waters. Actual adepts are the Alpine pioneers of the eighteenth century. For these early climbers, the mountain ice is a creation of a "white" magician. Embracing his frozen concoctions, the mountaineers feel his invigorating energy. They discover their origin and being far above their cottages and chateaux.

If "black" magic—"egocentric" magic—is narcissistic machinery that deceives and controls, then "white" magic—"cosmological" magic—constitutes a sacred art that reveals and opens. This latter form of magic is true to its Chaldean root *maghdim*, which means, according to Christian, "wisdom with the addition of the general sense we give to the term *philosophy*." The cosmological magus is a sage. He knows the inner significance of outward forms and deploys these meanings in a life that benefits others. This magus—appearing in the Hindu *Vedas*, the Persian *Zend-Avesta*, the Egyptian *Corpus Hermeticum*, Ficino's *De vita coelitus compara-nda*—discovers hidden connections among the physical, intellec-tual, and divine worlds and demonstrates these links in attractive forms. These bonds and their patterns, however, never exhaust the spiritual origin, which is ineffable and inexpressible, an abyss be-yond reason and language. The hope is that certain disciplines can vouchsafe brief intuitions of this hidden font, and that particular arts can gesture toward its grandeur.[43]

Yates agrees with Christian. The Renaissance magi, self-con-sciously grounding their activities on the wisdom of the Persian Zoroaster and the Egyptian Hermes, attempt to "guide or control the influx of *spiritus* into *materia*." Ficino, Pico, Paracelsus, and Bruno essay through their arts to recognize and express a spiritual flow that is always present yet hidden in all things. Through their magic, they try to remind the world of what it all-too-often and narcissistically forgets: Everything is a pattern of the world spirit.[44] These magicians thus counter egotists who view themselves as self-contained, separate entities able to dictate other isolated objects.

Cosmological magic is *any* discipline capable of revealing through intuition and intimating through expression the abysmal forces of life that cannot be disclosed by positivistic science, ortho-dox religion, or systematic philosophy.[45] For Christian, a primary form of such salubrious craft is "*Mountain Theology.*" Inspired by the "magnetism of solitary heights," this theology of the peaks is em-bodied by those who climb to the clouds to behold and channel the sacred[46]: by the ancient Chaldean, Indian, Persian, and Egyptian magi who ascended nameless heights to commune with universal spirit; by Abraham, who tests his faith on Mount Moriah; Moses, who on Sinai receives the law of God; the magus Zoroaster, who experiences Ahura Mazda atop Mount Alburz; Jesus, transfigured on a high mountain; Muhammad, who first experienced Allah on Jabal al-Nur, the Mountain of Light. To this illustrious list we can add Shelley, envisioning the abyss of being on the peak of Mont Blanc; Bryon's Manfred, conjuring the fates on the Jungfrau; Nietzsche's Zarathustra, in the heights observing the eternal recurrence; and Mann's Hans Castorp, seeing on the Magic Mountain sights inaccessible to those below.[47]

For these mountain theologians, peaks are a way of seeing, a fresh though vertiginous vision of the familiar towns and habits below as well as a new experience of new landscapes above the ice line.[48] The buildings and beliefs below, now defamiliarized, appear small and unimportant. The infinities above, slowly becoming familiar, seem to be everything. On the peak, suspended between heaven and earth, star and mud, the magus of the cosmos throbs on the threshold between space and form, spirit and matter. There he understands that he is an interpenetration of these two entities—a pattern of the invisible immensities, a part of the crag on which he stands. This new vision leads to a fresh mode of being. Realizing that he is a point on a circle whose center is everywhere and circumference nowhere, he no longer identifies solely with his body or the forms of time or space, nor exclusively with his soul, formless and ubiquitous. Rather, sensing the interpenetrations of spirit and matter, he consents his parts to the whole, chooses to submit his actions to the draft of being. Yielding, he is empowered to reveal to others, in words and gestures, the infinite in the finite.

One need not *literally* climb mountains to undergo such "cosmological" experiences. One can attain such heights *psychically*, as Wordsworth makes clear in book six of his *Prelude* (1850). Failing to ascend to the top of an Alpine peak, Wordsworth's pilgrim nonetheless apprehends the transcendent powers of his imagina-

tion. He realizes an unseen, infinite power, a universal mind animating and organizing the crags as well as the meadows. The
point is this: If one can understand that his home is not in sensual
attachment to matter but "with infinitude," "something ever more
about to be," then one becomes, even if he remains in the plains, a
mountain theologian, a *limen* between sky and earth, boundless
reaches and rugged forms.[49]

Crystal gazing and polar exploration—theology of jewels and
axles—suggest the same conclusion. One need not actually stare at
crystals to understand relationships between pattern and turbulence,
minute lattice and distributed force. Likewise, one is not required to
trek to the poles to apprehend the *axis mundi*. In both cases, the
adept, the aspiring cosmological magus, can meditate on interior
shapes—the geometries of mind, unconscious *terrae incognitae*. However, the frozen crystal, the Alpine glacier, the snowy pole constitute
sacred technologies that make spiritual travel less arduous.

Crystals, glaciers, and the poles form invitations to the uncanny, preludes to gnosis. The crystal gazer transforms the frost
on the window into strange attractions. The explorer converts the
unmapped pole into his inmost column. The climber transmutes
the moony ice into a revelation of the ground of being. In each
case, the beholder experiences a return of some repressed energy
that forces him to evaluate his habitual distinctions between familiar and unfamiliar. What he thought was homely and substantial—
his yard's frozen puddle or his cottage under the peaks, his ego or
his reason—turns out to be distant, unreal. At the same time,
strange happenings—flamings into the crystal's corridors or lunar
glaciers, unbounded winds or unconscious bubblings—appear to
be the foundations of everything. During this experience—a sublime moment of disturbance and exhilaration—the ego, formerly
stable and primal, metamorphoses into a bark floating on an ancient sea, while the unconscious depths, before barely recognized,
turn into the font of conscious existence.

This uncanny experience can begin in the familiar (as it does in the case of the crystal gazer); between the familiar and unfamiliar (as in the instance of the Alpine climber); or in an utterly unfamiliar realm (as in the case of the polar explorer). The result is the same. One realizes that the world is double—local and global, same and other, pattern and abyss. To embrace this uncanny fact is to enter the haunt of the cosmological magician: revelations of strange yet familiar powers that the world forgets. The magician of the cosmos knows that every familiar is the garment of the strange abyss, the boundless powers are common to all. He attempts in his works—charms, invocations, or poems—to reveal these relationships, to make the familiar strange and the strange familiar. This is why he is frequently feared, for he reminds that the ego is insubstantial, and that heaven is not ultimate.

To the early Alpinists the glaciers were regions of such uncanny visions. Drawn to the frozen giants as much for their *daimons* as their facts, these climbing pioneers offer a key to the esoteric history of glaciers, an arcane current that was not damned with the rise of glaciology. Even when hard scientists described glaciers as geological agents, these immense freezes remained magical demiurges. We can see this melding in the words of the first serious scientist of glaciers, de Saussure. In the midst of his empirical recordings, he proclaimed that in the frozen crags the "soul is uplifted, the powers of intelligence seem to widen and in the midst of this majestic silence, one seems to hear the voice of Nature and to become the confidant of its most secret workings."[50]

ICE AGE

The rise of geological science in the eighteenth century contributed significantly to a shift in sensibility among poets, theologians, and philosophers. During the classical, medieval, and Renaissance periods, men and women largely viewed mountains as

gloomy blights on God's otherwise beautiful world. In the eighteenth century, people began to see the peaks as special manifestations of the eternal laws shaping the globe.[51] The science of
glaciers was a major cause of this new sense. Glaciology dispelled
dark superstitions and revealed the principles by which the earth
had evolved. Arising from the enthusiasm of the early Alpine explorers, this science fit the sublime ejaculations of Deluc, Murith,
and Bourrit into verifiable theories.

De Saussure was closely connected to this Swiss circle of Alpine
pioneers. Like his climbing colleagues, he had a passion for the
magic of the mountains. Yet, at the same time, he possessed a sober
scientific mind. Hence, while his fellow Alpinists remained amateur
observers who wanted the thrill of the clouds, de Saussure developed into a serious scientist of the peaks' frozen grandeurs. In his
relentless exploring, recording, and advertising, he became what
Bourrit wished to become: the undisputed authority on mountains
for his age. (Indeed, de Saussure inspired the first ascent of Mont
Blanc. In 1760, at the age of twenty, he offered a reward to any man
who could reach the peak. In 1786, Michel-Gabriel Paccard and
Jacques Balmat succeeded and claimed the prize. De Saussure himself achieved the top the next year.[52]) From the time he was named
professor of philosophy at the Geneva Academy at twenty-two until
he died at fifty-nine, de Saussure collected copious data on the
Alpine environment, making significant contributions in topogra-
phy, geology, and glaciology. Filing these observations his four-vol-
ume *Voyages dan les Alpes* (1779–96), de Saussure provided for later
scientists and enthusiasts a wealth of information on which almost
all ensuing theories of glaciers were based.[53]

De Saussure himself did not achieve significant theoretical
breakthroughs on the movements of glaciers. Despite his acute eye
for observing facts, he remained bogged in conventional theories
on glacier motion and geomorphic function. His theory of glacial
motion was a rehash of a "gravitational theory" forwarded in 1760

by Gottlieb Sigmund Gruner in *Die Eisgebirge des Schweizerlandes*.[54] According to this theory, glaciers move by sliding down inclines on currents of water that flow between the glacier and the ground. Continuing throughout the year, this sliding slows during the winter and accelerates during the summer. For de Saussure, this gradual but persistent slippage accounts for the "heaps of ice in lowlands warm enough to produce great trees and even abundant harvests" as well as for the "moraines," large piles of rocks from the peaks that gather in the lower ends and edges of the glaciers.[55]

De Saussure's theory of glacial motion did little to improve upon the opposing theory, the "dilatation theory" offered by Scheuchzer in *Itinera per Helvaetiae Alpinas Regiones*. In this explanation, the cause of glacier movement is the water that flows down the sides of mountains and thus into the cracks and pores of the ice. When the water freezes again, it expands, and thus "causes the glacier to thrust forward and to carry with it sand and stones, some of great size."[56]

Although both of these theories accounted for the *fact* of glacier motion and for the glacier's transport of high altitude rocks to lower altitudes, neither explained two other phenomena that were soon after associated with glacier activities: the placement of huge boulders, called erratics, in valleys miles from the stones' mountain sources, and the shapes of rocky river beds that could not have been formed by the flow of water.

De Saussure, like Scheuchzer before him, did not believe that glaciers were powerful geomorphic agents. The likely reason for this limitation was this: Both men were "catastrophists" and thus believed that the present formation of the globe is the result of the flood described in Genesis. Suggested by Swedenborg in 1719 and later consolidated by Werner and his Neptunist school, this theory explained erratics and riverbeds by claiming that the ocean once covering earth was sufficiently powerful to move mountains and carve valleys. According to Werner, mountains precipitated during this primal ocean's gradual diminution, while valleys were carved later when this same sea forcefully withdrew. In a time when many believed that Creation took place in 4,004 B.C. and that species were fixed, catastrophism demonstrated that the formation of the earth is the product of a comparatively recent disaster and explained fossils as remnants of a global annihilation. For pious eighteenth-century scientists holding this reassuring vision, glaciers simply could not be the agents of geomorphism.[57]

Certain imaginative thinkers of the late eighteenth and early nineteenth centuries—such as Jean-Pierre Perraudin, a Swiss hunter; Ignace Venetz, a Swiss engineer; and, as we have seen, Goethe—speculated that glaciers, not oceans, were the agents of global formation. However, the most convincing early proponent of the glacial theory of geomorphism was James Hutton. In *Theory of the Earth* (1788), Hutton counters catastrophism with "uniformitarianism." He argues that the present shape of the globe, including its erratics and riverbeds, is a manifestation of geological laws that have been at work for immeasurable durations. These laws altering the present globe are *uniform* with the principles that changed it in the past and will transform it in the future. Under the direction of these laws, the globe is not a fixed form waiting for a new catastrophe but an evolving pattern expressing the constant pressure of immense forces. As Hutton concludes, the earth's revolutions are infinite, sublime, revealing "no vestige of a beginning, no prospect of an end." Applying this theory to the glaciological details in de Saussure's *Voyages*, Hutton suggests that erratics were once carried to their current sites by extremely powerful glacial movements still at work in the present.[58]

Hutton's work opened the possibility that glaciers are not merely isolated hunks of ice creeping in mountains but also vestiges of global demiurges potent enough to uproot huge masses of stone. Grasping this implication, John Playfair, Hutton's disciple, proposed in *Illustrations of the Huttonian Theory of the Earth* (1802) that glaciers are nature's "most powerful engines" for "moving large masses of rock." Playfair claims that glaciers are "in perpetual motion, undermined by the influx of heat from the earth, and impelled down the declivities on which they rest by their own enormous weight, together with that of the innumerable fragments of rock with which they are loaded." Though he (like Hutton) draws on the gravitational theory of glacial motions, he nonetheless claims for the glacier a power much greater than de Saussure granted. Describing these "great engines," Playfair strikes a pose of awestruck wonder when he beholds the Mer de Glace: "The immense quantity and size of the rocks thus transported [by the force of these glacial engines], have been remarked with astonishment by every observer, and explain sufficiently how fragments of rock may be put in motion, even where there is but little declivity, and where the actual surface of the ground is considerably uneven. In this manner, before the valleys were cut out in the form they now are, and when the mountains were still more elevated, huge fragments of rock may have been carried to a great distance."[59] Playfair did not attribute to glaciers erosive powers forceful enough to carve these valleys. Still, he set the stage for Jean de Charpentier and Agassiz to argue that glaciers are earth shakers, frozen deities who once ruled the globe in an Ice Age, not a golden one.

De Charpentier and Agassiz did not provide new information or ideas concerning glaciers. They synthesized existing facts and theories. By 1832 the principal elements of the "glacier theory" were established. Playfair had explained the glacial transport of erratics. Venetz, drawing from the observations of Alpine peasants, had claimed that glaciers are the formative agents of mountain landscapes. De Saussure and Scheuchzer had proved that glaciers persistently move. Jens Esmarch, a Scandinavian scientist, had in 1824 suggested that ancient glaciers dug out existing basins and fjords. Esmarch, Venetz, and Goethe had each speculated that an Ice Age, not a global ocean, was the primary geomorphic agent.[60]

With these principal features in place, all de Charpentier and Agassiz had to do was piece them together and publish them. To a large extent, this is exactly what happened. However, we cannot forget that this emerging glacial theory was faced with stern opposition from both uniformitarian and catastrophic fronts. Hence, de Charpentier and to a greater extent Agassiz not only had to synthesize existing ideas but also to overcome virulent criticism from the ruling geological schools of their time. On the surface, these criticisms are surprising. Ostensibly, the uniformitarians would embrace the glacial theory as convincing evidence for their own hypothesis. Would not a geomorphic Ice Age prove that the glacial dynamics at work in the present were also at work in the past? The answer is "yes," but a global Ice Age also presupposes a nonuniform alteration in climate—a period of *catastrophic* cold. Hence, for many uniformitarians, an Ice Age was as problematic as a universal deluge. Was this "nonuniform" upheaval of ice attractive to the catastrophists? Would not these scripturally minded geologists see in the Ice Age a more plausible version of the flood? The answer is "no," for the catastrophists found no Ice Age mentioned in the Bible—only a flood—and therefore dismissed the glacier theory as quickly as they rejected evolution.[61]

In the midst of these senses of glaciers and the controversies they occasioned, de Charpentier, a Swiss geologist, delivered in 1834 what is often considered the first scientific paper on glacial geomorphology. In "Sur la cause probable du transport des blocs erratiques de la Suisse," published in 1835, de Charpentier argues that virtually all of the geological characteristics of the Alpine landscape—including erratics, riverbeds, moraines, and peaks—are products of the movements of immense glaciers once covering the region. His coherent articulation of existing ideas, however, met with criticism, most notably from Agassiz himself. Already an internationally famous paleontologist at the age of twenty-seven, Agassiz was at that time in his career a catastrophist. In response to Agassiz's request for additional proof, de Charpentier published in 1841 *Essai sur les Glaciers*, in which he acknowledges that the glacier theory will only be accepted if erratics resting well beyond current glaciers can be shown to have glacial origins. In his conclusion, he lists the primary proofs for the glacial origin of erratics and thus for the glacial theory in general. Of these proofs, two are especially salient. One, the physics of existing glaciers does not contradict the notion that they once, when larger, bore huge stones over large distances. Two, the *only* way to explain erratics is to invoke a theory of glacial transport. These proofs point to only one conclusion: The Ice Age is a fact.[62]

De Charpentier's conclusions failed to foster widespread endorsement of the glacier theory. Only after the world-renowned scientist Agassiz offered his support did the theory begin to gain converts. After visiting de Charpentier at his home in 1836, Agassiz became convinced of the validity of the glacier theory. Immediately, he threw himself into glaciology, spending part of every year between 1837 and 1845 in Neuchâtel studying the ice. By 1838, he had produced the so-called *Discours de Neuchâtel*, in which he provides a history of glaciology and proofs for an Ice Age. Although he disagreed with de Charpentier in particulars, he on the whole endorsed his theory of the shaping powers of ice. After further research, he published in 1840 his *Etudes sur les glaciers*, which quickly put the glacier theory in the forefront of European scientific debates. This book is largely an extension of his early lecture and a synthesis of existing ideas. However, it nonetheless gained for Agassiz, perhaps unfairly, the title of "father" of the glacier theory, and made his name and the "Ice Age" forever associated. Whatever the merits or demerits of Agassiz and his book, the fact remains: After the release of this study, scientists less and less disputed the "what" of the Ice Age and more and more argued over its "how."[63]

Beginning with de Saussure and culminating with Agassiz, this history of early glaciology is marked by rapid development. From

1779, when de Saussure published the first volume of his *Voyages*, to 1840, the year Agassiz related his *Etudes*, the study of glaciers had grown from the simple gathering of Alpine facts to sophisticated theories of the formation of the globe. By the early years of the nineteenth century, thinkers viewed glaciers and their mountain habitats as central specimens in debates between catastrophists and uniformitarians. No longer aberrations of God's harmonious designs, the frozen peaks were now markers of nothing less than the destiny of the planet. To gaze toward the summits was not to see only static giants of ice but also to envision cataclysmic explosions, catastrophic creations, bewildering durations—the ice come to monstrous life, juggling mountains like baubles, carving rivers and lakes as if they were streams and puddles.

Bewildered by such conceptions, even the most staid scientist could not withhold from wondering if another catastrophe was silently rumbling under the quiet peaks, or if the stern stability above was but an illusion in a world uniformly flowing. This hypothetical scientist could surely not refrain from feeling an unsettling blend of terror and exhilaration as he underwent these visions. He was an insignificant speck before these horrible upheavals and inconceivable eons. Yet, he was also a humming pattern and bearer of these sublime forces and epochs. Feeling such contradictions, this early nineteenth-century geologist—a Playfair, say, or a Venetz or an Agassiz—surely understood how his prescientific forbears and amateur contemporaries could view frozen mountains as magical regions. Surely he shivered with the same stirrings as the mountaineers who approached the clouds hungry for angels. Certainly he felt the chill of those earlier villagers who avoided the demon-haunted glaciers and summits dangerous with dragons. Whatever this geologist felt, he probably could not perceive the glaciers he studied as mere hunks of matter following predictable laws. There were simply too many unexplained phenomena—creeping ice, enormous erratics miraculously moved—and too many unanswered questions—Is time finite or infinite? Does nature proceed in fits or gradually?—to leave him any conclusive comfort. The mountains he studied, in, say, 1816, might reveal some secure laws, but they remained as strange as the moon.

1816 was the year that Percy Shelley and Mary Wollstonecraft, along with Clare Clairemont, made a pilgrimage to Chamonix, where, under the frozen abysses of Mont Blanc, they were stunned into new insights. Aware of the peasants' superstitions, the occult appeal of mountains, de Saussure's *Voyage*, and the opposing theories of the uniformitarians and the catastrophists, Percy and Mary grasped the import and complexity of the glacial crags.[64] They realized that in those glowering giants was a mixture of geological necessities, supernatural creators, and demonic destroyers. Galvanized by their experience, both turned to their art forms to record their thoughts. The results of these exercises are "Mont Blanc" and important parts of *Frankenstein*.

SHELLEY MAGUS

Shelley spent his youth perusing the arcane pages of cosmological magi, training, though he did not know it then, to become a theologian of the glacier. In an 1812 letter to William Godwin, Shelley reports that his youthful studies were devoted to reading "[a]ncient books of Chemistry and Magic" "with an enthusiasm of wonder, almost amounting to belief" (*SL* 1: 227). As he explains in another letter to Godwin, posted the same year, these occult researches consisted of poring over the "reveries" of Albertus Magnus and Paracelsus (1:303). Though he admits that his "fondness for natural magic and ghosts" has abated (1:303), he nonetheless during his first meeting with Godwin in October of that same year expressed his admiration for Paracelsus as well as Cornelius Agrippa.[65]

Studying Albertus Magnus, Shelley encountered the leading medieval authority on science and magic. Committed to the laws of nature, Albertus in his comments on magic distinguishes between natural, good (cosmological) magic and unnatural, evil (egocentric) magic. Magics that manipulate the powers of the cosmos for their own selfish ends are evil. Necromancy, communing with the dead in hopes of controlling the future, violates God's providence. Conjuring demonic helpers is likewise pernicious, for it assumes that God's grace is not sufficient. Dangerous as well, astrology seduces the star-gazer to idolize the forces of the stars as autonomous deities. Opposed to demonical magic is natural magic. This brand of magic resembles demonic magic in channeling the forces of nature and the influences of the stars. However, it differs from its devilish opponent in desiring to heal, to increase the world's goodness. This "good" magic, gleaned largely from hermetic treatises, manifests and focuses powers that are always already present in nature and thus part of God's plan. Like prayers or meditations, this benevolent craft helps along what should happen anyway. It speeds healing or deters sickness; it accelerates metals into gold, and bodies into souls. The exemplars of this "good" magic are the magi of the Gospels—not evil sorcerers but great men participating in God's holy work.[66]

Praising the biblical magi, Albertus unwittingly celebrates a long tradition of ancient magic that was recovered during the fifteenth-century hermetic revival. As Ficino claims in *Theologia Platonica* (1482), this tradition of noble magic began before the days of Moses in Zoroaster's Persia and the Egypt of Hermes Trismegistus. Issuing from Zoroaster's *Chaldean Oracles* and Hermes's *Corpus Hermeticum*, this esoteric current quickly gave rise to a class of magi versed in and able to channel the energies of the cosmos. From these magicians of old sprang a line of *prisci theologi* including not only Orpheus, Moses, Pythagoras, and Plato but also the nameless wizards who followed the star of Bethlehem.[67] Ficino's canon of magicians—though, as we now know, erroneously dated (the *Oracles* and the *Corpus* arose ca. 200 A.D.) and incorrectly attributed (both texts were composed by anonymous hands)—was embraced by Renaissance magi anxious to harness wisdom and power still fresh from the world's dawn.

Agrippa was one such magus. In *De occulta philosophia* (1533), he details this tradition of noble magic, which begins with Zoroaster, runs through Plato, and thrives in Porphyry. Drawing from Ficino and his disciple Pico, Agrippa describes the magus's cosmos as threefold, consisting of an elemental, or natural realm; a celestial, or astrological region; and an intellectual, or angelic level. Each of these worlds shares affinities with and is influenced by the one above it. God's spiritual powers descend through the angels of the intellectual plane to the stars of the celestial world to the elements of nature. The magician's task is to channel and focus the salubrious currents of each realm onto the sick souls of the earth. To draw the powers of nature, he develops natural magic. Gleaned from studies of medicine and physics, this magic involves manipulating stones, plants, and animals to draw down to earth corresponding stellar powers. Celestial magic, associated with astronomy and mathematics, entails manipulating abstract elements—numbers and geometrical shapes—to fashion statues, columns, or pyramids that pull and direct sidereal energies. Ceremonial magic, more difficult, requires the magician to perform sacred rituals that attract angels. If he succeeds in conjuring these powers beyond the stars, he can perform miracles.[68]

Writing at about the same time as Agrippa, Paracelsus likewise celebrates a perennial tradition of magic early exemplified by Zoroaster. In *Aurora of the Philosophers* (ca. 1540), Paracelsus names the unfallen Adam the first magus and claims that his prelapsarian magic persisted in secret ceremonies of the ancient Chaldean, Persian, and Egyptian magi.[69] Instanced by Zoroaster and Hermes, this magic, as Paracelsus explains in *De occulta philosophia* (ca. 1540), is a way of knowing: a "power to experience and fathom things which are inaccessible to the human reason."[70] Distinct from

witchcraft, this wisdom—notably practiced by "the three Wise
Men of the East"—requires faith in the divine spirit immanent in
the cosmos. Practicing such faith, the magus becomes divine: "As
God awakens the dead to new life, so the 'natural saints,' who are
called magi, are given power over the energies and faculties of nature. For there are holy men in God who serve the beatific life;
they are called saints. But there are also holy men in God who serve
the forces of nature, and they are called magi."[71] The magus, far
from *violating* nature's laws, *consents* to them. Moving with nature's
spiritual flow, he directs this flux toward an ameliorative end.

Steeped in these Renaissance exemplars of the perennial philosophy, Shelley was also interested in Zoroaster. Around the time
that he announced his occult concerns to Godwin in 1812, Shelley
fell under the spell of Thomas Love Peacock, a scholar and poet
whose wide learning in the ancient world extended to Zoroastrian
magic. In his 1810 edition of *The Genius of the Thames*, Peacock included a long note on the ancient Persian religion (he would delete
the note in 1812). When he met Shelley in 1812, he was undertak-
ing *Ahrimanes*, a long narrative poem (never finished) that featured
Zoroastrian lore. By 1813, Shelley and Peacock were together in
Bracknell, where they met John Frank Newton. While Shelley and
Peacock likely found the extreme (and sometimes nudist) Newton
faintly ridiculous (Peacock satirized him in *Headlong Hall* and
Nightmare Abbey), they nonetheless discovered in him a stimulating
interlocutor on Zoroastrianism. In his book *Return to Nature* (1811)
and in four letters published in *The Monthly Magazine* (1811),
Newton had theorized that humans, now overly civilized and thus
separated from nature, were suffering under the reign of "Ahrimanes," the evil, dark, destructive deity in the dualistic Zoroastrian
religion, akin to the Hindu Shiva and the Greek Jupiter. However,
in a period soon to come, "Oromazes," the good Zoroastrian god
of light and creativity (similar to Vishnu and Apollo), would foster a
new age in which humans would live in harmony with nature.[72]

In the midst of their conversations with Newton, Shelley and
Peacock were also dipping into Count Volney's *Ruins of Empires*
(1791), a text that concisely explains Zoroastrianism. Describing
how a "Sovereign and mysterious Power of the Universe" indifferently razes civilizations and the tyrants that sustain them, Volney
provides a genealogy of religious ideas. He describes Zoroaster as a
prophet who, living five centuries after Moses, "revived and moral-
ized among the Medes and Bactrians the whole Egyptian system of
Osiris, under the names of Ormuzd [a common variant of Oro-
mazes] and Ahrimanes. He called the reign of summer, virtue and
good; the reign of winter, sin and evil; the renovation in spring,
creation; the revival of the spheres in the secular periods of the
conjunction, resurrection, and his future life." Volney further associated Ahrimanes with "the great lizard" of evil in Genesis, while
he linked Ormuzd with the Bible's "benevolent God of light."[73]

Peacock and Shelley were also at this time reading the *Zend-
Avesta*, the most ancient and sacred text of the Zoroastrian religion.[74] From Abraham Hyacinthe Anquetil-Duperron's 1771
translation of this text into French, they would have learned much
about Zoroaster as a magus, and, significantly, as a *mountain*
magus. The *Zend-Avesta*—a gathering of laws, commentaries,
liturgies, and rituals dating before the sixth century B.C. and possibly written, in part, by Zoroaster himself—reveals not only the
dualistic principles of the religion (Ormuzd the principle of light
and life, Ahrimanes the power of darkness and death) but also the
forms of magic connected with each deity. As Anquetil-Duperron
explains in "Vie de Zoroastre"—part of his introduction—when
Zoroaster received his prophetic message from Ormuzd, he was
dwelling in a Persia inhabited by evil magicians who worshipped
and conjured the dark powers of Ahrimanes.[75] As the *Zend-Avesta*
claims, these dark magicians saw Ahrimanes as an archmagician, a
cosmic thaumaturge bent on ruining the gorgeous creations of his
bright opponent. However, Zoroaster countered this dark magic
with "good magic"—recitations capable of drawing Ormuzd's

grace. He moreover instructed a class of magi in these secret arts of praise and elevation.[76]

This benevolent Zoroastrian magic partly originated in the clouds, close to the throne of Ormuzd. As Anquetil-Duperron reports, Zoroaster once ascended Mont Albordj, the cosmic mountain made by Ormuzd at the beginning of the world. At the summit, the earthly dwelling of his god, Zoroaster consulted with Ormuzd. He learned the truth and power of his prophetic message. He received a list of divine sayings to report to the Persians. (This story of mountain vision, according to Anquetil-Duperron, likely gave birth to the later mountain experience and nocturnal voyage of Muhammad.[77]) Inspired by their master's numinous mountain encounter, later Zoroastrian magi performed fire rituals on the peaks.

Soon after perusing Anquetil-Duperon's edition, Shelley drew from Zoroastrian imagery in *Laon and Cythna* (later entitled *The Revolt of Islam*), a political allegory composed just after he completed "Mont Blanc." In the opening of this poem, a youth despairing over the darkness ruling the world witnesses a sky battle between an eagle and a serpent. He later learns that the eagle and the serpent represent the "Two Powers" that rule the "world with a divided lot." The eagle figures the "Spirit of evil," which manifests itself in the world in the form of tyranny. The serpent embodies the spirit of good, the power of love. (Notice how Shelley revises Volney's association of the serpent with Ahrimanes; we shall soon find Shelley transforming Zoroastrian dualism more extensively.) The eagle now holds sway over the world. However, the serpent's benign power shall soon rise again. For now, the serpent persists, along with his worshippers, in a temple hidden in the ices of the South Pole (*SP* 2:113–29).

SHELLEY'S SUBLIME SCIENCE

Shelley's scientific studies, largely drawn from the works of Erasmus Darwin in the years between 1811 and 1813, were not separate from his magical explorations.[78] He found in science not a refutation of magic but a body of information that he could transform into a new craft: a magic not directed toward transcendent deity but grounded on physical necessity, a "poetic" magic that might transmute the currents of nature into ameliorative poems. Science for Shelley was sublime—a vision of infinite, dynamic, evolving energies (such as glacial power) that might animate the poet's spells (such as "Mont Blanc"), which in turn might enlighten those blinded by oppressive superstition.[79]

From Erasmus Darwin's *The Botanic Garden* (1791), a scientific poem, Shelley learned of William Herschel's "sublime" theory of "the construction of the heavens." Untold ages ago, an immense mass spanning the reaches of the heavens began to revolve, powered by a huge central force. Eventually, this primal nebula turned so rapidly that its outer areas broke away to form other spinning nebulae. This fragmentation constituted the first stars, and such breakages still generate new heavenly bodies.[80] Motivated by Darwin's description of this theory, Shelley in 1812 studied Laplace's account of evolving nebulae in *Exposition le Système du Monde* (1796), which claims that "[m]an now appears, upon his small planet, almost imperceptible in the vast extent of the solar system, itself only an insensible point in the immensity of space."[81]

As Shelley also gleaned from Darwin, geology is likewise sublime, for it demonstrates the earth's long evolution as well as the stupendous forces that shape the globe. As Darwin reports in *The Temple of Nature* (1803)—another poem on science—the earth likely arose from and was formed by a primeval ocean.[82] Yet, Darwin elsewhere describes a Vulcanist (and Huttonian) alternative to this Wernerian Neptunism, suggesting that subterranean fires caused primal earthquakes that heaved up continents and mountains.[83] In either case, immense catastrophes explode the globe into being. But Darwin is not a simple catastrophist merging geology and Genesis. Rather, he maintains that these upheavals are part of a harmonious rhythm of creation and destruction that has unfolded over millions of years. Shelley found this tension between uniformitarianism and catastrophism elaborated in another geological work he was reading in 1811, James Parkinson's *Organic Remains of a Former World* (1804–11). Though a catastrophist, Parkinson maintains that the globe has undergone numerous revolutions over immensely long periods of time. Thus, the earth *uniformly* experiences cyclical catastrophes, destructive and creative.[84]

From the immensities of heaven to the durations of earth, Shelley descended to the electromagnetic energies coursing through minute atoms. In *The Temple of Nature*, he read about electromagnetic energy pervading all matter and thus entertained the possibility that the cosmos is not solid and stable but a field of force. Although Darwin was writing before the discoveries of Davy, Oersted, and Faraday, he nonetheless prophetically conjectured that electricity and magnetism are manifestations of one force.[85] Turning in 1812 to Davy's *Elements of Chemical Philosophy*, Shelley found Darwin's speculation substantiated as well as the suggestion that matter is comprised of "points" of attraction and repulsion.[86]

Shelley experienced these connections in *Zoonomia* (1794, 96), a prose work in which Darwin argues that one galvanic spirit motivates *all* matter, animate and inanimate.[87] Hence, living and nonliving beings are different only in degree. Originating from a primal ocean, organic forms initially and spontaneously appeared as microscopic particles. Eventually, over long periods of time, these cells evolved into vegetables. After a longer duration, leaves metamorphosed into fins, feet, and wings. Hence, all extant flora and fauna have developed, over a period of millions of years, from oceanic spores.[88] Like Lamarck, Darwin believed that this evolutionary process is progressive. Species improve as they metamorphose, ascending from simplicity to complexity.[89] The driving force of this improvement—and here Darwin diverges from Lamarck and resembles the Neoplatonists—is divine love, electric

Venus. Matter and love are inseparable. The goddess creates atoms and endows them with "immutable properties" through which they grow and evolve. These innate principles *determine* the universe. Yet, Darwin still maintains that humans are free, responsible for their actions.[90]

Darwin does not explain how humans can be fated and free. Nor does the young Shelley. In *Queen Mab* (1813), he proclaims that the one "consentaneous love" that "inspires all life" will eventually create a world in which the "lion forgets to thirst for blood" and sports beside "the dreadless kid" (*SP* 1:284–5). Yet, like Darwin, Shelley is not clear on how this deterministic biological evolution—this "all-sufficing Power" of "Necessity"—translates into moral responsibility, social reform, or any other undetermined activity.

GLACIAL FATE AND FREEDOM

Shelley's problematic belief in necessity—in an infinite power organizing the universe over innumerable eons of time—is a primary outcome of his scientific studies.[91] For Shelley, the multitudinous heavens, the catastrophic earth, the sparks of chemical affinity, and the cells of life, love struck, are manifestations of an immutable cosmic law. Rather than lamenting over this universal determinism—as a Blake or a Coleridge might—Shelley embraces it for three reasons, expressed in *Queen Mab*. First of all, the principle of necessity is an established fact: Astronomy, geology, chemistry, and biology alike reveal an "unvarying harmony" holding all beings to an "all-sufficing Power / Necessity" (*SP* 1:273). Second, this incontrovertible fact is sublime, a vision of "an interminable wilderness of worlds" that "staggers" "even soaring fancy" (239–40). Third, these sciences of the sublime safeguard against tyranny by overturning the reductive myths that kings and priests concoct to scare their subjects (249–53).

Yet, there are problems with Shelley's (and Darwin's) theory of necessity. If everything is fated, is the tyrant, who appears to violate fate, determined as well? Or, does the tyrant detach himself from necessity in his programs to thwart its hum toward harmony? Likewise, what of the poet who, like Prometheus, counters tyranny and reforms the world? Is he simply an instrument of fate, a cog in a cosmic machine? Or does he self-consciously channel and focus the lawful currents of which he is always already a part? What is in play in these questions is the old debate between fate and freedom. Yet, as my questions suggest, these two terms are clumsy. Shelley believes that humans are fated and free, driven by inevitable natural laws—those principles of astronomy, geology, chemistry, and biology—and by unpredictable human desires—to control nature or to participate with its flows, to remain closed or open to others. The question is not "Are we fated or free?" but "How are we fated *and* free?"

These difficult questions growing out of Shelley's sense of scientific laws recall his interest in magic. Leaving for a moment the question of fate and freedom, we can see that for Shelley the tyrant, in somehow countering nature's laws for his selfish gain, is a version of the egotistical magician, while the Promethean poet, who in some way shapes necessity to benefit others, is an avatar of the cosmological magician. Shelley's Zoroastrian "dualism" might not in all cases distinguish between two opposing cosmic principles—as it does in *The Revolt of Islam*—but might rather draw a distinction between two contrasting dispositions toward one principle. These dispositions—the egocentric and the cosmological—would then feature contrasts of their own. The tyrannical magician would struggle between cosmic necessity and egotistical desire. The cosmological magus would oscillate between this same cosmic power and his endeavors to channel it in salubrious directions. In both cases, "magic" is an effort to relate to and alter necessity. Magic is an activity of the *mind*—a mental attempt to reshape the world.

These relationships are complex. They require further meditations on necessity and creativity, science and magic, dualism and monism, mind and matter. A place to undertake this meditation is Chamonix.

In the summer of 1816, the Glacier des Boissons and the Mer de Glace overwhelmed Shelley. As he explains in a letter to Peacock, the glaciers are vast engines of destruction, juggernauts indifferently exploding valleys and villages: "These glaciers flow perpetually into the valley ravaging in their slow but irresistible progress the pastures & the forests which surround them, & performing a work of desolation in ages, which a river of lava might accomplish in an hour." Moving at the rate of about a foot a day, these glaciers "drag with them from the regions where they derive their origin all the ruins of the mountains, enormous rocks, & immense accumulations of sand & stone. These are driven onwards by the irresistible progress of the stream of solid ice" (*SL* 1:498).

Yet, the ice is also beautiful. Describing the Glacier des Boissons, Shelley notices that its "surface is irregularly broken into a thousand unaccountable figures. Conical & pyramidal crystallizations, more than 50 feet in height rise from its surface, & precipices of ice of a dazzling splendour overhang the woods & meadows of the vale." Likewise, the Mer de Glace coruscates like blue waves. Its "mass of undulating ice" "exhibits an appearance as if frost had suddenly bound up the waves & whirlpools of a mighty torrent. . . . [T]he waves are elevated about 12 or 15 feet from the surface of the mass which is intersected by long gaps of unfathomable depth, the ice of whose sides is more beautifully azure than the sky." Struck by these undulations, Shelley likens the ice and its environs to a "living being," with "frozen blood forever circulat[ing] slowly thro' his stony veins" (*SL* 1:497, 500).

During these rhapsodies, Shelley reveals his scientific senses. He is especially interested in the relationship between the dynamic glaciers and the landscape surrounding them. Disagreeing with de Saussure, who believes that the glaciers undergo periods of "increase and decay," Shelley fears that the glaciers will continue to grow until they have destroyed the entire valley. Manifestations of scientific law, of the "terrible magnificence" of "necessity," the glaciers simply annihilate without prejudice. Yet, the catastrophic freezes can also create with equal indifference. They transform the landscape through their icy engines and generate life through their rivers of meltage. They are demiurges, divine beings, analogous to "the poet" (*SL* 1:499, 497).

Emphasizing the glacier's fitness to alter an entire region, Shelley, like Darwin, appears to be a catastrophist with a uniformitarian notion of time. Witnessing the geomorphic force of the glaciers, Shelley fears that their icy engines will one day ruin, like the "Deluge" of *Prometheus Unbound* (1819–20), an entire cycle of civilization (*PU* 4.283–317). Yet, this impending catastrophe, like the abolishing deluge, is not a manifestation of God's will in a finite temporal scheme. It is only one catastrophe among numerous catastrophes, past and future. For millions and millions of years, necessity has been creating and destroying world upon world. To quake under the glacier is to experience time opening into infinity and space changing into a giant poet at his cosmic drafts.[92]

Science, however, is not sufficient to account entirely for these floods of ice. Awed beyond the concepts of empiricism, Shelley grasps for magic. Thinking of Buffon's "sublime but gloomy theory" that the globe will eventually be "changed into a mass of frost" by glacial and polar ice, Shelley conjures "Ahriman." He pictures this dark magician—"[t]hroned among these palaces of death and frost, so sculptured . . . by the adamantine hand of necessity"—casting "around him, as the first essays of his final usurpation, avalanches, torrents, rocks, and thunders, and above all these deadly glaciers, at once proof and symbols of his reign" (*SL* 1:499). Yet, Ahrimanes is not a demonic magus to be overcome. On the contrary, as a personification of necessity, he is to be embraced. Though "a subject more mournful and less sublime," he is nonetheless a figure that "neither the poet nor the philosopher should disdain to regard" (513). Shelley wrests Ahrimanes from traditional religious contexts and redeploys him in a scientific one. No longer the tyrant of a fallen universe, he is now a necessary power in living cosmos. Not demon, he is *daimon*.

If Ahrimanes is a figure of necessity, then what is Ormuzd? Shelley does not mention the Zoroastrian magus of light in his letter to Peacock. However, he does suggest that the bright Persian potency thrives in human creativity—in the power of men and women to *turn* necessity. First beholding the glacial mountains, beautiful yet dreadful, Shelley is overwhelmed by "a sentiment of ecstatic wonder, not unallied to madness" that agitates his "regard" and his "imagination" (*SL* 1:497). What particularly stokes his empirical and creative faculties is an insight into how the mind relates to matter. While he watches the Alpine region unfold before him—with its "vast" and "snowy pyramids," its ravine overflowing with the "untameable Arve"—he realizes that this scene is as much created in his own mind as it is discovered in his sight, for the impressions in his mind will one day produce the scene in the minds of others. His mental images of the Alpine glaciers are creations in their own right, powerful enough to *replace* Mont Blanc in the minds of others (1:497). This power to turn, or trope, nature's necessities into mental images is the virtue of Ormuzd.

If Ahrimanes personifies indifferent, inhuman necessity, then Ormuzd is a figure for the process by which humans channel the currents of cosmic determinism into ameliorative patterns. If Shelley's Ahrimanes is strict fate, then his Ormuzd is limited freedom. If Ahrimanes is a line, Ormuzd is a slight bend. If Ahrimanes is blind matter, Ormuzd is conscious mind.

This inflection of Zoroastrian magic through the problem of the relationship between mind and matter generates two questions. First, if Ahrimanes as necessity and Ormuzd as creativity are no longer enemies in a dualistic universe, then how do they relate to one another? Second, if Ahrimanes is no longer mere evil and Ormuzd no more simple good, then what are their respective relationships to good and evil?

Shelley provides a clue to the relationship between matter and mind—Ahrimanes and Ormuzd—at the end of his rhapsody on mental powers. After exploring the possibility that his mind creates the Alpine scene, he claims that "[n]ature was the poet, whose harmony held our spirits more breathless than that of the divinest" (*SL* 1:497). This statement suggests that nature creates the human minds that in turn reshape its forms. Necessity creates undetermined patterns. Creative minds adhere to fate. Nature as a poet is mind as much as matter. Poet as nature is matter as much as mind. How can nature be necessity and creativity? How can the poet be free and fated?

In "A Defence of Poetry" (1819), Shelley speculates on the relationship between internal imagination and external reality. Employing a favorite Romantic image of the poetic mind, Shelley compares "Man" to "an instrument over which a series of external and internal impressions are driven, like the alterations of an ever-changing wind over an Aeolian lyre, which move it by their motion to an ever-changing melody" (*PS* 277). The wind is necessity. Everything in the universe is, like man, an Aeolian harp, a passive instrument through which this power flows. However, as Shelley continues, "there is a principle within the human being, and perhaps within all sentient beings, which acts otherwise than in the lyre, and produces not melody, alone, but harmony, by an internal adjustment of the sounds or motions thus excited to the impressions which excite them. It is as if the lyre could accommodate its chords to the motions of that which strikes them; even as the musician can accommodate his voice to the sound of the lyre" (277). The fated harp can yet freely turn the winds in new directions. Although it responds

passively to the currents, it—the harp, the human, possibly any sentient being—still activates its own powers. The wind strikes the
strings into sound. The strings turn the air into harmony. On a basic
level, all sentient beings transform the raw information of their environment into meaningful messages concerning food, shelter, or
sex. On a simple human level, most everyone translates the droning
"tick-tick" of a clock into a more harmonious "tick-tock." In a more
complex fashion, the poet receives external and internal impressions
that he renders back into images appropriate to his own disposition.

All beings that feel—and this category may include rocks and
plants as well as humans and animals—are similar in kind. They
are determined to be moderately undetermined. However, despite
this common element—the ability to differentiate slightly from
necessity and thus bend law in one direction or another—sentient
beings are distinct in degree. Some are able to gain greater distances than others from the flows of fate. These freer beings are
thus able to entertain wider arrays of possibilities for turning these
flows. An amoeba in a stream barely distinguishes itself from the
current on which it floats. A fish, too, is almost continuous with
the water but yet navigates in more complex ways than the
amoeba. An otter, though immersed in the flood, peeks its head
above the surface to see more clearly where it wants to go. But a
human, though he requires water and must return to it often, for
certain periods stands on the shore, surveys the waves, and concocts complex plans of navigation.

Hence, Ahrimanes as fate or matter and Ormuzd as freedom
or mind are not mutually exclusive. They are two aspects of one
process. This process is "life." In "On Life" (1819), Shelley claims
that materialism—a belief that mechanical matter is all that exists—is limited, for it discounts the ability of humans to transcend
mentally the "change and extinction" that rule the physical realm.
Man distances himself from his immediate material context (Ahrimanes's chains) by sending his thoughts (wings of Ormuzd) to the

past, to the future, and through eternity. He simply cannot imagine his own annihilation, for "there is a spirit within him at enmity with nothingness and dissolution" (*PS* 173). Hence, "life" is not mechanical matter but a thriving organ in which "[e]ach is at once the centre and the circumference" (173). This organ is a mental unity, a universal "mind."

Shelley reaches this conclusion through a blending of Humean empiricism and Platonic idealism, a strange marriage the poet discovered in William Drummond's *Academical Questions* (1805).[93] Following Hume, Shelley explains that casual relationships among empirical events are not necessary connections but arbitrary links based on habitual mental associations. If "[n]othing exists but as it is perceived" (*PS* 173), then the mechanistic worldview is a product of a certain habit of mind. This Humean skepticism does not lead Shelley to cynicism. It inspires in him a Platonic vision of a universal mind. If the divisions of the mechanistic philosophy—like subject and object, cause and effect, self and other—are based on mental habits, then the opposite could just as well be true: subjects and objects, causes and effects, selves and others could well be "merely marks employed to denote the different modifications of the one mind" (174).

Shelley proposes such a possibility for three reasons. First, the human mind yearning for holistic powers beyond the divisions of time and space perhaps recollects an origin in an eternal consciousness. Two, if the divisions of space and time are illusory, based on arbitrary mental habits, it could follow that a mental principle beyond space and time generates life and being. Three, if "to be is to be perceived," then an intuition of a universal mind is just as valid as an empirical perception of mechanism.

Ultimately, Shelley realizes that we cannot know if a collective mind exists. In meditating on this "intellectual philosophy," "[w]e are on the verge where words abandon us, and what wonder if we grow dizzy to look down the dark abyss of—how little we know"

(*PS* 174). Even if we could intuit an immense mind that organizes cosmic matter into harmonies—just as individual minds arrange perceptions into meaningful relationships—we could not grasp this mind's cause. We can conclude only this: The universal mind—the power of life—originates in an abysmal realm beyond our ken.

Shelley's concept of life presupposes two aspects: an abysmal cause and an organizing mind. Though Shelley does not explain how these two powers relate, he offers clues in "On Life" and in "Defence of Poetry." In the former work, as we have seen, he claims that each being is simultaneously the "centre and circumference." To exist as middle and periphery, an organ must inhabit a cosmos whose center is everywhere and circumference nowhere. In such a paradoxical sphere—circumscribed and uncircumscribed—each part is finite and infinite, discrete and distributed, itself and not itself, differentiated and indifferent, unique and common. Each being is identical with every other living thing because the same circumference, the same unbounded space, binds all things. Yet, each being is also different from every other being. Each is its own unique center, its own place on the sphereless sphere. The circumference resembles the mysterious cause, the ungraspable necessity. The center is analogous to the differentiating mind, the power to distinguish and organize. The cause, or necessity, is indifferent, undifferentiated force—gravity, electricity, instinct—a power that every living thing shares. The mind is the cosmic faculty of differentiation, of distinction, of individuation—that which divides gravity into galaxies, galvanic flows into lightning, instinct into species. Thus, in the context of Shelley's image of the Aeolian harp, undifferentiated necessity is the wind, and differentiated mind constitutes each individual harp. Every sentient being as a harp depends upon the wind for its existence as a harp but at the same time turns the wind to create an individual harmony. Dependence on an indifferent, unseen cause is necessity. Power to divide the wind into meaningful patterns of sound is mind. Ahrimanes is wind. Harmony is Ormuzd.

As the power of differentiation, the universal mind resembles the mental organization described by Gregory Bateson in *Mind and Nature* (1979). Bateson argues that a mind is not simply a mass of nerves inside a human skull but rather the capacity to differentiate. Hence, a mind is not one thing or another but the power of relationship—the capability to divide and relate—and thus the "metapattern" that connects all patterns.[94] In this way, Bateson's mind is akin to the organic power that differentiates parts while relating them to wholes. At the same time that Shelley was envisioning mind as one aspect of life, Coleridge in *Theory of Life* (1816) defined life as "*the principle of individuation* or the power that unites a given *all* into a *whole* that is presupposed by all its parts*" (*CC* 11:510). Life is a relationship, a power that unifies and separates, that divides a one into a many and combines the many into a one. Thus, life, like Bateson's mind, is polarized, exhibiting a tendency "*at once to individuate and to connect, to detach, but so as either to retain or to reproduce attachment*" (510).

But the power to differentiate requires as its own complementary opposite an indifferent force. The rhythmical waves require a faceless ocean. Darting amoebas must be shot through with instinct. Imagination needs nerves. Necessity and mind; energy and form; fate and freedom: These are the right and left hands of life. As Emerson explains in "Fate" (1860), these two primary forces of the cosmos, fate and intellectual power, are never separate: "If Fate follows and limits power, power attends and antagonizes Fate." Hence, the "jet of chaos which threatens to exterminate us," can be converted by "intellect into wholesome force." The "water drowns ship and sailor, like a grain of dust. But learn to swim, trim your bark, and the waves which drowned it, will be cloven by it, and carry it, like its own foam, a plume and a power." Likewise, the "cold is inconsiderate of persons, tingles your blood, freezes a man like a dewdrop. But learn to skate, and the ice will give you a graceful, sweet, and poetic motion."[95]

NEGATIVE GNOSIS

To digress, quickly: Unlike Emerson, who on the crepuscular common directly perceives the currents of the universal being, and unlike Thoreau, who before the thawing bank intuits the playful demiurge drafting coral and crystal, Shelley is skeptical of achieving a "positive" gnosis—an immediate and indubitable experience of the whole informing the parts. Rather, as Shelley suggests in "On Life" and as he will intimate in "Mont Blanc," the most that the visionary can hope for in this world is a "negative" gnosis—a sublime yet skeptical sense that no empirical form or psychic intuition reveals the deep cause of existence. Emerson and Thoreau maintain that palpable patterns, properly perceived, *open* into the abyss of being. Shelley, on the contrary, believes that these same discrete parts, no matter how they are observed, *veil* their origin. Emerson and Thoreau enjoy *direct* apprehensions of their identity with the abyss—the *tat tvam asi*, thou art that. Shelley, however, *indirectly* comprehends the same abyss through difference, through what it is not. It is not this, not that. *Netti, netti.* It must be something else.

Yet, this difference between positive and negative gnosis is one of degree and not of kind. Like Emerson and Thoreau, Shelley believes that origin of the cosmos is not Jehovah but an abysmal spiritual energy; that this abyss does not manifest itself in the world as good as opposed to evil but rather in pairs of mutually interdependent opposites; that each being in this cosmos is a pattern of this abyss—not a unit of fallen matter separated from God—and thus a coincidence of opposites, a microcosm of the macrocosm; and that this abysmal energy can be revealed and channeled by certain arts, such as alchemy or poetry.

Shelley is simply less willing than Emerson and Thoreau to proclaim with intuitive certainty that this deep cause definitely exists. Like Hume, he suspects that things and thoughts are quick ephemera that cannot disclose stable truths. Yet, like Plato, he conjectures that beyond these brief glitters and glooms is a transcendental yet immanent plenitude of being. Skeptical, he cannot be sure of either surmise. However, informed in the sublime sciences limned by Darwin and studied in the magical conjectures of Paracelsus, he can believe that the cosmos of the perennial philosophers—the material universe as a polarized precipitation of a spiritual abyss—is the most reasonable to the positivist, the most amenable to the poet, and the most ameliorative to the reformer.[96]

TYRANNY AND LOVE

To return to the current: If Shelley's Ahrimanes and Ormuzd are not evil and good deities forever at odds but complementary opposites, then how is one to differentiate between good and evil? For Shelley, evil exists in efforts designed to *violate* the mysterious cause of life; good inheres in actions meant to *direct* this same cause into ameliorative directions. The basis of evil is tyranny—the egocentric attempt to divide the world into controllable bits. The ground of good is love: a desire to connect with others in such a way that the ego is blurred, merged, and unified with some power greater than itself. In the former case, the tyrant trying to turn necessity to his own selfish purposes entraps himself, ironically, in a deterministic scheme. In the latter, the lover desiring to merge with others unexpectedly finds himself free to create.

Shelley instances these ideas in *Prometheus Unbound*. He explores the tyrant in Jupiter and the lover in Prometheus, and meditates on how both of these forms relate to necessity, a power that Demogorgon appears to personify.[97] Whether Jupiter is a separate entity or a projection of Prometheus's mind (both readings are valid),[98] this cosmic tyrant wants to control the universe, to turn all things into doubles of his selfish desires. Yet, his assumption that his separate ego rules other things and egos reveals his ignorance of two primary facts of nature. One, there is an abysmal cause that generates all acts and thus refutes the ruler's conviction that he is *causa sui*. Two, this cause pervades and unifies all phenomena; therefore, it unveils hierarchies as illusions.

Jupiter demonstrates his blindness of this deep cause in a long speech in which he asserts his supreme power. Like Oedipus in *Oedipus Rex*, he proclaims his knowledge and potency in lines that ironically show that he is ignorant and powerless. On his heavenly throne and surrounded by his subjects, the tyrant states that he is "omnipotent." He has "subdued" everything but the reproachful soul of man. He will soon "trample" this soul through the agency of his child by Thetis. This "fatal Child" will be the "terror of the Earth." He will grant Jupiter total control. However, Jupiter soon finds that this child is in reality Demogorgon. This enigmatic being, akin to fate, arrives in the midst of Jupiter's speech, dethrones the tyrant, and pulls him into oblivion. Thinking himself master of all, Jupiter is in fact a slave, not only to the fate that undoes him but also to those whom he thinks he rules. What he does not know is that the main cause of his fall is his slave's renunciation of hatred. When Prometheus recalls his curse of Jupiter and begins to pity his oppressor—in essence no longer acknowledging him as a tyrant but as a living being—then Jupiter simply disappears (*PU* 3.1.1–83).

Three illuminating elements emerge from Jupiter's fall. One, in trying to alter fate to fit his own ends—in attempting to play the egotistical magician—the tyrant psychically separates himself from necessity. He thus persists in perverse fantasies: He believes that his subjectivity is distinct from and superior to the objects he beholds, that he absolutely knows and controls the laws of nature, and that he is totally autonomous. Two, in psychologically dividing himself from the currents of nature (he cannot physically distinguish himself), the tyrant, ironically, enslaves himself between the Scylla and Charybdis of desire and fear. He is obsessed, and thus controlled, by his yearning for a complete power that he can never attain; yearning thus, he is haunted by a fear of losing the power he thinks he possesses. Three, attempting total ascendancy, the tyrant secures his fall, for his strict measures inspire his subjects to question his power, to demystify him, to humanize him, and thus to strip him of his identity as dictator.

Prometheus counters Jupiter. Initially, Prometheus believes in Jupiter's fictions of tyranny and thus proves a double of his oppressor. Hollowed by hatred toward his alleged master, he becomes himself a tyrant, even though he appears to be a slave. Like Jupiter, he is blinded by revenge and thus imprisoned in his obsessed mind. Yet, when Prometheus denounces hatred and replaces it with pity, he recalls his curse (*PU* 1.1–71). Fittingly, this curse is recited to him by the shade of Jupiter, an event that again shows that hatred is tyranny. Soon after beholding his former tyranny (in the same way that the "Magus Zoroaster" once "met his own image walking in a garden"), he fully repents his former transgression (1.191–261). He admits: "I wish no living thing to suffer pain" (1.306). Ruled by love, he reconnects with Asia, a multifaceted figure for his beloved, for his "feminine," "emotional" side, and for life in general. Thus implicated lovingly in an "other"—another person as well as the distributed power of life—he descends—indirectly, through the agency of Asia—into the lair of Demogorgon and thus also merges with abysmal fate itself, the cause of life. Connected thus, he frees himself from his chains, reunites with Asia in body as well as mind, and creates the world in his own image of harmony and democracy (1.804–834).

From this sketch of Prometheus arise three salient points. First, the person ruled by love escapes the oppressive fictions of the tyrant. Merging with others, he understands that his identity is not separate from and superior (or inferior) to the objects he beholds but part of a larger current of life. He becomes humble before the mystery of being, content to work *with* the grain of life though he may not know certainly its origin and laws. Second, the loving person, in relinquishing the fiction of a separate, autonomous ego, is liberated from the shackles of fear and desire. If "I" and "you" are illusions, false divisions in a cosmos unified by life, then there is no substantial "other" to fear or desire. Freed to flow with the current of being, the loving individual is, third, capable of directing this current into patterns—poems and gardens—that enrich his environment. Prometheus the cosmological magus—like a harmonizing Aeolian harp or an organizing mind—shatters oppressive fictions, experiences the vigor of the currents of life, and bends these flows into forms that nourish the world. As Demogorgon proclaims during his dialogue with Asia, "[a]ll things are subject" to "Fate" but "eternal Love" (*PU* 2.4.120).

What do these digressions on fate and freedom, matter and mind, evil and good, have to do with glaciers and "Mont Blanc?" In the snowy Alps Shelley finds these relationships revealed and illuminated. He discovers in the frozen floods the powers of the universal mind, his relationship to this mental force, and the possibility of mountain magic capable of redeeming the world.

FROZEN FLOODS AND THE WITCH POESY

"Mont Blanc" opens with an image that appears to have nothing to do with glaciers and mountains.[99] Instead of detailing his Alpine surroundings, Shelley's poet paints a relationship between mind and matter.

> The everlasting universe of things
> Flows through the mind, and rolls its rapid waves,
> Now dark—now glittering—now reflecting gloom—
> Now lending splendour, where from secret springs
> The source of human thought its tribute brings
> Of waters,—with a sound but half its own.
> Such as a feeble brook will oft assume

In the wild woods, among the mountains lone,
Where waterfalls around it leap for ever,
Where woods and winds contend, and a vast river
Over its rocks ceaselessly bursts and raves. (*MB* 1–11)

The "everlasting universe of things" and "the mind" engage in Wordsworth's "ennobling interchange." The stream of things like a strong river—now shimmering, now shadowy—flows through the mind, nourishing it and stimulating it with flickering golds and browns. Yet, the mind like a channel directs and alters the river, bending its currents, resounding its roar, and contributing its own waters from "secret springs." So blended are mind and the flow of things that they are almost indiscernible: The "its" in the phrase "with a sound but half its own" could refer to either the "everlasting universe of things" or "source of human thought." If the stream of experience is a river, then the mind is a brook bed generated by its own spring but welcoming the river's flow. If experience is the wind, the mind is a gathering of trees inhaling the wind and transforming its current into nourishing air.[100] In each case, the mind—which could be an individual human mind or the universal mind—is shaped by and shapes the flow of things while the currents of experience form and are formed by the mental power. Yet, importantly, both powers are part of one process, one living whole. The woods and wind could not exist without each other, nor could the riverbed and the water. These seemingly different powers are two aspects—like necessity and mind, fate and freedom—of the process of life.[101]

But why does Shelley's poet open "Mont Blanc" with a description of mind and experience that ostensibly has little to do with glaciers? He foregrounds the powers of his mind. He transforms—like a bed its river, like a leaf the air—the flowing data of the Alpine scene into a pattern significant to his human concerns, into a symbol of the connection between mind and matter. This pattern in turn enriches his relationship with the frozen Alps, empowering him to embrace them as stunning manifestations of living processes that he shares. Beginning the poem with the conclusion of his Alpine experience, the poet prepares himself and his readers to envision the seemingly inhumane, indifferent peaks not as evil, threatening "others" but as strange familiars, homely monsters. But in what way do the glaciers inspire such a theory of mind and matter?

Shelley's poet opens the next stanza by personifying the Ravine of Arve. Calling the gorge "thou," he familiarizes it, connects it to human experience, merges mind and matter. Further, he imaginatively transforms the ravine into a more expansive version of the creek bed pictured in the first stanza. Not a meaningless mess of rocks, the ravine is a symbol of a universal mind through which necessity—the wide Arve—thunders.[102]

The ravine as mind is a "many-coloured, many-voiced vale." It is filled with "pines, and crags, and caverns" over which sail "cloud shadows and sunbeams" and through which courses the Arve and a "Power in likeness of the Arve" descending from the "ice gulphs." These icy abysses—the frozen peaks and the glaciers—"gird" this power's origin, a "secret throne" from which a hidden being sends down forces that flash through the ravine like "lightning through the tempest" (*MB* 12–19). Hence, the winds, waters, and invisible power issue from the abysmal, "awful" cause. Yet, this necessity is not a principle of crass materialism. It generates creative minds to shape its currents.

This mountain "Power" courses its "chainless winds" through the ravine's "giant brood of pines." These ubiquitous breezes "drink" the odors of the needles and hear the harmonious sounds of the swinging branches. Like the woods of the first stanza, these trees, elements of an expansive mind, thus relate to the wind, the power of necessity, in two ways. First, in their blowing and whistling, they manifest to sight and sound a wind that would otherwise remain invisible and soundless. Second, in exhaling a current of their own, they alter and enrich the wind. Moreover, the "Power" from the icy gulps cascades through the valley in the form of waterfalls whose prismatic droplets generate "earthly rainbows" in the ravine. These rainbows, like the trees, reveal and transmute the unseen power. In refracting into diverse hues the invisible currents of this power, these multi-colored bows gesture toward the power's hidden presence while altering its composition (*MB* 19–27). Finally, the descending power produces in the ravine a "strange sleep / Which when the voices of the desert fail / Wraps all in its own deep eternity" (27–8). Necessity originates even the dreams of those who people the ravine. These dreams block the physical sounds of the icy desert above but nonetheless, lulled by whistling trees and the roar of waters, open into a mysterious eternity that inspires fresh waking thoughts.

Agitated by these echoes and commotions of the ravine, Shelley's poet explores his own relationship to these immense processes.

> Dizzy Ravine! And when I gaze on thee
> I seem as in a trance sublime and strange
> To muse on my own separate phantasy,
> My own, my human mind, which passively
> Now renders and receives fast influencings,
> Holding an unremitting interchange
> With the clear universe of things around;
> One legion of wild thoughts, whose wandering wings
> Now float above thy darkness, and now rest
> Where that or thou art no unbidden guest,
> In the still cave of the witch Poesy,
> Seeking among the shadows that pass by
> Ghosts of all things that are, some shade of thee,
> Some phantom, some faint image; till the breast
> From which they fled recalls them, thou art there! (*MB* 34–48)

Discovering in the ravine hints of a cosmic mind, the poet looks to his own psychic constitution. He finds that his mind resembles the universal one in receiving and rendering—passively accepting and actively translating—the stream of experience, in engaging in a perpetual "interchange" between the necessity of things and its own mental powers. In this present case, his mind is in the process of converting the powers of the Arve itself into coherent images. Initially, his "phantasy" is overwhelmed by the river's force, able to generate only "wild thoughts" that flap aimlessly over the "darkness." However, he calms his mind by imagining for it a place of repose separate from the flux: "the still cave of the witch Poesy." This mental *topos*, generated but yet sequestered from the flow of experience, is the site of poetic creation. It houses the secret springs of the individual mind, the currents that contribute to the floods of necessity. It proffers a tranquil bank from which one can select, reorganize, and harmonize certain streams of life.

This mental space is witchy, magic, the region of Ormuzd where humans fashion their own forms to alter the laws of Ahrimanes. If the mind is an Aeolian harp, this witch is its capacity to convert melody into harmony. If the mind is a prism, she is the ability to arrange driving white light into quiet rainbows. As powers of the Arve course through the mind, "Poesy" stands aloof from the amorphous images of experience and looks for images that she favors, that she might clarify and polish into a symbol, a poem.

Yet, just as the images of necessity can flood the poet's mind, so they can withdraw. While the poetic witch is exploring the flow, the ghostly waters return to their origin, the "breast" from which they issue. Following this flow to its source, the witch faces again the Arve, which could be the cause of the mental images or a particular manifestation of an even deeper cause. Whatever the ultimate origin of the universe of things, the point is this: no matter how powerful the magic of the witch, her craft is dependent always on the indifferent necessities of "all things that are."

The third stanza opens with the poet deflated by this withdrawal of images. He suggests that, like some dreamer, he has experienced in the witch's cave "gleams of a remoter world"—a nonphysical region that even the dead might see in their eternal sleep. Then, looking "on high" to the frozen peaks, he wonders if he has been abruptly awakened from such a dream or even from death, for the "unknown omnipotence" of the icy towers seems to have unfurled a "veil" separating his life from the visions of the dead. If he has not been flung back to the limits of wakefulness, then perhaps, he conjectures, he is still in a dream and surrounded by an inaccessible realm of mighty sleep (*MB* 54–7).

Despair and doubt beset the poet. His magical power, his witch Poesy, no longer rests in a stable cave. She is "[d]riven like a homeless cloud from steep to steep / That vanishes among the viewless gales." The poet's mental powers are failing. He does not know if he is alive or dead, awake or asleep. He is insubstantial, a fading cloud (*MB* 57–9).

How to account for this poet's sudden exhaustion, coming so quickly after his sublime vision of his place in the cosmos? Possibly, the poet pulled too intensely into his psychic interiors. He became overly enamored of his own imagination. He went too deep into the cave of poesy. Thus, he narcissistically disconnected himself from the nourishing flows of things. Unmoored, he is now impotent, confused.

To shock himself back into an awareness of his place in the world—to reorient himself to things or to search more deeply for the "breast" from which mental images issue—the poet turns outward. He stares at the peak of Mont Blanc. Yet, cowering under the "unearthly" ice of the peaks and before the glacial "floods" below, he feels further fear. He beholds indifferent forces of annihilation: a "desart peopled by storms alone," a "rude," "bare," and "ghastly" region, hideously "riven" and "scarred." Quaking before this ostensibly meaningless scene—one that escapes his powers of interpretation—he can only wonder about its nature. Is it the place "[w]here the old Earthquake-daemon taught her young / Ruin?" Is it a site where "a sea of fire" once enveloped "this silent snow?" (*MB* 60–74).

If the poet during his earlier deflation and disorientation suffered from too much interiority, then here he suffers from excessive exteriority. Horrifying forces overwhelm his mind. The witch Poesy flounders in the current. Earlier, he could familiarize the Arve by discovering in its shape and function homologies with his own mind. Now, he cannot find words to connect himself with the frozen peak and glaciers, to pattern them as "others" that are somehow the "same." Aloof and inaccessible, the icy gulphs strike him as entirely "other." They are therefore threats not only to his identity but also to all human systems of meaning. Shelley's poet is on the verge of demonizing the icy peaks.

To repeat: Going to one extreme of self-admiration, the poet severs his mind from the nourishing flows of things and thus undergoes disorientation and despair; pushing to the other extreme by focusing on natural processes devoid of human significance, he feels diminished as a creative agent, afraid of an environment over which he has no control. What the poet needs is a restoration of balance, a new interchange between the fast influencings and his separate "phantasy." This he achieves by reorienting himself to his glacial environment. After asking if the icy flows are sites of earth-rending quakes and snow-scorching fires, he experiences a "negative" intuition. He realizes that these questions cannot be answered. Therefore, the mountain freezes can be interpreted positively as well as negatively. If the peaks are always beyond understanding, then why not interpret them not as devils but as manifestation of the abysmal cause?

This appears to be the poet's reasoning. After admitting that no one can answer his questions, he claims, skeptically yet idealistically, that "all seems eternal now." Assuming that the Alpine ice embodies a power beyond the categories of space and time, the poet embraces the ice as a check on tyranny and an inspiration for charitable poetry.

The wilderness has a mysterious tongue
Which teaches awful doubt, or faith so mild,
So solemn, so serene, that man may be,
But for such faith, with nature reconciled,
Thou hast a voice, great Mountain, to repeal
Large codes of fraud and woe; not understood
By all, but which the wise, and great, and good
Interpret, or make felt, or deeply feel. (*MB* 76–83)

The obscure language of the ice need not be a demonic incantation. It can be a sublime oracle encouraging a healthy skepticism, a respect for cosmic powers beyond human ken, and a tentative faith, a hope that the ungraspable energies are as salubrious as they are ruinous. If one is noble enough to feel, interpret, or render the mountain ice in this way, then one sees it as a resounding voice against the corollaries of fraud and woe—an overturning of the oppressive "certainties" of the tyrant, a therapeutic expansion for the depressed. Interpreting the ice thus—patterning its mysterious currents with his own mind, with the "witch Poesy"—the poet overcomes his own tyranny and woe: his oppression of himself by his own ego and the consequent despair. He merges what was sundered—his own separate "phantasy" and the "clear universe of things." Like the ravine as universal mind, he submits to—flows with—the mysterious sources beyond his cognition. Yielding, he trusts these springs to nourish him. Empowered, he directs the channels. He lovingly focuses them on oppression and sadness.

Regaining a balance between his own fate and freedom, his personal Ahrimanes and Ormuzd, the poet in stanza four rises to consider the cosmic balance, the universe's vast relationships between power and poetry. Meditating on the "deadal" earth—its intricate imbrications of life and death, spring and winter, flux and stasis—he concludes that some indifferent, unchanging, ungraspable "Power" must cause the ephemeral reticulations. His poetic

witch revived, he finds an appropriate pattern by which to image
the two aspects of this interdependent relationship: the unseen
peak of Mont Blanc and the glaciers that flow down from the
heights. The "primaeval mountains" "teach" the "adverting
mind"—the attentive mind—that the "far fountains" of the hidden
peaks originate frozen shapes: "glaciers" that roll and "creep like
snakes that watch their prey," "frosted precipices" that "scorn
mortal power," and icy pinnacles that resemble "cit[ies] of death."
These manifestations of the hidden power, epitomized by the glaciers, constitute a "flood of ruin" that "[r]olls its perpetual stream"
like a juggernaut, destroying rocks, trees, insects, birds, beasts, humans, and villages. Yet, these glacial powers are also creative: the
ice carves the ravine of Arve, through which nourishing waters
rush with "restless gleam" to provide the "breath and blood of distant lands" (*MB* 99–125).

The glaciers are no longer mere agents of death but revelations of the universal mind. They divide indifferent power into
oppositions—life and death, creation and destruction—that generate the rhythmic process by which nature thrives. Differentiating and identifying, these oscillating flows of ice—like the
currents of the Arve—translate unity into diversity. Without them,
the undifferentiated power (the peak) would remain unmanifest.
With them, it realizes its potential in palpable forms that conceal
and reveal its obscure distances.

Energized by his glacial image of the relationship between
cosmic power and poetry, Ahrimanes and Ormuzd, the poet re-
considers his imagination. After witnessing the glaciers' organizations of the peak's power, he speculates on how his mind arranges
the forces of the heights—on how his mind is *glacial*. He again
gazes at the peak. He tries to picture what occurs on its unseen
heights—the sounds, the lives and deaths, the "calm darkness of
moonless nights," the "lone glare of day." Yet, again, he skeptically
concedes: "[N]one can behold" the qualities of this peak, and none

can hear its silence. All one can say of this power is that it is the dwelling of "the secret strength of things / Which governs thought" and determines the laws even of the "infinite dome / Of heaven." Still, though this necessity remains beyond knowledge, it is not beyond interpretation. The poet has grown. He can now familiarize the formerly foreign peak. He calls it "thou," personalizing it as he earlier personified the ravine. He realizes that this mysterious force is a law of his own being. He understands that he shapes this law. He inquiringly concludes: "And what were thou, and earth, and stars, and sea, / If to the human mind's imaginings / Silence and solitude were vacancy?" (*MB* 142–4).

The human mind, this rhetorical question suggests, is essential to the existence of the Mer de Glace. If the human mind did not interpret—did not make meaningful and moral—the powers of nature, then these energies would remain insignificant—vacant, barren. Amoral powers and indifferent laws energize the mind. The mind forms these potencies and principles into moral imperatives and differentiated organizations. Recalling Blake's proverb of hell, "[w]here man is not, nature is barren,"[103] Shelley's poet proposes, cautiously (he does not relinquish his "awful doubt"), that human minds are not separate from nature but an integral part of its functions. The glacier turns the peak's power into a polarized force of creation or destruction. The poet's mind—all poetic minds—trope the glacier, the river, the frozen pinnacle into symbols as essential to existence as air. The poet *creates* Mont Blanc. He realizes its invisible, aloof silence in familiar and palpable rhythms. He makes it a significant stranger, an exotic cipher of his innermost concerns, an uncanny range.

Properly seen, viewed scientifically as well as magically, the glacier, like the mind, like Shelley's poem, is a river or an ocean, a current of periodic waves, as much as a durable solid or a steadfast chunk.[104] To the egotistical magus, it may appear to be an undeviating, threatening other. To the cosmological magician the glacier is as fluid and salubrious as the Ganges or the Adriatic. It is Asia's "many winding River" on which the soul as "enchanted Boat" rides down to the "Ocean," and then to the "Sea profound, of ever-spreading sound" (*PU* 2.5.74–84). It is the "Wild West Wind" billowing to existence winter and spring, spring and fall.

POETICS OF INFINITE REGRESSION

The poet's mind is a glacier, creating and destroying as it flows with the universe of things. The form of its expression is also glacial, endlessly oscillating back and forth between opposing tendencies. Shelley's poet throughout this lyric undulates between elation and despair, interiority and exteriority, below and above, arrogance and humility. In the same way, the poem itself is a beginning and an end. Its opening is a conclusion, a theory of the interdependent relationship between mind and things that could only have come at the end of the poet's experience under Mont Blanc. Likewise, its ending is a beginning, a question about the relationship between mind and things that refers back to the theory at the beginning. Like Joyce's *Finnegans Wake*, which begins with the ending of the last sentence, like a Möbius strip, as an ouroboros, Shelley's poem revolves, each of its parts simultaneously forming a start and a finish, a life and a death. Moreover, the poem is both finite and infinite. On the one hand, it is a limited system of words and lines, contained on about three pages. On the other hand, it opens into an unlimited regression of signification, for Shelley's poem "Mont Blanc" contains Mont Blanc which itself is the law of all things in the universe and therefore includes the poem "Mont Blanc" that contains Mont Blanc, which includes "Mont Blanc," and so on, ad infinitum. The poem is like a set of all things that includes therefore the set of all things. It, like the glacial peaks, is simultaneously stable and dizzying.

The crystal embodies and reveals a poetics of self-organization. The glacier instances and intimates a poetics of infinite regression. One unlearned in glaciology experiences the Mer de Glace as an immovable mountain of white matter. Yet, one versed in the facts of glaciers knows that behind the bluish blanchings are frozen interiors that open into untold millennia. The present glacier turns vacuum, sucking its observer back millions of years to an unimaginable Ice Age, a world covered in blinding white. But even this juggernautical ice, on the verge of exploding deserts to mountains, peaks to rivers, is not the source of the Ice Sea under the White Mountain. This primeval freeze is itself an agent of ageless laws of global formation that fade into a beginningless prehistory, an origin that infinitely recedes. A forward moving vertigo matches this backward one. The present Mer de Glace is also a portal to endless futures: the Alps deflated into valleys of new oceans, London reduced to a few stones, humans turned fossils. This is the uniformitarian sublime: Agents of geomorphic transformation become windows to interminable laws of metamorphosis that admit "no vestige of a beginning, no prospect of an end." As a powerful and prominent organ of such laws, the Mer de Glace, like all glaciers, stuns its observer into the vertigo of infinite regress—origins that have origins that have origins, ad infinitum, and ad infinitum, ends that point to ends that open to more ends.

In another mood, one witnesses the Mer de Glace as a catastrophist would. The ostensibly still ice becomes a snapshot of the crest of an immense wave—a brief pause in the universal vacillation of creation and dissolution, a calm before the crest crashes into the trough, crushing the cosmos into new birth, a beginning that already contains its own decay. The catastrophic vision transforms everything, no matter how seemingly stable, into but a pulse of the eternal rhythm of terror and tranquility. Solid foundations become soup bogs, which in turn become again granite. Nothing is as it seems. All being is unbeing. Matter does not matter. This is the spatial sublime suggested by the catastrophist theory: Something is really nothing, foundations are unfounded, mountains are waves. A primary agent of catastrophe, the Mer de Glace, as all glaciers, is a powerful revelation of this spatial vertigo.

Synthesizing both views of the glaciers—seeing it as an agent of interminable laws as well as an organ of universal creation and destruction—Shelley experiences one primary sensation throughout his glacial vision: vertigo, the simultaneous fear and love of falling through empty space or unclocked time. This dizziness—caused by floating in the nothing that is everything—agitates the form of Shelley's poem, an endlessly churning Möbius strip (a microcosm of the catastrophic cosmos) and an infinitely regressive set that contains all sets (an image of the uniformitarian universe). Revealing in form these energies, Shelley has fashioned in his verse a glacier.[105]

A glacier is a special revelation of what is true of everything in Shelley's cosmos—everything is potentially a portal to infinite time or boundless space. In the same way, the crystal in the context of Thoreau's work is a unique disclosure of what is ubiquitously present in the universe: Each event is a self-organized pattern of the whole. A crystal, like a glacier, opens into infinite regressions. A glacier, as a crystal, is a site of self-organization. Still, the crystal's shape tends to reveal autopoesis, while the form of the glacier is prone to disclose unending regression, and progression.

FRANKENSTEIN'S DUALISM

"Mont Blanc" features a mountain poet negotiating between fate and freedom. *Frankenstein* and *Manfred* explore Alpine magi unable to reconcile necessity and creativity. Victor and Manfred long to achieve the vision of Shelley's glacial poet, yet their egocentric desires thwart their abilities to flow with and thus trope the mysterious cause. Unable to relinquish their fictions of an autonomous ego, they cast fate as a current to be countered. Psychologically divorced from necessity, they become dualists. They endorse a division between fated matter and unfettered mind. Embracing this latter pole while demonizing the former one—placing Ormuzd and Ahrimanes at odds—they find themselves tragically separated from the nourishing current of things.

While Percy stood awed under the ice in 1816, Mary was beside him, registering her own impressions. She published the Alpine visions of her husband—his "Mont Blanc" and his letters to Peacock—in her 1817 *History of a Six Weeks' Tour,* and exposed her own mountain images in 1818, in *Frankenstein.*[106] In this novel, she composes her own version of "Mont Blanc," opening her second volume with a distraught Victor straining to find solace in the sublime ice. Aware that the monstrous outcome of his violation of fate—his magical overcoming of the necessity of death—has murdered his brother and caused his friend Justine to be executed for the crime, he rides to Chamonix for a slight respite from his mental torture. Ironically, given his earlier perversion of nature's rhythm between life and death, he praises the glaciers for their "silent workings of immutable laws."

> The weight upon my spirit was sensibly lightened as I plunged yet deeper into the ravine of Arve. The immense mountains and precipices that overhung me on every side—the sound of the river raging among the rocks, and the dashing of the waterfalls around, spoke of a power mighty as Omnipotence—and I ceased to fear, or to bend before any being less almighty than that which had created and ruled the elements, here displayed in their most terrific guise. Still, as I ascended higher, the valley assumed a more magnificent and astonishing power. Ruined castles hanging on the precipices of piny mountains; the impetuous Arve, and cottages every here and there peeping forth from among the trees, formed a scene of singular beauty. But it was augmented and rendered sublime by the mighty Alps, whose white and shining pyramids and domes towered above

all, as belonging to another earth, the habitations of another race of beings. (*F* 91)

Continuing, Victor reaches the valley of Chamonix proper, above which he no longer sees castles but "immense glaciers" descending from "the supreme and magnificent Mont Blanc." These mountain powers pull him from his despair and thus grant him the relief of oblivion. Heartened by this escape, he spends the next day attending to glaciers.

> I stood beside the sources of the Arveiron, which take their rise in a glacier, that with slow pace is advancing down from the summit of the hills, to barricade the valley. The abrupt sides of vast mountains were before me; the icy wall of the glacier overhung me; a few shattered pines were scattered around; and the solemn silence of this glorious presence-chamber of imperial Nature was broken only by the brawling waves or the fall of some vast fragment, the thunder sound of the avalanche or the cracking, reverberated along the mountains, of the accumulated ice, which, through the silent working of immutable laws, was ever and anon rent and torn, as if it had been but a plaything in their hands. These sublime and magnificent scenes afforded me the greatest consolation that I was capable of receiving. They elevated me from all littleness of feeling; and although they did not subdue my grief, they soothed and tranquillised it. In some degree, also, they diverted my mind from the thoughts over which it had brooded for the last month. (93)

Like Shelley's poet, Victor admires the frozen peak as a site of the "power mighty of Omnipotence" and the descending glaciers as polarized patterns of this power's laws. Flowing ice appears to Victor as a revelation of fate itself. Yet, for Victor, unlike the poet of "Mont Blanc," this indifferent energy is not connected to mind or consciousness. The glacier's rhythms do not make him more creative and wise by elevating him from his separate "phantasy" to an awareness of the universal mind. They do not inspire an ennobling interchange between his individual powers and the more holistic ones of the cosmos. The glaciers are to Victor oblivion, the *absence* of human thought. Their icy movements decenter human cares. They calm anxious men to unthinking stones.[107]

This dualistic vision of ice as fated matter distinct from fallen mind grows out of Victor's earlier relationship to universal law. Merging his youthful interest in magic with an adult knowledge of anatomy, Victor created a living being. Yet, this breakthrough did not constitute a cosmologically magical submission to fate. It proved an egocentrically magical violation of necessity. The experiment grew out of Victor's resentment toward the negative pole of the world's primary relationship, that between death and life: "Life and death appeared to me ideal bounds, which I should first break through, and pour a torrent of light into our dark world. A new species would bless me as its creator and source; many happy and excellent natures would owe their being to me. No father could claim the gratitude of his child so completely as I should deserve theirs. Pursuing these reflections, I thought, that if I could bestow animation upon lifeless matter, I might in the process of time . . . renew life where death had apparently devoted the body to corruption" (*F* 52–53). Nature's laws are the chief agents of a "dark world." Hating this world because it burns with death, Victor takes revenge upon it. His attack not only separates the human from the natural. It moreover transforms nature into a double of his egocentric desire. Notice that Victor is motivated less by a yearning to make other humans happy than by a longing to be ruler of appreciative subjects. His alleged impulse to "renew life" is a selfish fantasy to vanquish the world of what he most fears— death—and to rise to a dictator over a race of slaves. Trying to fulfill this wish, he supposes that the human mind in general is separate from and superior to the laws of matter and that his mind in particular is distinct from and better than those of the subjects he will rule.

By the time Victor reaches the Alps in despair, he remains such a dualist but reverses his hierarchy. Before he elevated his creative mind over deathly matter. Now he demonizes his mind and aggrandizes nature. This new relationship toward fate issues from the monstrous result of Victor's mental machinations. Victor's mental effort to overcome death ironically produces *more* death—a murderous being. Realizing this on the glacier, he loathes his consciousness as he formerly hated fate, and views fate as an escape from his guilty psychic disposition. His admiration for the ice does not grow from an impulse to embrace life but from a craven yearning to escape responsibility. Not a *topos* that inspires awareness of his connection to the cosmos, Victor's ice is an excuse to avoid awareness, to block insights that might explode into cosmic consciousness.

Victor's dualism blinds him. Praising mind, he neglects matter (recall the *ugliness* of his being). Lauding matter, he thwarts self-awareness (note the *naiveté* of Victor's escapist fantasy). Oscillating between these poles—now emphasizing the powers of his mind, now focusing only on the agencies of matter—Victor knows neither.

This double darkness is revealed on the glaciers. Still on his escapist excursion to the glaciers, he walks over the Mer de Glace. Suddenly, he feels this "river of ice" flowing through his own being and swells with "something like joy" at the prospect of merging with its majestic flux. Yet, just as he senses his unity with matter, he perceives bounding over the ice the monster itself, his creation. His despair returns. He curses the being and attempts to kill it. If Victor had possessed a deeper understanding of the "silent working of immutable laws," he might have realized that the creature's appearance on the glacier is not a violation of his sense of unity with fate but a consummation of the marriage. He perhaps would have embraced the creature as an outcome of his mental activities. He might have taken responsibility for the consequences of his limited freedom. He would have celebrated the being as an opportunity to restore to balance his increasing split between mind and matter.

Unable to welcome his creation, Victor tragically spends the remainder of his days oscillating between praising immutable laws as agents of forgetfulness and condemning fate as the cause of all of his woe. This contradiction—manifested by his closing speeches to Walton, in which he vacillates between condemning scientific hubris and rallying the crew to risk death for polar discovery— could have been avoided had Frankenstein, like Shelley's Alpine poet, been attuned to the lesson of the glacier. Yet, his dualistic theurgy condemns him in the end to take his place in a long tragic line of Faustian overreachers.

MANFRED, CLIMBING, AND TRANSCENDENCE

Like Shelley in *Frankenstein*, Byron in *Manfred* rewrites "Mont Blanc." Composing his drama in the wake of the summer of 1816—during which he was "half mad" with Mary and Percy, "metaphysics," and mountains"[108]—and soon after he wrote the Alpine scenes in *Childe Harold's Pilgrimage* (1814–17)—which are characterized by paeans to "throned Eternity in icy halls / Of cold sublimity"[109]—Bryon in this piece features an egocentric magus struggling in the snowy peaks.[110]

As Manfred explains to the Witch of the Alps—whom he has conjured in the Swiss Alps—throughout his life he climbed icy summits in hopes of transcending fate.

> . . . . From my youth upwards
> My Spirit walked not with the souls of men,
> Nor look'd upon the earth with human eyes;
> The thirst of their ambition was not mine,

> The aim of their existence was not mine;
> My joys, my griefs, my passions, and my powers,
> Made me a stranger; though I wore the form,
> I had no sympathy with breathing flesh,
> Nor midst the creatures of clay that girded me
> Was there but one who—but of her anon.
> I said, with men, and with the thoughts of men,
> I held but slight communion; but instead,
> My joy was in the Wilderness, to breathe
> The difficult air of the iced mountain's top,
> Where the birds dare not build, nor insect's wing
> Flit o'er the herbless granite. (*M* 2.2.50–65)

Presupposing a dualism between his spirit and his flesh as well as between his magical powers and the aims of ordinary folks, Manfred invokes the frozen peaks as realms worthy of his transcendental powers. His "breathing" the "difficult air" of the "iced mountain's top" symbolizes his overcoming of the limitations that beset other men. Hence, the glacial slopes are markers of fate. To climb the mountain ice is to battle with necessity. To reach the top is to vanquish the foe. As Manfred explains in his speech to the Witch, this climbing is inseparable from his other primary activity: the study of "sciences untaught / Save in the old-time," which has made him equal to the ancient "Magi" in perceiving and manipulating "Eternity" (2.2.83–96).

Climbing and conjuring: both offer respite from the conflict that troubles Manfred throughout the play—an *agon* between spirit and flesh. As he exclaims earlier, while hiking one morning on the frozen slopes of the Jungfrau, he, like all humans, is "[h]alf dust, half deity/ Alike unfit to sink or soar." Thus "mixed" in "essence," he contends always between "low wants and lofty will," "degradation" and "pride" (*M* 1.2.39–44). In Manfred's case, this dualistic conflict is instanced by his inability to overcome guilt. As he claims in his opening speech, which takes place in the high Alps, insight into and power over eternal energies, figured by the "Tree of Knowledge," is not tantamount to freedom from the pain, the tree of eternal "Life." His magical powers, his abilities to perceive and alter fate, have not enabled him to forget "that all-nameless hour" when he destroyed his beloved blood relative Astarte through committing a horrible crime with her, likely incest. Like Victor, Manfred has attempted to free himself from the shackles that moor ordinary men. Yet, also like Victor, he has remained tethered to the most common of chains: a guilty conscience.

The main action of the play involves Manfred's four attempts to employ his magic—associated with spirit, freedom, and Alpine peaks—to overcome this guilt—connected to matter, fate, and mountain glaciers. In the first extended scene, Manfred conjures the "Spirits of Earth and Air"—among whom is the spirit of Mont Blanc and the "Glaciers's cold and restless mass" moving "onward day by day"—to convince them to release him from his destiny: perpetual suffering over the tragedy of Astarte. For Manfred, this liberation will come with "forgetfulness." However, the spirits inform him that this oblivion cannot be granted, for even they do not forget. Like the glacier spirit he desires to transcend, he must remain tied to the events of his past, present, and future. This first failed attempt to achieve oblivion—not, as in Victor's case, by merging with fate but by overcoming it—ends with Manfred falling senseless at the sight of an image of Astarte (*M* 1.1.26–261).

Failing to find oblivion through his mind—he finds that his mind is tied to memory even when separated from a body—he, like Victor, attempts to annihilate his consciousness by merging with matter. In the next thaumaturgic scene, Manfred, overwhelmed with guilt, ascends to the "toppling crags of ice" and the misty "glaciers." In contact with the fateful powers he had earlier tried to reject, he commands the ice to crush him. His magic failing to accelerate the glaciers, he decides to leap from the peaks. He hopes to crash his "atoms" into those of the earth. However, just as he springs from the cliff, a hunter restrains him. Ironically, another child of the flesh he would throw off or destroy retains him still within the icy hoops of destiny (*M* 1.2.1–125).

With his own mental and corporeal powers impotent to violate fate, to free him from his past, he next conjures the Witch of the Alps—beautiful like "twilight" "rose tints" on the "lofty Glacier's virgin snow"—hoping that she might grant a "pardon to a Son Of Earth." He requests that she pardon him for Astarte's death; bring Astarte back from the dead; or allow him to die. To the first request, the Witch expresses astonishment. Why should a powerful magus be concerned with a "recreant mortality" that he should have transcended long ago? After Manfred explains his plight, likening himself to the Wandering Jew condemned to suffer without dying, the Witch softens and offers her help. Though she cannot revive Astarte or kill him, she might aid him if he will swear obedience to her will. This request outrages Manfred. He rejects the part of fate-battered wander and rises to his other pole of being—that of the arrogant magus who will bow before no one. He refuses her aid and commands her to retire (*M* 2.2.13–163). Hence, his encounter with the glacial Witch fails because he is overly weak and too brash: overly servile to the weaknesses of the flesh and too prideful to bend to the powers of another. Like Victor, he is doubly blind—unable to understand his material limitations, unwilling to grasp the extent of his mental powers.

Desperate, Manfred next tries to conquer the ruler of earthly fate, "Arimanes," who dwells on the summit of the Jungfrau. Reaching the peak of this mountain—having mastered the glaciers on its slope—Manfred again shows himself equal in power to the spirit world. He invokes the energies of an "overruling Infinite"— ostensibly Ormuzd—to constrain Ahrimanes to conjure a speaking image of Astarte. Standing before this phantom lover, come from a realm beyond that of Ahrimanes and his destinies, Manfred asks if he is pardoned or condemned. He receives no answer but discovers only that tomorrow his "earthly ills" will end. At the height of the Swiss Alps, above the cruising glaciers, Manfred, it seems, has been released from his suffering. Yet, we must note that only his "earthly ills" will cease—perhaps his spiritual ones will persist. Likewise, in the wake of his interview with this phantom, he is not empowered but "convulsed," shocked back into his own "mortality" (M 2.4.26–167). Though he has, like Shelley's poet, ascended to the origin of the earth's cause, he nonetheless remains, like Victor, split between a desire for control—an impulse to reduce the world to his double—and a penchant for subjection—for relinquishing his mental kingdom to become a slave to rocks.

This mountaintop vision calms Manfred's suffering. He feels tranquil knowing he has glimpsed eternal beauty. Yet, his bodily death, which occurs the day after his revelation, shows that he in the end remains a tragically minded dualist. Unlike Shelley's poet, he never embraces fate as the nourishment of his freedom, matter as the food of his mind. He continues to demonize powers that threaten his tyrannical ego. Cloistered in a tower—a symbol of his fantasy of an impermeable ego—he awaits his death. At the moment of his demise, demons appear to drag him to hell. He asserts his ego, defying the devils. A powerful magus to the last, he rejects them, and claims to die through the agency of his own will. Yet, this conviction is likely an illusion growing from his arrogance. His earthly death was prophesied, so how could he control it? Still, even if this belief concerning control is ungrounded, it nonetheless provides comfort. When Manfred slips away, he tells the attending priest that "tis not so difficult to die" (M 3.4.1–151).

⋆⇒◉⇐⋆

Manfred's tragedy is more complex than Victor's. Still, in the end it is a symptom of the same cause: the inability to embrace the glacier as an uncanny agent—familiar as a revelation of holistic law, strange as a sublime invitation to expand. Trapped in an "either/or" logic—the perverse logic of all tragic figures—both men split the cosmos in two—fire or ice, life or death—and pit one side against the other. They set going a battle within themselves, a competition between the unconscious and consciousness that reduces them to half-men. Rejecting the ice, they become ice men. Could they only see the glacier as a living mind of which their own thoughts form an integral part, they would again thaw, and find in the revolving crystals a thousand flames, or a portal to the staff of life itself, the central pole, the *axis mundi*, the omphalos, the caduceus—the esoteric Antarctic.

THREE

THE POLES

There was . . . no recognizable three-dimensional space in the Arctic. There was also no time. The sun never set, but neither did it appear. The dim round-the-clock light changed haphazardly when the lid of cloud thickened or thinned. Circumstances made the eating of meals random or impossible. I slept when I was tired. When I woke I walked out onto the colorless stripes and the revolving winds, where atmosphere mingled with distance, and where land, ice, and light blurred into a dreamy, freezing vapor that, lacking anything else to do with the stuff, I breathed. Now and then a white bird materialized out of the vapor and screamed. It was, in short, what one might, searching for words, call a beautiful land; it was more beautiful still when the sky cleared and the ice shone in the dark water.

—Annie Dillard, *"An Expedition to the Pole"*

POLAR DREAMS

In "Tlön, Uqbar, and Orbis Tertius" (1940), Jorge Luis Borges, deeply read in Poe, explores the consequences of creating fantastical fictions. In Borges's parable, a hermetic society has produced over two centuries a multivolumed encyclopedia of an imagined

world called Tlön. Appropriately, given Tlön's purely mental existence, the inhabitants of the realm are idealists. Believing that "to
be is to be perceived," they discredit scientific inquiry and embrace immediate intuition as the only reality. The language of
Tlön excludes nouns, which presuppose substance enduring
through change, and deploys only impersonal verbs and adverbs,
which express the ephemeral nature of unmediated contact.
Though this world interests Borges's narrator for its philosophies,
it most strikes him for a different reason: Tlön, a "fantastic
world," eventually becomes *actual* and intrudes into the "world of
reality." A vibrating compass whose case is etched in the script of
Tlön appears in a package from Poitiers. Later, a native from Tlön
materializes in Chucilla Negra. After a night of raving, he dies.
Coins from the corpse's belt are intolerably heavy. They effuse a
lingering oppressiveness. At the story's conclusion, reality has
yielded to the dreams of Tlön. Its fictitious history and philosophy
have erased other pasts and ways of thinking. Its language has
usurped familiar tongues.[1]

This tale is a testimony to the powers of the mind, suggesting
that an imagined world, if pictured with sufficient concreteness,
can become real. This possibility is not untroubled, for mental
systems that replace the real can be pernicious. As Borges's narrator observes, Tlön is similar to "dialectical materialism, anti-Semi-
tism, Nazism." Like these ideologies, it is a "symmetry with a
semblance of order" concocted by men to embody their narrow
dreams of harmony. The invasion of Tlön into the real is a form of
tyranny, an onslaught of the dreams of the few onto the thoughts
of the many. Significantly, a major force behind the encyclopedia
of Tlön was one Ezra Buckley, a nineteenth-century millionaire
slave owner from Memphis, Tennessee.[2]

A fantastical mental picture can also liberate. If "reality" is already imperialistic—a concoction of an evil demiurge (a Buckley
or a Hitler)—then a way of escaping such a world is to imagine a

more democratic, heterogeneous universe that might replace the current ideology. The vocation of the liberator is to counter the petty dreams of the tyrant with his own fantasies of an alternative universe more richly attuned to the variety of lived experience. Though initially foreign, this communal vision may prove a more accurate picture of an undying cosmic reality.

Fantastical worlds can become real in two ways—in the systems of the tyrant or the visions of the liberator. Likewise, real spaces can become fantastical in a twofold fashion. On the one hand, a tyrant might fictionalize a physical space so that he can exploit it. For instance, a developer desiring to transform a forest into profit might metaphorize the wooded ecosystem into raw material fit for human consumption. On the other hand, a liberator might transform a humanized region into the sublime laws sustaining the cosmos. A poet might release chthonic energies underlying city grids.

Unmapped spaces are most likely to inspire such fantasies. The virginal ices covering the poles have for centuries stimulated robust visions, serving as blank screens on which men have projected deep reveries—tyrannical narcissisms and spiritual sublimities. Ernest Shackleton expresses this relationship between reverie and *terra incognita* in a response to a journalist who once asked him how he first became obsessed with polar exploration. Surprisingly, this man noted for common sense claimed that his desire for the ice might have first emerged from an occult draft, or perhaps even from a dream.

> I think it came to me during my first voyage . . . I felt strangely drawn towards the mysterious south . . . we rounded Cape Horn in the depth of winter. It was one continuous blizzard all the way. . . . Yet . . . even in the midst of all this discomfort, my thoughts would go out to the southward. . . . But strangely enough, the circumstance which actually determined me to become an explorer was a dream I had when I was twenty-two. We

were beating out to New York from Gibraltar, and I dreamt I
was standing on the bridge in mid-Atlantic and looking north-
ward. It was a simple dream. I seemed to vow to myself that
some day I would go to the region of ice and snow and go on
and on till I came to one of the poles of the earth, the end of the
axis upon which this great round ball turns.[3]

Coming from a pragmatic explorer, this response sounds strange,
for it associates the poles not with glory or gain but with curious
attractors and somnambulistic visions. Yet, Shackleton's words express the spiritual impulse in almost all polar explorers: the longing to discover at the *axis mundi* the eternal center of oneself and
the universe—fantastic and unfamiliar to the rationalist, real and
intimate to the visionary.

However, in a more imperialistic disposition, Shackleton
enunciates other dreams of the polar ice as a surface to be exploited. In his dedication to *South* (1919)—his account of his last
and most dangerous expedition in the Antarctic continent from
1914 to 1916—he claims that he and his crew were engaged in a
"White Warfare of the South" while his British fellows were
falling in the "Red Fields of France and Flanders."[4] The South
Pole is not a portal to the mystery of life. It is an enemy that is
feared as a threat and desired as a possession. Shackleton's fantasy
of ice as an "other" to be transformed into a commodity embodies
another yearning that has driven men to the fields of ice from the
time of Pytheas to the days of Peary: the keen hunger to impose
something onto nothing, orderly grids onto indifferent plains, the
words of man onto silent nature. Not surprisingly, the Nazis with
whom Borges associates Tlön were interested in the poles as
mythological supports of Aryan hallucinations.[5]

Accounting for Shackleton's two tendencies—exoteric and esoteric—a spiritual history of the poles is a narrative of the relationships that emerge when the human mind contends with an abyss

beyond mental mapping. If the crystal is the microcosm revealing in its lattices the oceans of life and if the glacier is the mesocosm throbbing between earth and sky, then the poles are the macrocosm, undifferentiated life thriving beyond its heterogeneous forms. The poles are more threatening and more sublime than crystals or glaciers—more menacing because they invite and mock man's fantasies of complete order, more grand because they inspire explorers to transcend the discrete ego and dive into the distributed current.

Coleridge and Poe inflect in their work these polar powers, horrible yet holy, reality and dream. In *Rime of the Ancient Mariner* (1798), Coleridge sends his Mariner deep into the Antarctic Circle, where he is haunted by several reveries: violent dreams of monstrous ice, scientific fantasies of perfect maps, disturbing visions of a void that lives. Likewise, Poe in *The Narrative of Arthur Gordon Pym* (1838) ships his protagonist into the Antarctic outland. There Pym oscillates between a drive to dominate and yen to merge. In the end, he undergoes a terrific vision of a milky cataract, above which hovers an immense figure, fully white, fabulous as an angel.

ANTIPODES

In the ancient Western world, the poles appeared as blank screens on which men projected conflicting desires—their yearning for polarity, a harmony between opposites, and their longing for hierarchy, a relationship between unequal antinomies. Probably drawing from Parminedes or Thales, Aristotle speculates in *Meteorology* (ca. 330 B.C.) that the earth is a sphere divided into northern and southern zones that mirror one another. Both are comprised of a habitable region bounded by two uninhabitable ones—a fiery band near the equator and a frozen field at the pole. The cold realm to the north is *Arktikos*, for it rests under the constellation of *Arktos*, while the icy zone at the southernmost point is *Antarktikos*—the opposite of its northern counterpart.[6] In this view, the planet is balanced on

either end by interdependent antipodes unified by the axis on which
the heavens turn. However, these poles are nonetheless inferior
wastelands. They are thus central and peripheral, same and other,
desirable and repulsive. As the head and feet of the planet and points
on the world axle, they harmonize and turn the earth and its inhabitants. As frozen unknowns, they are different from the temperate
regions, "others" that help define the mapped regions as the "same."

Aristotle's speculative vision of the poles is not original. This
view arose as early as 400 B.C. and persisted throughout ancient geography until the time of Ptolemy (150 A.D.). Crates of Mallos (ca.
150 B.C.), a geographer associated with the Stoic school and often
credited with constructing the first globe in recorded history,
agrees with Aristotle, except that he claims that an ocean, not a
continent, circles the globe near the torrid equator.[7] Cicero follows
Crates in his "Dream of Scipio" sequence in *De Republica* (ca. 50
B.C.). Inspired by Plato's stunning vision of earth as seen from
above in his own *Republic* (ca. 380 B.C.), Cicero elevates Scipio into
the heavens, where he looks down upon an earth "rigid with ice" at
either end, torched with unbearable sun in the middle, and inhabited in two small zones crammed between fire and frost.[8] (Significantly, Cicero, like Plato, intends this vision to be a sobering lesson
to ambitious men who despite their arrogance know only a sliver of
a vast globe roiling and freezing with inhuman energies.[9]) Strabo in
his *Geographia* (ca. 10 A.D.) likewise invokes the mirroring-hemi-
sphere theory. He assumes like Crates that the two realms are forever divided, this time by an impassable desert.[10] Culminating this
geographical tradition, Ptolemy in his own *Geographia* (ca. 150
A.D.) explains the five-zone theory and wonders if there might be
below the torrid equator a vast *terra australis incognita*, an unknown
southern land, in which a civilized race lives forever separated from
the northern lands of Egypt, Greece, and Rome.[11]

Most ancient geographers agreed on this model of the globe.
However, disagreement arose over whether the southern region

was inhabited. Aristotle claimed that the unknown southern zone *could* sustain life but never speculated on an Antarctic civilization. However, Cleomedes, a second-century Greek astronomer and geographer influenced by Crates, argued in *On the Circular Motion of the Heavenly Bodies* that "life-loving" Nature fills the world "wherever possible." Hence, life exists in the southern realms just as it does in the northern ones.[12] What beings inhabit these unfamiliar spaces? For Strabo (ca. 64–18 A.D.) and the Stoic school, creatures *exactly* dissimilar to those dwelling in the known north people the mysterious south. When the sun rises in the south, it sets in the north. People below plant their footsteps in opposite directions from those above. This theory of opposing worlds inspired geographers to call the southern region the "Antipodes," "with the feet opposite," or "Antichthon," "counterworld."[13] Eratosthenes in *Hermes* (ca. 240 B.C.) countered this notion. Inspired, like Cicero, by Plato's astronautical view of the earth, Eratosthenes details Hermes's vision from the sky of a globe balanced on either end by races dwelling in fecund paradises: "Five encircling zones were girt around it: two of them darker than greyish-blue enamel, another one sandy and red, as if from fire. . . . Two others there were, standing opposite one another, between the heat and the showers of ice; both were temperate regions, growing with grain, the fruit of Eleusinian Demeter; in them dwelt men antipodal to each other."[14]

From these theories emerge two dichotomies concerning the southern continent that persisted until James Cook crossed the Antarctic Circle in the eighteenth century. First of all, for many ancient Europeans inhabiting the northern temperate zone (termed the *oikoumene*, or "known world"), the unknown southern hemisphere was the dark other, the alien planet—the antihuman, the monstrous. The reasons for this classical interpretation of the southern hemisphere are obvious. Geographers were empirically familiar with moderate tracts of the northern region, even receiving reports from Pytheas (ca. 300 B.C.) on the Arctic ice, and were thus bound to ground their Arctic cartographies on facts, however incomplete. However, these same mappers knew little of the spaces below the equator. Therefore, they projected upon this southern void images of their deepest phobias. This prejudice concerning the south likely caused Antarctic exploration to lag far behind forays into the Thules of the north. By the fifteenth century, when European geographers were gaining an accurate picture of the Arctic Circle, the bottom of the world remained a blank expanse or a precinct of freaks. Until Cook penetrated its outer ring, the South Pole was the world's unconscious, a reservoir of its repressed terrors. If the North Pole was horrifying, with its crushing bergs and ghostly floes, the *terra incognita australis* was literally dreadful *beyond* words, haunting men with utter darkness or unrelieved glare.

However, some classical geographers projected onto the southern void fantasies of paradise or visions of the sublime. This positive interpretation of the unknown pole suggests a second dichotomy of classical geography: that between positive and negative interpretations of the southern zone. While most members of the so-called Stoic school of geography, instanced by Crates and culminating with Strabo, viewed the south as a waste, Eratosthenes envisioned both poles as paradises beyond the clotted ignorance of the familiar world. Likewise, Cicero cast the unknown regions of the planet, including the poles, as sublime correctives to the ambitions of man. In both cases, the southern region is not monstrous but ameliorative. This favorable reading of the South Pole also outlived the classical age, sporadically surfacing until the eighteenth century, when geographers hoped that the Antarctic fostered El Dorado.

This portrait of classical geography introduces positive and negative currents of polar representation that endure through the Middle Ages, Renaissance, and eighteenth-century. Present in the age spanning from Aristotle to Ptolemy are the hierarchies that will concern medieval cartographies: bifurcations between civilized north and monstrous south. Likewise, blinding the ancient geographers are the polar blanks that later scientific explorers will yearn to map and consume. Further, the classical mappers also sense that the southern abyss is a portal to rich life.

BRUMAE AND BLEMYAE

St. Basil in the fourth century urged Christians to ignore unknown lands and instead to meditate on souls. St. Augustine at about the same time denied the existence of a habitable continent to the south. Yet, medieval geographers could not relinquish troubled dreams of an *alter orbis*.[15] Even though pious theologians condemned theories of an Antarctic race, the dream survived, primarily in the work of the Venerable Bede (673–735), who in *De natura rerum* divides the world into a northern pole "uninhabitable by reason of cold," a temperate zone, a torrid zone at the equator, an inhabited southern winter zone, and an "austral zone around the southern turning point which is covered with land and is uninhabitable by reason of the cold."[16]

Inspired by Bede's classical speculation, several medieval mapmakers turned to the south. One anonymous fifteenth-century cartographer labeled the southern hemisphere with one word, *brumae:* fogs—mists reducing waves and whales to blobs. Terse, terrifying descriptors of the *antichthon* also haunt an anonymous 1489 *mappa mundi: frigida*, frozen, and *perusta*, burned—the icy hell of Dante, and Milton's brimstone. Another geographer adds to these unsettling images, maintaining that the oceans below the equator endlessly boil under an unbearable sun.[17] In each case, the counterworld is the pernicious "other"—the contrary to order, light, and life. As pervasive fog, it recalls the abyss in Genesis, the chaos that Jehovah rectified; as ice, it likewise evokes an indifferent plain of white on which "this" and "that" are meaningless; like fire, it also reduces particular growths to flat ash; boiling water, it is nothing, again, but primal soup.

What could thrive in such a landscape but inhuman, inhumane creatures? When medieval geographers imagined the denizens of such inhospitable zones, they conjured monsters, giants, and demons. Lambert, the twelfth-century Canon of St. Omer, includes in his *Liber Floridus* a *mappa mundi* that devotes an entire half to an *australis terra incognita* inhabited by unimaginable aliens. Drawing from the five-zone theory, Lambert features two hemispheres: a northern one comprised of a temperate realm sandwiched between a polar freeze and an equatorial boil, and a southern one made, literally, of nothing—a large white blank containing only bloodless words. Depicted only in language, the southern region is

> unknown to the sons of Adam, having nothing which belongs to our race. The Equatorial Sea [Mediterranean] which here divided the [great land masses or continents of the] world, was not visible to the human eye; for the full strength of the sun always heated it, and permitted no passage to, or from, this southern zone. In the latter, however, was a race of Antipodes (as some philosophers believed), wholly different from man, through the difference of regions and climates. For when we are scorched with heat, they are chilled with cold; and the northern stars, which we are permitted to discern, are entirely hidden from them. . . . Days and nights they have one length; but the haste of the sun in the ending of the winter solstice causes them to suffer winter twice over.[18]

Like Strabo, Lambert in this version of "negative geography" conceives of the south as a forbidden planet harboring a race of aliens that are simply *not* what known humans are. Although one might fault Lambert—and Strabo's Stoic school—for lack of imagination, one must concede that his thin depiction of the southern realm reveals an important psychological insight: When humans are faced with an unknown quantity, they often assume that it is the *exact* opposite of the known. This unconscious mirroring is at the core of imperialism, spiritual or material. The Christian mapper must conceive of alien space as a zone of everything that he and his godly brethren are *not*, just as the political colonizer must represent the colonized as nonhumans who must be humanized. In both cases, the "other" mirrors—opposes, reverses—the "same" and thus solidifies by opposing the narcissistic identities of cultures who think themselves superior.[19]

If Lambert sketches his antipodal doubles with the abstract "not," his more imaginative contemporaries rise to more "positive" geographies of the south, painting blank spaces with uncouth monsters doubling unconscious fears and desires. Take the Hereford map, drawn by Richard of Holdingham in the 1280s and still hanging in the Hereford Cathedral in England. Based on the "T-O" model of many medieval maps—a circle divided by a "T" figure into the three continents of Asia, Europe, and Africa, with Jerusalem placed in the center—this map places Europe and the top half of Asia on the left, or northern side while it locates the bottom of Asia and Africa on the southern, or righthand side. The strip bordering the southernmost arc of the map is replete with no less than eleven Antarctic monsters. Among these are the Blemyae, with eyes and mouths on their breasts; the Himantopodes, who crawl on the ground with four legs; the Sciopods, a one-legged species notable for holding their single foot above their heads as an umbrella; and the Philli, who test the chastity of their wives by exposing babies to serpents (the "legitimate" infants are left unbitten while the "bastards" are instantly killed). These species are part of a group of fourteen monstrous peoples living along the South Pole, which includes, in addition to those mentioned, men with the heads of dogs, a horde who consumes serpents, and a species that suffers from such a small mouth that it must suck food through a reed.[20]

In depicting these *autre* beings, Richard was likely drawing from the Psalter *mappa mundi* (ca. 1250), one of the first medieval maps to feature in its southern corner all fourteen races, first described in Solinus's third-century *Collection of Marvels*.[21] These Antarctic races are likewise pictured in Higden's fourteenth-century *Polychronicon*. In addition to detailing some of the monsters already mentioned, Higden marvels over the Anthropophagi, a race of cannibals; the Garamantes, who thrive in waters that freeze in the night and boil during the day; the Virgogici, who eat insects; and the Antipodes, dancers with sixteen fingers.[22]

Culminating these medieval traditions is Sir John Mandeville, who in his *Travels* (ca. 1370) brings together the "negative" geography of a Lambert and the more troubled "positive" imaginings of a Richard or a Higden. On the one hand, he describes the antipodal nature of the southern region. At its polar bottom dwell men who are "foot against foot to those that dwell even under the Pole Arctic," a race and a land that runs contrary to those of the north. Yet, one the other hand, Mandeville peoples his southern regions with monsters: "giants, horrible and foul"; "men of figure without heads"; "dwarfs" with no "mouths"; "folk whose ears hang down to the knees"; beings that "are both men and woman." In both cases, Mandeville fills the empty hemisphere with European fantasies of the "NOT ME," assuming that that which is unfamiliar must be utterly different: a reversal of the north or a violation of what is taken to be human.[23]

The monsters of the "positive" speculators share a common thread. They embody a persistent Western fear of the loss of meaningful distinctions and stable hierarchies. For these geographers, the *oikoumene* is ruled by the law of noncontradiction and the great chain of being. In a hemisphere ruled by these principles, humans are separate from and superior to animals, men are distinct from and better than women, heads are above feet. Deploying the "either/or" fallacy, the geographers of the monstrous

assume that if the known world is organized by such orderly principles, then the unknown world is ruled by opposing powers: a
(non) law of contradiction and (non) principle of anarchy. Hence,
in the *terra incognita*, the graded distinctions between humans and
animals, men and women, head and feet collapse. Men crawl like
snakes and eat raw flesh. Androgynes possess the genitals of both
sexes. Freaks use their feet to shade their heads. These collapses of
logic and hierarchy recall an even more horrifying chaos: the primal void, the leviathan, Satan. The foggy, the frozen, and the
burning are no different in kind from the Sciopods, the Garamantes, or the Anthropophagi. All are not human, not heaven.

Yet, though these monsters are ciphers for the "other," they
are also secretly the "same." As images of the unfamiliar, they constitute doubles of fear and desire. Thus, they mirror the geographers' aversions to anarchy as well as their narcissistic wish to be at
the center of the significant world. In the former case, the monsters are outward projections of deep terrors. In the latter, they are
images of the other that constitute the pleasure of the same. These
monsters symbolize the complex of the colonizer, the tyrant of
space. He requires that those he colonizes be in conflict and complicity with him. He represents the colonized space so that it
counters him—and thus comprises an object to be feared—as well
as constitutes him—and therefore serves as a desideratum.[24]

Toni Morrison in *Beloved* (1987) exemplifies this process in a
tragic context: the oppression of African slaves in nineteenth-century
America. In the words of her narrator, white people—the colonizers
in this case, tyrants of African regions and bodies—represent races of
color as jungle beasts, believing that "under every dark skin [is] a jungle," "swinging baboons, sleeping snakes, red gums ready for their
sweet white blood." Yet, this jungle originates not in the blacks but in
the whites. The whites make the jungle in their own breasts but plant
it in the bosoms of the blacks. They—the "whitepeople"—look for
the eyes of apes in the blacks they would oppress when in reality the

"screaming baboon [lives] under their own white skin; the red gums [are] their own."[25] The whites project their animal instincts—a part of themselves that they fear and would like to ignore—onto those they desire to colonize and thus demonize. This projection of fear, however, also fulfills the whites' desires to view themselves as humans in contradistinction to animals over which they are superior. In casting blacks as monstrous enemies to be ruled, the whites mirror a repressed region of their own being—creating an other that is really the same—as well reflect themselves to themselves in flattering light—thus fashioning a same that is actually an other.

The medieval geographers' colonizations of blank spaces on maps are somewhat trivial when compared to American slaveholder's tyrannies over actual bodies and villages. However, though this distinction in degree should be registered, a similarity in kind remains. In both cases, a fantastic mental geography is imposed onto an intractable reality—unknown southern regions and unfamiliar ethnicities. This cartographical tyranny did not cease when explorers began to experience the Antarctic with their own eyes—when freaks gave way to floes. Rather, this colonization persisted throughout the seventeenth and eighteenth centuries—not so much in the name of Christian piety as in the guise of scientific investigation and capitalistic gain.

SOLOMON'S GOLD

In 1409, a momentous event occurred in the history of voyaging: Jacobus Angelus's translation into Latin of Ptolemy's works on astronomy and geography. The dissemination of Ptolemy's theory of a spherical globe and his lists of longitude and latitude opened the door to expeditions below the equator and offered the possibility of global circumnavigation.[26] Inspired by Ptolemy, a new school of geographers arose, bent on replacing monsters with grids and keen to send ships to the points on their accurate maps. Among the earliest of Ptolemy's disciples was Pierre d'Ailly. In his 1413 *Cosmographic Compendium*—which would influence Columbus— he claimed that "[t]he earth is spherical, and the Western Ocean is relatively small."[27] To sail west is to reach Indian wealth.

The spices and other treasures of the Indies as well as of Cathay constituted the primary motivation for the famous expeditions of the fifteenth, sixteenth, and seventeenth centuries. Eager to expand their empires, countries like Spain, Portugal, England, and Holland financed voyages in search of new materials and fresh trades, hoping to find in the "New World" and the "East" substantial boons for state coffers. Thus, the spiritual imperialism of the Middle Ages—the Christianization of all space—becomes in the Early Modern period a material imperialism—a desire to own and exploit "unclaimed" lands.[28]

This mercenary impulse inspired explorers to choose expediency over the slow probing of unknown regions. Hence, for English and Dutch explorers, the more familiar regions of the Arctic provided the best route for a passage to the east. By the beginning of the fifteenth century, British fisherman had already for years been sailing through the waters above Iceland and around Greenland. Likewise, in about 1360, Nicholas of Lynn sailed north from Norway. He found a frosty land (likely Greenland) littered with ruined settlements (probably left from the Vikings) and peopled with inhabitants only four feet tall (Eskimos). Upon his return, Nicholas wrote an Arctic geography that included a picture of the pole as a black magnetic obelisk shimmering in the midst of a whirlpool. At about the same time, Niccolo and Antonio Zeno, two Venetian brothers, sailed deep into the Arctic (allegedly) and later produced a map, published in 1558. Though this map is inaccurate, it inspired confidence in early Arctic voyagers, reassuring them that they were not navigating a region of monsters but of ordinary and trodden, if cold, ground. Even earlier, beginning in the ninth century, Vikings had settled the zones of the Arctic Circle.

In sum, by the fifteenth century, northern European explorers viewed the Arctic seas not so much as horrifying wastelands as conduits to Asian treasures.[29]

The voyagers of Spain and Portugal searching for a southern passage to the East were likewise more interested in wealth than exploration. When Bartholomew Diaz in 1488 became the first European to reach Africa's tip, he did not continue south but turned east, toward the spice. Likewise, in 1497, Vasco da Gama relinquished the opportunity to chart the oceans south of Africa and gave sail to India. Meanwhile, in 1492, when Columbus landed on what he thought were the East Indies, he sensed an immense mass to the south but did not enjoy the funding to find such a continent. By 1520, Ferdinand Magellan, bent on discovering the bottom of a vast southern continent explored by Amerigo Vespucci in 1501, found the Strait of Magellan, which flows between the southern tip of Chile and Tierra del Fuego. Instead of pushing further south, he turned west. His ship eventually circumnavigated the globe.[30]

Hence, although the age of capitalistic exploration increased empirical knowledge of the Arctic, it offered little new information on the Antarctic and actually inspired a renewal of Etratosthenes's fantasy. In the words of L. P. Kirwan, while seventeenth-century visions of the Arctic were becoming increasingly familiar and accurate, the Antarctic remained "in the realm of academic argument and speculation about the existence of a fertile southern continent."[31] Throughout the so-called scientific revolution, the South Pole endured as a blank screen on which Western fears and desires were cast. Only now, in a more secular age, fogs and monsters gave way to gold and ice.[32]

Opening in Portugal in 1418 his school of geography, Henry the Navigator first motivated European sailors to push below the equator, where they found not a bizarre world that reversed their own but a tropical coast. Henry's mid-century explorers speculated that Africa was Ptolemy's notorious southern continent. However, by the end of the century, Diaz proved otherwise, reaching Africa's tip. Some years later, Vespucci opined that Brazil was the famed antipodal mass. However, Magellan soon disproved this theory by rounding the tip of South America. Yet, even though Magellan denied this possibility, he sparked in geographers the idea that the torrid Tierra del Fuego might be the northernmost tip of the south polar region. In their respective world maps of 1536 and 1570, Oronce Fine and Abraham Ortelius feature a vast Antarctic continent crowned by the Land of Fire. Although both geographers' cartographical images are bounded by detailed borders—suggesting well-explored coastlines—their interiors remain blank, empty whites broken only by abstract diction—*terra australis recenter invento sed nondum plene cognita* (the southern land newly discovered but not yet fully known) and *terra australis nondum cognita* (the southern land not yet known).[33]

This cartographical combination of alleged knowledge and admitted ignorance concerning the South Pole reflected and influenced the mercenary concerns of the age. Contemplating and exploring the south in search of wealth, the geographers and explorers of the age welcomed the idea that the southern region was not an icy waste but a fertile zone. If the Antarctic's theoretical torrid border—the Land of Fire—could concretely fire dreams of paradise, then its blank interior could spark more general fantasies of splendid comfort—reveries of a vague El Dorado. This blend of (alleged) lucrative fact and (admitted) ignorance perfectly doubles the "logic" of capitalistic desire. In wishing to transform space into commodity, the capitalist requires that the space feature a modicum of attractive concrete qualities. Yet, this same capitalist needs for the space to be vague so that its "value" can be imposed from without by the marketplace. A region transformed into a commodity is a seductive fact and a blankness waiting to be priced, an object of desire and a cipher of how much consumers are willing to pay, a potential paradise and a *tabula rasa*.

This "logic" is revealed by the example of Alvaro de Mendaña de Neyra, a Spanish Captain, and Pedro Fernandez de Quirós, his Portugese pilot. Fueled by speculations of such geographers as Fine, the Spanish Viceroy of Peru sent these men in search of the fertile polar land. They did not find such a continent but happened upon some islands near what is now New Guinea. Assuming that the southern continent must be tropical, Mendaña and Quirós thought that their fecund islands bounded the southern paradise. Moreover, they also theorized that the monetary worth of this unseen Arcadia was as immense as the wealth of Solomon.[34] They called these lands Solomon Islands, mooring them to a concrete image of paradise—Solomon's kingdom as described in the Bible—and abstracting them into a system of numbers—the monetary wealth of gold.

The history of Antarctic exploration throughout the sixteenth, seventeenth, and eighteenth centuries is crowded by sailors like Mendaña and Quirós—entrepreneurial explorers casting the South Pole as a double of capitalistic desire. Although scientific curiosity partially drove such pioneers, the monetary fantasies of their funding countries constituted the primary impulse. In 1577, Francis Drake, funded by Sir Richard Grenville and quietly supported by Queen Elizabeth, sailed south to break into the growing Spanish empire in the Pacific. Grenville and the Crown wanted from Drake specifically a passage to the Indies and Cathay and generally "the discovery, traffic, and enjoying for The Queen's Majesty and her subjects, of all and any lands, islands, and countries southwards beyond the equinoctial, to where the Pole Antarctic hath any elevation above the horizon."[35] Reaching in 1578 Magellan's Strait, Drake sailed past the Land of Fire and into the waters below Cape Horn. For Drake, this voyage dispelled the theory of Tierra del Fuego as the northern tip of the southern continent as well as suggested that there was no *terra incognita australis* at all but only a "South Sea" expanding in "large and free scope."[36] However, geographers in Europe ignored Drake's notions—as they earlier ignored Magellan's—and continued to translate data into a double of desire. Following George Best, a geographer who wrote in 1578 that the "Terra Australis" was a "great" polar "land" of "fruitful soil," mapmakers believed for the next two centuries that a bountiful southern soil could be discovered and exploited.[37]

Indeed, even though Dirck Gerritz of the Dutch East India Company likely saw in 1599 the snowy mountains of the South Shetland Islands (which lie below Cape Horn and Drake Passage), Quirós in 1605 thought he had discovered the southern Eden after striking land south of the Solomon Islands. He named his find Australia del Espiritu Santo and believed that this land, later called the New Hebrides, was a zone of "gold and silver, cattle and grain, the richest fruit and the healthiest climate, a land without venomous beasts or insects, peopled by gentle natives."[38] Likewise, although in 1615 two Dutchman of the Dutch East India Company rounded Cape Horn and, like Drake, found no land, in 1642 Anthony van Dieman, governor of the Dutch Indies and connected with the company, commissioned Abel Janszoon Tasman to search for a southern Arcadia. Tasman found no gold but pushed the alleged southern Eden even further south by discovering New Holland (later called Australia) and Van Dieman's Land (eventually termed Tasmania). In the same way, the English merchant Anthony de la Roche in 1675 demonstrated that if the southern "Eden" did exist, it was not only much further south than anyone had imagined but also a frozen waste. In the next twenty years, several British pirates confirmed la Roche's vision, reporting only icebergs in the southern seas. Nonetheless, in 1694, William Dampier published *New Voyage Around the World*. This book—dedicated to the Royal Society—again envisioned a southern paradise. The scientists of the society welcomed this publication. The dream persisted.[39]

UNKNOWN AND ICY SEAS

Yves Joseph de Kerguélen-Trémarec's 1772 Antarctic expedition exemplifies a major change that took place in polar exploration during the eighteenth century. Sailing for a France that had lost most of its North American holdings during the Seven Years' War (1756–63), Kerguélen hoped to take possession of a new land mass. Aware that English explorers had already tried to claim the South Pole—in 1764 and 1766 the British Admiralty had respectively sent Charles Byron and Philip Carteret in search of the undiscovered continent—Kerguélen knew that time was against him. Driving his vessels below the Horn, he on February 12 reached a misty land, which he dubbed "South France." He returned to Paris to report that he had found "the central Mass of the Antarctic continent," replete with "wood, minerals, diamonds, rubies, precious stones, and marble." Commissioned to ship to South France in 1773 to trade with the polar natives, Kerguélen found that he had been wrong. He discovered on his island no jewels but only snow. Disappointed, he renamed South France the Land of Desolation.[40]

Alexander Dalrymple's career extends to a quarter of a century the transformation that took place in one year in Kerguélen's case: the metamorphosis of Antarctic dreams from Eden to freeze. After becoming an employee of the East India Company in 1752, Dalrymple spent the next decade traveling in the East, where he mastered international trade and southern geography. Eventually, driven by mercenary greed and scientific curiosity, he built his prodigious researches into a grand theory in favor of the fertile polar garden. After returning to England in 1765, Dalrymple, now a fellow of the Royal Society, published his polar hypotheses in *An Account of the Discoveries Made in the South Pacific Ocean* (1767) and *A Historical Collection of Voyages ... in the South Pacific Ocean* (1770–71). These studies argue that the unknown continent is an immense land mass where the scientist will find new facts and the speculator will enjoy a cornucopia "sufficient to maintain the . . . dominion . . . of Britain."[41]

While Dalrymple was composing these works, the members of the Royal Society were planning to chart the transit of Venus across the sun, a mapping that might confirm the circumference of earth and reveal the distance between earth and sun. Half a century earlier, Edmund Halley had predicted that Venus would next cross the sun in June of 1769 and had suggested that this transit would be best observed from stations across the globe. Drawing from Halley, the Royal Society decided to situate observers in the Hudson Bay, the North Cape, and the South Pacific, near where the pole allegedly rested. Dalrymple applied to lead the southern expedition, requiring a command of a naval vessel and a guarantee that he would receive a second ship if he lost the first before reaching his goal. He moreover announced that he was more interested in the pole than in Venus. Offending the navy with such presumptions, he was deemed unfit for the job.[42]

This rejection would not have been important had it not set the stage for James Cook. It was he that was chosen to sail south in Dalrymple's place, not only to mark the passing of Venus in the name of science but also to search for the pole, in the name of both science and the emerging British Empire. Shipping in August of 1768 in the *Endeavor*, Cook was instructed by the society and the navy to sail to Tahiti and record the transit. After performing this service, he was to "put to Sea without Loss of Time, and carry into execution the Additional Instructions contained in the inclosed Sealed Packet." This hermetic package contained directions to search for the fabled continent, and, failing that, to explore New Zealand.[43]

Returning to London three years later, Cook made his report to the navy and the Fellows. As Alan Gurney observes, Cook's "astonishing account" is an intoxicating blend of fantastic romance, accurate science, and financial appraisal.[44] The Admirals, the Fellows, and eventually the inhabitants of England read in Cook's unadorned style of a shipwreck, exotic isles, and the perils of the waves; of the transit of Venus, the surveying of New Zealand coastlines, and a southern continent not yet found; of tropical southern islands replete with plants, fish, mammals, and natives.[45]

Hence, Cook's first voyage only fueled dreams of southern Eden, troubling the sleeps of the Royal Society, the navy, and the general public. Far from excluding the possibility of a subequatorial paradise, his report made its existence seem more plausible and desirable. With curiosity over Antarctica at an apex, the navy, with encouragement from the Royal Society, funded another Cook-led voyage, this time instructing the captain to do nothing but find the pole.[46]

Introducing his account of Cook's penetration into the Antarctic Circle and his ensuing sight of ice and more ice, Gurney alludes to Thomas Huxley's claim, delivered almost a century after Cook's expedition, that "one of the great tragedies of science is the slaying of a beautiful hypothesis by an ugly fact."[47] This thoroughly anthropocentric claim—grounded on the idea that notions that give pleasure to humans are beautiful while indifferent facts are unattractive—nonetheless accurately captures the consequence of Cook's second voyage: a shattering of the humanizing dreams of the European psyche before the inhuman ice.

Driving the *Resolution* and the *Adventure* toward the Antarctic Circle in December of 1772, Cook encountered not Blemyae or bounty but instead "high hills or rather Mountains of Ice . . . within Field ice and many islands of Ice without in the open Sea." Billowing around these towers were numerous whales, while scores of penguins perched on the ice and several sorts of birds screamed above. As the ships neared the circle, these glowering pinnacles became covered in "Hazy" snow, through which white albatrosses emerged.[48] His ships rigged with icicles, his men fighting frost on their beards, how could Cook discern between this and that? In this region, bird and man and ship become nothing but snow. Even if one were to happen upon the southern continent, how would he know if the frozen mass was an immense berg or stable land?

As he entered January, Cook raised this issue. Approaching a large plane of ice, Cook claimed that what an earlier explorer "took for Land . . . [is] nothing but Mountains of Ice surrounded by field Ice." He admitted that he and his crew were likewise "deceived by the Ice Hills" when they first "fell in with the field Ice," for many had thought that the ice was a land mass that "join'd to land to the Southward." However, by the third of January, two weeks away from being the first European to penetrate the Antarctic Circle, he was able to discern between field ice and land. So prevalent wass the ice and so scare was the land that he concluded that only floes and bergs exist in this southern sea. He confessed that he was "sorry" to "have spent so much time" "searching after . . . imaginary lands." After several more days of cruising through the gloom, he was convinced: there is nothing at globe's bottom but indifferent white.[49]

On January 17, at 11:15 A.M., Cook crossed the circle, leading "the first and only Ship that ever cross'd that line." There he saw nothing but ice.[50] As he wrote later in *Voyage Towards the South Pole and Round the World* (1777), when he passed the line, the weather cleared into a vision of "only one island of ice," a vista that expanded later that day into "the whole sea in a manner covered with ice."[51] By the next day, as he complained in his *Journal*, he "could see nothing to the Southward but Ice." This "immence Field was composed of different kinds of Ice, such as high Hills or Islands, smaller pieces packed close together and what Greenland men properly call field Ice, a piece of this kind, of such extent that I could see no end to it." This extensive freeze turned his ships north.[52] His first push to the polar continent—if it existed—had failed.

A year later, after spending time in New Zealand, Cook again tried to sight a southern land mass. On the twentieth of December 1773, his ships once more transversed the circle. Navigating among dangerous bergs two hundred feet high, he was again thwarted in his quest for land. Not defeated, in January of 1774 he made another push into the circle, reaching the farthest point south achieved in the eighteenth century. Still, he sighted no land. Meanwhile, the crew had become weary and worn. Cook, ever solicitous of his men, returned to England without having established the continent.[53]

Yet, Cook reached a conclusion: The ice covering the circle must extend "quite to the Pole" and is "perhaps joined to some land to which it had been fixed from the earliest time."[54] Hence, if a southern continent exists, it is not a paradise but must

> lay within the Polar Circile where the Sea is so pestered with ice, that the land is thereby inacessible. The risk one runs in exploreing a coast in these unknown and Icy Seas, is so very great, that I can be bold to say, that no man will ever venture farther than I have done and that the lands which may lie to the South will never be explored. Thick fogs, Snow storms, Intense Cold and every other thing that can render Navigation dangerous one has to encounter and these difficulites are greatly heightened by the enexpressable horrid aspect of the Country, a Country doomed by Nature never once to feel the armth of the Suns rays, but to lie for ever buried under everlasting snow and ice.[55]

If this blunt account of the monotonous ice was not unsettling enough to those who dreamed of Eden, Cook emphasized that this ice-doomed land, if it does exist, will grant its discoverer no fame, for "the world will not be benefited by it."[56]

Cook did not prove or disprove the existence of the *terra incognita australis*. However, he did show that if such a southern land does exist, it will remain intractable to human desires, metaphysical and utilitarian. As Stephen J. Pyne astutely observes in *The Ice* (1986), "Cook thus became the great practitioner of 'negative discovery'," an explorer whose greatest achievement was the revelation of "Refusal," the disclosure of "No."[57] Given these negations, Cook's portrait of the ice is, in a certain way, both more horrifying than the demons of the medieval mapmaker and more desirable than the Eden of the Renaissance cartographer. While the monsters of the medieval mind are terrifying "others," they are at least products of a dualistic worldview that pits goodness against evil. These beings fit within a familiar, stable system of categories and are thus recognizable and predictable. In contrast, the unmapped ice is *indifferent* to human fears of evil, existing beyond dualistic categories, outside of normalizing concepts. To the mapper hoping to impose some order on the unknown, the pervasive ice can only be—*nothing*, no-*thing*, not this or that. While the devil can cause nightmares, the void, as Pascal knew, keeps one sleepless. Likewise, although the Renaissance vision of a southern Eden pleased the dreams of speculative geographers, this paradise is necessarily bounded, inevitably delimited by the fallen world that is its opposite. Reveries of Eden always emerge from and dissolve into nightmares of pain, corruption, and death. Cook's ice below the circle, however, is unbounded, a trackless white expanse, virginal, on which one can project *infinite* desire. The empty ice fields are plenitudes of ever renewed yet never fulfilled longing.

HOLE AT THE POLE

The Antarctic ice as void or plenitude, annihilator of meaning and generator of significance: These connotations of the frost reveal an esoteric spirit of ice beautifully expressed in the early eighteenth century by the third Earl of Shaftesbury: "In places most remote from man's works and occupations we encounter the manifestation of the divine Mind pure and undefiled."[58] Victoria Nelson, in a recent essay, explicates: "what is farthest away and most hidden is, paradoxically, always what is most important: the journey to the poles is a journey to the center of the soul."[59] To wander in polar weirdness is to rest in the house of spirit.

In sounding the esoteric pole, one best begins not on the actual polar ice but in the deserts of ancient Egypt. During the second century, the Peratae, a Gnostic sect whose name roughly means "those who pass through," abandoned on clear nights the walls of Alexandria, and walked into the desert. In the dry air, thousands of miles from the Antarctic ice, these visionaries strained toward the boreal sky. Directly to the north, they lighted on Draco, the serpent coiled around the pole star. For these spiritual adepts, this polar dragon was not evil or chaos. It was a threshold between matter and spirit, time and eternity—a portal leading to the original abyss, the unknowable monad from which life springs.[60]

Maintaining that the cosmos is a triad unified by this polar serpent, this Gnostic sect, surprisingly optimistic toward matter, is not dualistic, close to the Manichees, but monistic, near the Neoplatonists.[61] According to Hippolytus in his third-century *Refutation of All Heresies*, these heretics perceived the snake's crystal scales in everything: stars and sand, bodies and souls.

> The universe is the Father, Son, (and) Matter; (but) each of these three has endless capacities in itself. Intermediate, then, between the Matter and the Father sits the Son, the Word, the Serpent, always being in motion towards the unmoved Father, and (towards) Matter itself in motion. And at one time he is turned towards the Father, and receives the powers into his own person; but at another time takes up these powers, and is turned towards Matter. And Matter, (though) devoid of attribute, and being unfashioned, moulds (into itself) forms from the Son which the son moulded from the Father. . . .
>
> No one . . . can be saved or return (into) heaven without the Son, and the Son is the serpent. For as he brought down from above the paternal marks, so again he carries up from thence those marks roused from a dormant condition and rendered paternal characteristics, substantial ones from the unsubstantial Being, transferring them higher from thence.[62]

The Father is the unmoved, unbegotten origin, an ineffable, infinite fountain of energy—unnameable to language, unknowable to reason. Out of this source flows the Son, the organizing spiritual *logos*, the serpent coiled around the celestial pole. From the serpent emanates matter, formless and opaque but for the imprint of the snake who secretly flows through the muck, spreading light and grace. Those who see through the coatings of matter to these invisible slithers, these luminous interiors, awaken to their true home—the fatherly abyss beyond the polar portal. Alert, the Peratic Gnostic realizes that Draco coiled above is not only in the sky but also in the earth: each material event, viewed as a bearer of the Sonly light, is a serpent, a door to the abyss distributed in all beings, a terrestrial version of the celestial pole. Hence, everything mundane—from grains of dirt to albatross wings—is a terrestrial reflection of the sidereal portal, itself a mirror of the transcendent spirit. But—as the Gnostic further knows—the snake also coils in the human heart. Vertically gathering sky and earth, horizontally merging mundane differences, the Peratic serpent is the still point of the turning self: a psychic pole marrying opposing pulls—matter and spirit, reason and emotion. The cosmic axle is the spinal column. Earth's magnets turn in the mind.

The primary symbols of this esoteric pole—celestial, terrestrial, and psychical—are three: *axis mundi*, omphalos, caduceus. The world axle—variously figured by the Arctic and Antarctic pole stars, sacred trees and mountains, holy cities and aligned spinal columns—flows upwards and downwards and side to side. It directs the descent of the spiritual abyss as well as the ascent of the enlightened soul; it organizes mundane matter into graceful polarities—east and west, right and left, male and female. If this axle is a cross harmonizing all four directions, the omphalos is a threshold joining matter and spirit, pattern and abyss. Represented in the polar portals at the apex and nadir of earth and sky, in sacred oracles and dark caves, in actual belly buttons and inner doors of perception, the world navel is present wherever the adept crosses from many to one, surface to depth. Synthesizing the virtues of axis and navel, the caduceus is a stable center of the revolving world as well as a *limen* gathering the world's oppositions.[63] Symbol of the alchemical Mercurius, the snake-entwined staff reveals, as Jung notes, that the "heart of Mercurius" is the "Pole," present in all three stages of the alchemical work: boiling black (*nigredo*), congealed white (*albedo*), and distilled red (*rubedo*); matter as chaos, material organized by spirit, matter turned divine elixir; lead, crystal, gold; body, psyche, and spirit. As the principle of transmutation, Mercury is also the *psychopompus* who guides men, Jung continues, "on the perilous voyage over the sea of the world" to the "*Deus absconditus* (hidden God) who dwells at the North Pole and reveals himself through magnetism."[64]

Each of these symbols reveals what is always already true of all places and all beings. In an infinite cosmos whose center is everywhere and circumference nowhere, each point, properly seen, is the world axle, the cosmic navel, and the entwined staff. Yet, most people, asleep, prone to nestle to the nearest part and forget the whole, need shocking reminders. Hence, some require sacred representations—images of trees, caves, snakes—to recall them to their home. Others, bolder, desire to go to the thing itself: the actual pole or mountain or bubbling alembic. These pilgrims undertake exterior and interior quests, hoping to discover correspondences between landscape and soul, palpable bergs and inner ices. If such a quester can see through the sharp floes to the *terra incognita* within, he rises to more than mapping. He floats in a sea forever gridless.

A polar esotericist on such a journey would not have to go to the earth's ends without a symbolic map. Just as adepts have transformed unvisited trees, mountains, and caverns into symbols for placeless sacred powers, so visionaries have turned the actual poles, unbeheld, into figures of the figureless. Though he never reached the North Pole, Nicholas of Lynn envisioned it as a black obelisk towering in the midst of a cataract. This whirlpool,

Nicholas opined, would suck toward chthonic interiors any ship that cruised within its vortices. While Nicholas proved scientifically prescient in regard to the polar currents—which indeed swirl in circular loops—he had somewhere a sense that the pole is a portal to an abysmal unknown. In the same way, Athanasius Kircher in his 1665 *Mundus Subterraneus* conjectured that the North Pole opens into a whirlpool through which currents of seawater descend into an interior channel running the length of the earth. After flowing to the bottom of the globe, these currents gush outwards at the South Pole. This geographical speculation is a vision of the poles as points along a cosmic axle, thresholds between outer and inner, gatherings of opposing streams.[65]

In ensuing centuries, this theory of holes in the poles persisted in esoteric geographies. Thomas Burnet in *Sacred Theory of the Earth* (1681) supposed that waters from an interior source flow through an opening in the North Pole. In 1721, an anonymous French novelist in *Passage du pôle arctique au pôle antarctique par le centre du monde* imagined a ship being pulled into a vortex at the North Pole and reemerging in Antarctic waters.[66] By 1818, John Cleves Symmes, a retired Army captain from St. Louis, consolidated these trends, claiming that "the earth is hollow and habitable within" and "open at the poles." Some years later, in 1826, a disciple named James McBride expanded this thesis into *The Symmes Theory of Concentric Spheres*. Meanwhile, in 1820, an author dubiously named "Captain Adam Seaborn" published a novel entitled *Symzonia: A Voyage of Discovery*, which features a utopia of rational, pale beings dwelling at the Antarctic orifice.[67]

These theories, while fantastic from an exoteric point of view, are accurate from an esoteric angle of vision. While these imagined holes at the poles are on one level purely fictional occurrences little different from the medieval monsters or the Renaissance El Dorados, on another level, they are exact descriptions of each event in a universe whose center is everywhere and whose circumference is nowhere. It is this esoteric science, this imaginative empiricism, that Coleridge, versed in Burnet and Cook, and Poe, schooled in Kurguélen and Symmes, explore in their respective polar tales.

THE MARINER'S POLAR NIGHTMARE

If the ice at the pole discloses the core of being,[68] then what are we to make of the Mariner's violence toward the Antarctic whiteness? His initial aggression results from a tyrannical desire to impose upon life his dream of control. Yet, if the Mariner begins the poem as Ezra Buckley, a fascist of the imagination, he ends as an itinerant poet revealing to hylic wedding guests the pneumatic history of man and bird and beast.

Beginning the poem with the logic of dream, in which things unpredictably appear—"It is an ancient Mariner"—Coleridge has his Mariner plunge the wedding guest into a polar tale as dreamy as the poem, beginning simply with the line, "There was a ship." This "logic" of reverie is appropriate, for the Mariner's narrative opens in the region of dreams, the Antarctic. Versed in numerous accounts of Antarctic exploration,[69] Coleridge sends his sailor to a frozen sea hidden under layers of human representation—Strabo's classical geographies, Higden's medieval monsters, Quirós's Renaissance Edens, and Cook's eighteenth-century wastes. Under the spells of these "imperialistic" visions, the Mariner loathes the intractable ice.

As the Mariner tells the stunned guest, he and his crew do not enter the Antarctic by choice: They are driven by a "storm-blast," "tyrannous and strong," that strikes them south with "o'er taking wings." Since the Mariner navigates for his living, this meteorological affront threatens his identity. That this storm drives him into an unmapped land freighted with monstrous superstitions only deepens his fear of losing his place. The details on which he focuses once he is hurled into the circle reveal precisely this: a man panicky before potential erasure, and thus bent on holding some order.[70]

> And now there came both mist and snow,
> And it grew wondrous cold:
> And ice, mast-high, came floating by,
> As green as emerald.
>
> And through the drifts the snowy clifts
> Did send a dismal sheen:
> Nor shapes of men nor beasts we ken—
> The ice was all between.
>
> The ice was here, the ice was there,
> The ice was all around:
> It cracked and growled, and roared and howled,
> Like noise in a swound! (*AM* 51–62)

The imagery conveys the Mariner's initial desire to embrace the icescape as a magical realm of verdurous wealth. Though the region is covered in mist and snow, he claims that the cold is "wondrous"—a curious adjective suggesting not chill but marvel and admiration—and that the icebergs are "as green as emerald"—a simile invoking fertility and jewels. Yet, the ice is resilient to comfortable reveries. Finding only inhuman white, the Mariner quickly experiences bergs and floes as disturbing monsters. A "dismal sheen" replaces the emerald green. No known "shapes of men nor beasts" appear. Unable to discover the familiar, the human, the Mariner encounters the freakish *opposite* of the normal. Yet, the Mariner soon realizes that not even the medieval paradigm of the monstrous south can categorize the ice, for the Antarctic freeze is no*thing*—no discernible shape at all. Not the hellish opposite of Eden or the monstrous contrary of the humane, the ice is *beyond* pairs of opposites: not this or that, a monotonous whiteness that annihilates representations and individuals. Bereft of adjectives, similes, or synonyms, the Mariner is reduced to repetition: ice is here, ice is there, ice is all around.[71]

This ambiguous space reduces the Mariner to nothing but fear. Yet, salvation emerges. From the abyss appears a difference and a name, an albatross, *fiat lux redivivus*.

> At length did cross an Albatross,
> Thorough the fog it came;
> As if it had been a Christian soul,
> We hailed it in God's name.
>
> It ate the food it ne'er had eat,
> And round and round it flew.
> The ice did split with a thunder-fit;
> The helmsman steered us through!
>
> A good south wind sprung up behind;
> The Albatross did follow,
> And every day, for food or play,
> Came to the mariner's hollo!
>
> In mist or cloud, on mast or shroud,
> It perched for vespers nine;
> Whiles all the night, through fog-smoke white,
> Glimmered the white moon-shine. (*AM* 63–78)

The Mariner hails the bird as a cipher of a familiar worldview, Christianity. Like a Christian soul, the bird seems to impose order on the cold mist. Its presence offers an orienting difference, and its circular flying pattern coincides with the opening of the ice. The bird further reinforces an anthropocentric paradigm in concurring with a south wind salubrious to the crew and in submitting to the sailors' calls. Moreover, the bird appears to be pious, perching each evening for vespers.

Yet, the bird's nature resists the Mariner's familiarizing concepts. Although the Mariner and his fellows hail the bird "as if" it were a Christian soul, the bird nonetheless is a being of murky mist. Crossing into the sailors' view, it flies "thorough" the fog—cuts *through* it as well as proving *thoroughly* of it. Likewise, despite being continuous with a comforting breeze, the albatross is ultimately a foreign species—it eats unfamiliar food—and violates the principle of non-contradiction—it flies in a spiraling pattern and thus blurs centripetal and centrifugal forces. Also, though the albatross appears to "perch for vespers," it is simply sitting in the "mist or cloud," the "fog-smoke white" or "white moon-shine" that is its proper element.

The Mariner wants the bird to conform to human rules, yet the bird's nature challenges his anthropocentric desires. Hence, the albatross is both a potential symbol of orientation and a synecdoche of the disorientating power of the icescape. In the former case, the bird recalls the customs of Mariner's familiar world, now under threat. In the latter, it bears the qualities of the abysmal ice that annihilate reveries of human centrality.

How else is one to account for what happens next, when the Mariner, with no explanation, kills the bird with his crossbow? The bird as synecdoche for the desolate ice, as microcosm of chaos, threatens all that the Mariner holds sacred. Hence, he notches his arrow, takes his revenge on this offense to good order, and thus finds his place in a long line of cosmic hunters: Marduk, Jehovah, Zeus, Beowulf. When the Mariner fires his point, the bird is to him what Moby-Dick is to Ahab—an uncolored cipher of the forces that threaten the supremacy of man, a pasteboard mask behind which may be a nameless malignancy, or, worse, nothing at all. (Significantly, Ishmael likens the sperm whale to a "scarred iceberg."[72]) The Mariner and Ahab read the bird and the whale as signs of all factors that chagrin men's dreams of superiority, security, and control. These intractable elements—ranging from unanswerable questions to indifferent physical forces—betoken to these sailors the return of the first slop: dragons, serpents, hurricanes. Like Nietzsche's earth-hating metaphysicians, these seafarers work to stem the tide. They take revenge against time's unruly beings, reducing them with weapons to literal corpses, flattening them with concepts to danger-ous illusions or spiritual deaths.[73]

The polar ice as cipher for unimaginable waste: This is a mat-ter of perception. The man raging for order projects an image of chaos onto *anything* that does not fit within his egocentric grids. In Blake's *Book of Urizen* (1794), Urizen, the faculty of reason and the figure for the rational demiurge (Marduk and Jehovah), *produces* the void when he fashions his orderly cosmos. When Urizen splits Eternity into his own vision of order (a "solid without fluctua-tion") and everything else that does not fit within this view (such as unpredictable energy), the former realm becomes rational real-ity while the latter region turns unreal chaos. However, by split-ting the interdependent polarities of form and energy into a hierarchical relationship between valid organization and invalid turbulence, Urizen ironically ends up actually *creating* the anarchi-cal waste he wants to exile. Pattern without energy flattens to static indifference; unity with no diversity is blank. Urizen's uni-verse is in the end a rocky desert, Ulro.[74]

Shelley's Frankenstein likewise exemplifies this Urizenic de-sire. Like Blake's demiurge, Victor loathes the mutual arising of opposites, the complementarity between life and death. Yearning to vanquish death, and thus to create Urizen's "joy without pain," Frankenstein reanimates a corpse. Ironically, however, this crea-ture meant to vanquish death does nothing but make death. A fig-ure for the absence of the relationship between life and death, the creature reduces difference to the same, particular identities to pu-trefaction. Victor's rage for order at the expense of turbulence re-sults in the exact opposite of his desire: total chaos. That Victor dies in the Arctic ice is fitting, for he has existed (not lived) in an undifferentiated flatland ever since he shocked a cold body into motion. The ice is simply an externalization of his static interiors.

Mimicking Urizen and Victor, the Mariner suffers the same fate. Dividing and conquering, he creates an Ulro of his own. Soon after he kills the bird, he and his crew reach a windless, waveless ocean where they grow parched and unalive, as "idle as a painted ship / Upon a painted ocean" (*AM* 117–8). This realm is a fitting image of the Mariner's deepest though unconscious wish for utter order, total stasis. Yet, this monotonous plane is not a heaven of unchanging bliss but a region of "Death" and "Life-in-Death." Only corpses and zombies reside in a realm devoid of polarity. Ironically, the Mariner now inhabits the world that he most feared when he struggled below the circle. He finds himself enervated in an undifferentiated landscape where nothing and something, life and death, blend and blur. Complete order creates complete disorder. Life without death produces death without life. His murder of the albatross—his attempt to destroy the void—results in a flat ocean, the death of his crew, and the desiccation of his heart.

An isolated ego in a desert of undrinkable water, the Mariner still psychologically dwells in the polar ice. For seven days, he languishes in Ulro, frozen indifference. He wears on his neck the corpse of the albatross, a synecdoche of the pole as inhuman threat. He is possessed by the white Queen, "Life-in-Death." He sees in the water only "a thousand thousand slimy things," monsters of chaos. He is surrounded by dead men, pallid and unmoving as the ice. His throat, "dry as dust," a desert of ice, is unable to utter a human sound. Confined within a psychic prison of his own making, he is thus unable to connect with anything "other" than his alienated self: He is "[a]lone, alone, all, all alone / Alone on a wide wide sea." In this condition, he assumes that the environment outside his skin is an oppressive weight—the sky and sea "[l]ay like a load"—or an aggressive enemy—the dead eyes of the crew appear to "curse" him (*AM* 143–263).

Yet, the Mariner's relationship to the Antarctic ice has changed. Earlier, when sailing below the circle, he expressed his fear of the frozen otherness by reacting murderously. Now, however, above the circle but in the South Pole of the mind, he translates his anxiety into a desire for his own death. This transformation from murderous aggression to suicidal languishing is a logical consequence of the Mariner's self-fashioned Ulro. In a universe in which subjects and objects are persistently set against one another, one must take the role of either murderer or suicide. The subject in this dualist cosmos can either exert his will violently or relinquish his egocentric wish for control. Realizing that he cannot defeat his environment with his crossbow, the Mariner turns to the other extreme—he assumes that he is a passive victim of a deadly region and wants only to die. One spectrum of an "either/or" fallacy—either complete control or no control, either subjective activity or objective passivity—this suicidal attitude often abruptly returns to its murderous opposite. However, in the Mariner's case, the suicidal drive produces sudden charity toward the polar landscape he formerly demonized.

WINDOW TO THE WORLD

How are we to account for the Mariner's sudden embrace of the ice hounding him beyond the circle? To understand his transformation, we note two ways of suffering. The dualist (the Urizenic man) suffers solipsistically. He views the world *only* in relation to his pain and thus sees external objects as either therapies or causes for his hurting. He faces two options—he can actively transform the environment into a balm or passively endure its intractable irritations. The Mariner suffers in this way while below the circle, when he attempts to alleviate his physical and psychological ills by removing what he views as their cause: the snowy albatross. However, by the end of his seven days of suicidally suffering above the circle, caught in psychic Antarctic of his own making, the Mariner turns from his ego to the external world. His suicidal thoughts have weakened his ego. He realizes that he is not the only being who suffers. He understands that *all* creatures suffer. He charitably envisions a world hurting beyond his ego.

That the Mariner awakens to this shared biology—that he is converted from solipsistic to charitable suffering—is signaled by his appreciation of natural events that he earlier loathed. The abruptness of this transformation cannot be overemphasized: in an instant, the Mariner turns from lamenting the curse of the corpses and the fact that he cannot die to praising the beauty of the world. He *leaps* from seeing the world as Ulro to perceiving it as Blake's Generation—a thriving organic system generated by the interplay between interdependent polarities. Fittingly, this transformation recalls to the polar ice: Languishing in Ulro, the Mariner is really stuck in his vision of the ice as threatening indifference; now, on the verge of embracing an organic cosmos, he likewise views the world through the filters of the freeze, but in this case the ice is *alive*.

This conversion begins with the moon. While enduring his seven days of suicidal suffering, the Mariner scarcely attended to this nocturnal glow. When he did notice it, he associated it with the cruel influence of the stars and the curse of the dying crew. Now, however, he perceives the moon climb gracefully to illuminate the arid mainmast: "Her beams bemocked the sultry main, / Like April hoar-frost spread." Reminiscent of polar ice and prophetic of rebirth, the moon is now uncannily double—positive and negative, life and death, mocking and bright. As with the moon, so with the sea. Before, during his week of pain, the Mariner viewed the ocean as waste. Now the waves transform in the light of the icy moon: Within the shadow of the ship, the "charmed" water burns a "still and awful red." The current is obscure and burning, turbulent and calm, dreadful and wonderful. It too recalls the paradoxical polar ice, which was "dismal" and "wondrous," vague and green. Moving outward—from himself to mainmast to ship's shadow and beyond—the Mariner attends to the water snakes that he formerly found a horde of "slimy things." Now he sees them swim in "tracks of shining white" in the midst of "hoary flakes" of "elfish light." Interested in these bright whirls, he observes the snakes within the ship's shadow, finds them equally intriguing: coiling patterns of "glossy green" and "velvet black," like "golden fire" flashing. On the edge of a shadow, the Mariner again perceives duplicities he before repressed: the snakes are glimmering and gray, pied and golden, polarized vortices (AM 267–81).

In all three cases, the Mariner converts from the single vision—phenomena as either one thing or the other—to a double science: events are polarized. His hierarchies are uncannily upset by polarities he formerly repressed. Fittingly, each image is a traditional symbol for ambiguous energies ignored or demonized by most Western men.[75] There is first the icy moon: traditionally a symbol of Hecate, the triple-headed goddess of hell, earth, and heaven, of witchcraft, madness, and wild love. Then there is the burning sea, a perennial figure for chaos. And finally there is the serpent power itself: Tiamat, Satan, Leviathan. Each of these elements is analogous to the polar ice. The frosty moon, the bewitched water, and the snakes that are white are cognates to the empty-full, wondrous-dismal, blank-green crystals of ice. Hence, though the Mariner still views the unfrozen world through the filters of ice—he still wears the dead albatross—he is beginning to understand that the ice is not an opaque stuff to be subdued but a *window* to the polarities by which beings oscillate.

The Mariner has converted from narcissism to a more charitable curiosity. Immediately after comparing the snakes to a "flash of golden fire," he declares them—and ostensibly the moon and sea that preceded them—"happy living things." With this declaration, the Mariner elevates fully to Blake's second level of seeing—the world is an organic system thriving in polarized rhythms. Yet, this twofold vision is itself dependent on the onefold, on Ulro.

The two levels are themselves polarities. They are not separate but differentiated, not hierarchical but *holarchical*.[76]

As Coleridge explains in *Theory of Life* (1816), life—the polarized power of difference and identity—manifests itself in increasingly complex scales of being resembling "concentric circles" that grow more vigorous with each expansion. As Owen Barfield has noted, Coleridge casts these gradations into four categories: "absolute dependence of the parts on the whole," "additional dependence of whole on parts," "greatest number of integral parts presupposed in whole," and "parts themselves possessing character as wholes."[77] The first three categories fall under the rubric of inanimate matter (exemplified, respectively, by metals, crystals, and geological processes) and thus are driven by the primary polarity of "magnetism." The fourth category—animated matter—is likewise structured by magnetism but also contains the more complex process of "reproduction." The magnetic four-fold gives rise to a more complex reproductive quaternion, with the fourth stage of the magnetic and the first of the reproductive overlapping and forming an intermediate link between inanimate and animate. The reproductive four-fold is comprised of levels of sensibility (plants), motion (insects), consciousness (more complex animals), and, finally, self-consciousness, which would be the first link in a new quaternion, the human, motivated by self-consciousness on the individual level, interdependence in political life, independence in the moral realm, and genius in intellectual life (*CC* 11:510–532). Each level, from stone to poet, holarchically depends on the less complex scales it contains and is contingent upon the more complex scales including it.

The appearance of these scales of being depends upon one's angle of vision. As Coleridge complains in *Aids to Reflection* (1825), the observer with materialistic presuppositions—assuming a universe of impenetrable stuff moved by some force—will see the world as a machine, ignore the immanent power of polarized and polarizing life, and flatten four-fold pattern into single vision. Yet, as this thinker moves outward from his narcissistic tower and becomes interested in the external world, he interprets the world differently. He blesses "happy living things," polarized intensities (*CC* 9:398–9).

THE BELOVED'S MIRROR

When we left the Mariner, he had attained this level of seeing. Yet, one should not rest at this stage, for though humans include biology, they also transcend it. Growing from organic life is imagination, akin to Blake's Beulah, which is associated with dreams, reveries, gardens of symmetrical design. Excited by the vital hum, the Mariner quickly achieves this more complex realm of vision.

> O happy living things! no tongue
> Their beauty might declare:
> A spring of love gushed from my heart,
> And I blessed them unaware:
> Sure my kind saint took pity on me,
> And I bless'd them unaware. (*AM* 282–87)

Experiencing biological joy in the shimmering snakes, the Mariner also apprehends their aesthetic forms and at the same time feels a spontaneous gush of affection. This unwilled geyser, aptly originating from a spring beyond his fearing and desiring ego, inspires him to bless these beings unconsciously. Acknowledging their holiness, he further feels as if an invisible power, a "kind saint," benevolently influences him. With a striking abruptness, the Mariner has been transformed into a new way of seeing, able now to sense in the moon, waves, and snakes virtues beyond the visible—beauty and holiness—as well as to apprehend in his own being powers beyond his conscious control—fonts of love and generous saints.

How has this fresh conversion occurred, and what is its relationship to his experience of the ice? The Mariner now perceives the
snakes and their surroundings not simply through empirical curiosity
but also through emotional fervor. What before were only interesting external events are now both captivating occurrences and objects
of aesthetic delight. As aesthetic sites, the happy living things appear
to the Mariner as gatherings of difference—scintillating others that
engage his attention—and identity—reflections of his innermost
sense of beauty. Reflecting his interior harmony, the snakes and their
moony habitat stimulate a flow of affection. The perception of the
beautiful, Kant contends, is comforting and charming, for it, unlike
the sublime, is grounded on an apprehension of concord.[78] Noticing
such a solacing pattern in the sea, the Mariner—and this is a second
salient element of his conversion—falls in love: his heart leaps up
when he beholds the familiar in the other, when the glistening serpents *mirror* to him his aesthetic ideals.

For Coleridge, the faculty that combines perception, beauty,
and love is the imagination. Distinct from the understanding, Coleridge's term (borrowed from Kant) for the empirical modality
that gathers facts, the imagination translates facts into feelings,
senses into symbols. As Coleridge explains in *Biographia Literaria*
(1817), the poet is distinct from the scientist insofar as he shapes
the world to reflect his emotions: "[I]mages however beautiful,
though faithfully copied from nature, and accurately represented
in words, do not of themselves characterize the poet. They become proofs of original genius only as far as they are modified by a
predominant passion; or by associated thoughts or images awakened by that passion; or when they have the effect of reducing
multitude to unity . . . [or] when a human and intellectual life is
transferred from the poet's own spirit" (*CC* 7.2:23). The poet, like
the Mariner, takes the "faithful" images pictured by the understanding, such as snakes turning brightly, and transmutes them
into patterns of his passions. He charges biological occurrences

with human significance. He translates the visible world into a double of his interior energies.

This aesthetic doubling differs from the anthropocentric doubling that the Mariner earlier practiced. The latter form of doubling is narcissistic, a perception of the external world only in relation to the ego. The former way of duplicating is more charitable, based on an intuition of a distributed wholeness coursing through discrete parts. Think of the Concord farmer Emerson describes in *Nature* (1836). Although this farmer believes that his deeded lands are entirely his, he really possesses only his narrow idea. He commodifies the elm into twigs that can be consumed for fuel and thus does not perceive the reticulated bark or serrated leaves. He sees only his own comfort during the winter. Emerson's poet is the true possessor of the farm. He apprehends the tree as a part of whole in which he himself participates. He discerns in the roots and trunk and limbs a deeper self, what Emerson in "Self-Reliance" (1841) calls the "aboriginal self," the invisible power animating visible organs (*EW* 2:37). This self of nature unifies diverse phenomena, enabling self-conscious beings to discover in others the same. It is this revelation—that everything in the world always doubles everything else—to which Emerson refers when he claims that we should make the world a "double of man" (*N* 57).

Seeing the snakes as a double of a spring of life gushing even in his own breast, the Mariner transforms the water serpents into a symbol, defined by Coleridge as a part that reveals the whole, a translucent conduit through which ubiquitous life flashes. The Mariner accomplishes this elevation of the particular to the universal through the spontaneous activation of the two primary modalities of the imagination. Through an involuntary intuition of the *primary* imagination, he apprehends in his finite mind the "eternal act of creation in the infinite I AM" (*CC* 7.1:304)—that is, he grasps a harmonious principle of life coursing through the waves. Sensing on impulse this beautiful concord gathering the different patterns, he then activates the *secondary* imagination, the modality that "dissolves, diffuses, dissipates, in order to re-create," that, in all cases, "struggles to idealize and to unify" (7.1: 304). He produces a linguistic pattern that expresses the hidden relationship between subject and object, difference and identity. He *represents* the moon, waves, and snakes as humming eddies of living harmony. For Coleridge, this is the middle way of the imagination, the "reconciling and mediatory power" that incorporates the holistic intuitions of reason (Coleridge's term, also from Kant, for the extrasensory faculty) with the empirical data of the understanding. The marriage of these two powers engenders "symbols, harmonious in themselves, and consubstantial with the truths of which they are conductors" (6:29).

A form of vision and voicing that lies between the under-standing and the reason, the imagination apprehends and enunci-ates an intermediate realm between visible and invisible.[79] Instinctively lifting the snakes into interfaces between waves and deep, the Mariner aptly experiences an intermediary himself: a "kind saint" who takes pity on him. A saint, like a Coleridgean symbol, is a concrete harbinger of the immaterial. When believ-ers pray to a saint, they picture a familiar intercessor between their habitual senses and strange spirits. They fashion a sacred technology, an imagistic instrument for intuiting a power beyond their empirical faculties. When this technology is effective, it glows with uncreated light, blossoms into an unexpected aureole, a numinous sphere, and eventually is consumed in its own fires, disappearing before the invisible power that it bears to earth. The proper office of the saint, and the symbol, is to function as vehi-cle—valuable during the journey but useless once the destination is achieved.

Before turning to the moment when the Mariner passes through his saintly symbols to the imageless nothing that nonethe-less gives rise to all things and images, we ask: How does the Mariner's elevation from sense to symbol in the unfrozen sea relate to his earlier negative experience below the Antarctic Circle? The Mariner is becoming *conscious* of a vision that he *unconsciously* experienced in the polar ice. Below the circle, the Mariner registered the pole as a wasteland and reduced the bird to a cipher of this void. Yet, the images he chose to detail the pole and its synecdoche in such negative lights reveal positive undercurrents. The dismal yet gleaming appearance of ice as well as the spiraling flying patterns of the bird overtly strike the Mariner as violations of logic yet covertly suggest that the ice and the albatross are special revelations of dynamic polarities that create and conserve the universe. Likewise, blank freeze and foggy bird chagrin the Mariner as patterns of emptiness; however, these bland pictures more secretly unfold into the colorless all-color of being. If the Mariner below the pole could have renounced his narcissistic and anthropocentric obsessions, he then would have experienced the ice and the snowy bird as he now apprehends the moon, the waves, and the snakes: as eddies of the abyss of life. At that time, though, the Mariner had not yet been refined in the alembics of suffering, had not descended into the dark *prima materia* to have his ego dissolved. In the present instance, however, with his solipsism vanquished, he opens to the qualities of the ice that he formerly repressed, to the virtues hidden in the very language he employed to detail the frozen region.

His present experience is uncanny. His repressions of polar powers return to organize his current perception. These unloosed repressions flood into his sight and pervade moon, wave, and snake with the qualities of ice. This does not mean that these unfrozen phenomena do not already bear these virtues, that they are not always polarized patterns of the ungraspable abyss. It means that the uncanny return of the ice acts as a special lens—a crystalline scope—that empowers the Mariner to see in the moon, waves, and snakes beauties he might have otherwise ignored. Looking through the image of "hoar-frost," he discerns in the moon a vigor suggesting spring; glimpsing the water through thoughts of awful frozen wonder, he finds in it a fire; and staring through pictures of snowflakes and white vortices, he discovers in the water serpents flashes of gold. Thus, when the Mariner is struck by the beauty in these "happy living things," he is indirectly stunned by the beauty of ice. When he blesses these phenomena, he is belatedly sanctifying the pole. He sees double, inhabiting and perceiving both a figurative Antarctica and a literal oceanscape above the circle. The snakes as slime are the ice as chaos; these same serpents as living things are also ice as a window to generation; and, yet again, the snakes as instances of the beloved are the ice as a mirror of aesthetic passion.

NOTHING THAT IS NOT THERE

The Mariner during these conversions still wears the albatross. Yet, the bird is on the verge of falling away. This shedding will signal the Mariner's passage from the realm of natural beauty, the ice as reflection of harmony (Blake's Beulah—nature as a garden of gorgeous dreams and amorous delights) to the boundless energy of the sublime, the ice as no*thing* (Blake's Eden—the invisible power of life within and beyond nature). With amazing alacrity— the Mariner's conversion is miraculously abrupt, as almost all epiphanies are—the Mariner leaps from the imagination to the imageless. Immediately after he feels the pity of his saint and for a second time blesses the slithering ocean he does what he longed to do but could not in his earlier Ulro: pray.

> That selfsame moment I could pray;
> And from my neck so free
> The Albatross fell off, and sank
> Like lead into the sea. (*AM* 288–91)

The albatross is a cipher of the pole in all of its guises—waste of Ulro, window to Generation, and mirror of Beulah. Its disappearance suggests that the Mariner has passed beyond his crass ego, his charitable understanding, and his doubling imagination into a fourth faculty capable of apprehending invisible powers stripped of *visibilia*. This transcendence of representations is revealed in the following, in which the Mariner enters into a *mystical* state—a condition in which he *sees* though his eyes are closed.[80]

> Oh sleep! It is a gentle thing,
> Beloved from pole to pole!
> To Mary Queen the praise be given!
> She sent the gentle sleep from Heaven,
> That slid into my soul.
>
> The silly buckets on the deck,
> That had so long remained,
> I dreamt that they were filled with dew;
> And when I awoke, it rained.
>
> My lips were wet, my throat was cold,
> My garments were all dank;
> Sure I had drunken in my dreams,
> And still my body drank. (292–304)

Inaudible, this prayer not a spoken petition. Rather, it is akin to what Evelyn Underhill in *Mysticism* (1955) calls an "orison," a "mystical prayer" that "is not articulate" and "has no forms." Unseeing and mute, the mystic engaged in orison yearns to merge with the groundless ground of all beings. He relinquishes his understanding because its concepts falter before the totality for which he quests. He lets go of his imagination, for its pictures fail to depict the invisible energy he seeks. Left with his reason—the intuitive faculty—he hopes to experience what is beyond experience: life devoid of its beings.[81]

This *negative* movement is analogous to the process by which one experiences the sublime. An experience of beauty falls within the domain of the understanding and the imagination. The understanding represents a beautiful object that it cannot conceive while the imagination transforms this representation into a symbol. However, an encounter of the sublime occurs when the mind is overwhelmed with abysmal powers that it cannot conceive or image. Yet, inspired by this conceptual and imagistic failure, the mind's reason transcends ideas and pictures to intuit, partially, the nature of the ungraspable powers. Painful in its failure, pleasurable in its transcendence, the sublime vision is negative and contradictory: It presents the unpresentable, is informed by the formless, is blind but sees, conceives nothing but knows, esoterically, absolutes.

The Mariner's orison frees him from the albatross and releases him into the abyss. Liberated from concepts and images, the Mariner sleeps, closing his eyes to the visible in order to "see" invisible events. Significantly, his visionary sleep is "beloved from pole to pole." It gathers opposites into concord as well as merges Antarctic and Arctic into one immense staff of life—*axis mundi*, omphalos, caduceus. Issuing from "Heaven" by way of "Mary Queen," this "gentle sleep" vouchsafes a vision of formerly empty vessels ("silly buckets") overflowed with originless water ("dew") and therefore made holy ("silly" derives from *sely*, fortunate, holy).

This heaven and its queen are not only Christian figures for the New Jerusalem and the Mother of Jesus. Associated with the poles—both the North and South Poles of the universal axle and the individual polarities of all beings—and with boundless waters—dew flooding over the forms it fills—this heaven also suggests the Peratic plenitude and its polarized emanations. Witnessing this fullness overflow holy forms, the Mariner experiences the creation of the cosmos, the original and ongoing process by which the unknown monad flows outward into an ideal form, which itself emanates into the polarities of matter. Rising from his early embrace of snakes, the Mariner in his sublime orison beholds the Peratic father, the uncreated deep, cohering into

the serpentine eddy of the son, which itself overflows into the secret currents of living matter. If these speculations are valid—and
they are, given Coleridge's "darling studies" of traditional Hermetic and Gnostic texts[82]—then "Mary Queen" is not only the
orthodox virgin but also an avatar of the numerous Gnostic females analogous to the son in the Peratic myth. Ranging from
Barbēlo to Sophia, these intermediary figures bridge the spiritual
plenitude and fallen matter, distributed water and discrete
eddies.[83]

Knowing in his mystical dream the process by which the cosmos was and is created, feeling the holy serpent power slide into
his own breast, the Mariner awakes to discover that he, like the
queen, is a principle and agent of the currents of life. Like the
dew, the uncreated water of the plenitude, he causes the world to
grow—his dreams of moisture create nourishing liquid. As the
holy bucket, he is a vehicle of the floods he helps to fashion—his
body drinks the rain, transforming its drops into nourishment.
Fortified by this liquid bounty and now moving around the deck,
he for the first time fully understands his place in the cosmos: "I
was so light—almost / I thought that I had died in sleep, / And was
a blessed ghost" (*AM* 306–7) Having died to the controlling ego
that urged him to kill the bird, he is indeed "light," unattached to
matter either through extreme hate or possessive love. He has now
achieved the level of knowing attained by Thoreau before the
Walden ice and Shelley under Mont Blanc: a realization that he, as
a bright pattern of the ubiquitous abyss, is as unattached and insubstantial as the wind. Apprehending his distributed nature—but
not forgetting his discrete form, his limbs and body—he aptly
hears a "roaring wind" and watches the "upper air" burst into
"life." In the midst of the bold wind and the soaking rain, the sky
explodes into lightning—"a hundred fire-flags sheen." The ship
moves, escaping Ulro. The dead men rise, showing that nothing is
ever really dead (313–34).

QUATERNION

Liberated from the albatross, the Mariner has become a latter-day Peratic, a monistically minded Gnostic, sliding through the hidden portals of matter into the plenitude. To reach this vision, he has struggled through Ulro, Generation, and Beulah, finally to reach Eden, the transcendent yet immanent energy that creates and conserves all beings. Exceeding yet including all scales of existence—the physical, the biological, and psychological—as well as each level of seeing—Ulro, Generation, and Beulah—this realm of being is the totality, as Blake calls it, the "Four-fold." Far from stiffening into a rigid anatomy, as the medieval hermeneutical fourfold often did, this Blakean fourfold is a term for a heightened vision of the rich complexities of being—a name for a perception of the polar ice as a plane of opaque matter, a transparent window to thriving polarity, a mirror of gorgeous harmony, and a portal to the *no*thing without which no*thing* is. This fourfold vision redeems Urizen's demonizations of Ulro into valuable physical processes required for the growth of Generation's vegetable organizations; it elevates biological energies from mere violences (nature "red in tooth and claw") to fecund springs necessary for harmonious gardens; it opens Beulah's delights into portals of the invisible abyss. Hence, Blake's holarchical hermeneutic restores Urizenic machines to vigorous manifolds.

Coleridge, like his Mariner, is likewise fixated on the number "four" for holarchically expressing life's manifold. In his marginalia to Boehme's *Aurora*—drafted in preparation for his philosophical magnum opus, never written—Coleridge maintains that the cosmos begins in a "prothesis," an undifferentiated chaos, circumference without a center. From this primal energy, analogous to the Gnostic plenitude, emerges a "thesis," a difference in the abyss, a contraction into a center, a pattern of identity and difference. This first polarity—center and circumference, difference and indifference—recalls the Peratic Father contracting into a discernible Son. This thesis next organizes itself into an "antithesis," marked by the center expanding outward, irradiating its polarized rhythms into forms spreading throughout infinity—an expansion that resembles the serpentine Son undulating through the matter that overflows from his being. The whole—the entire cosmos, the manifold totality—created by this interaction among prothesis (indifference), thesis (difference in indifference), and antithesis (difference and indifference merged) is the "synthesis" (*CC* 12.1.562–3).[84]

Yet, this synthesis is not a static system. Because this whole is inseparable from its parts, it is at any one time the chaos of the prothesis, the struggle for form that is thesis, the coincidence of opposites that comprise the antithesis. Viewed from a diachronic angle of vision, the whole cosmos is perpetually evolving toward more complex syntheses, toward richer instances of consciousness. What appears to be complete is a seed for further development; synthesis dissolves again into prothesis only to cohere again later into a more manifold whole. Seen from a synchronic aspect, the synthetic whole is simultaneously unbounded energy, an *agon* between opposites, a harmonious conflict, and the relationship among all three levels. What is true of the cosmic whole is true of each individual *holon* (simultaneous part and whole)[85]: Each discrete form of the universe is an evolving heterogeneity—indifferent energy (gravity, electricity), tensed difference (cells and organs), harmonious interaction (organism and environment), and the relationship among all three (a part/whole participating in larger parts/wholes).

A man aware of such manifold existence can perceive the palpable patterns around him from any one of these levels of vision as well as from the perspective of all of the levels combined. To understand the cosmos and its beings in the latter way—from the synthetic aspect—is to know that life is the power of identity and difference (an unseen relationship), that this power is eternal (not subject to the decays of time and space), that it is abysmal (nothing to the concepts of the understanding or the pictures of the imagination, everything to the intuitive reason). Gaining this synthetic intuition, one further grasps that matters and forces indifferent to human comfort are not wastes but necessary forms of being; that a nature that lives by killing is not a violent monstrosity but a creative *agon*; that the harmonies between part and whole, self and other are not ends in themselves but gardens opening to unseen seeds and blooms.

That the Mariner experiences such an insight is further evidenced by the optical activities in which he engages after his vision. As his ship is driven homeward by a salubrious wind and a resurrected crew, the Mariner experiences the hums of matter with a new delight. No longer feeling vengeful, he delights in the "sweet jargoning" of "all little birds that are" as well as in the sound of the wind, which recalls the "pleasant noise" of a "hidden brook / In the leafy month of June" (*AM* 358–62; 368–72). What once the Mariner murdered—a bird—becomes mirthful harmony; and what he once cursed as a tyranny—the wind—is now a summer spring. This transformed sight inspires the Mariner's "moral" at the end of his tale—not a Christian chestnut but the result of a complex vision of serpent and abyss: "He prayeth well, who loveth well / Both man and bird and beast" (612–3).

Not only is this insight complex; it is also consuming. Briefly after his synthetic gnosis, the old sailor realizes that a polar spirit haunts him. As his ship tacks north in the billows of a mysterious wind, he understands that this spirit of ice drives the ship, bent on punishing him for murdering its beloved albatross. Even after the "curse" from the dead men's eyes is expiated when he approaches his home harbor, the Mariner nonetheless feels like he is a traveler on a lonesome road dreading some unseen fiend. This feeling of unease continues long after he witnesses the souls ascend from the bodies of the dead sailors, after he has confessed his "sin" to the Hermit, after his docking in his own country. As the Mariner admits near the close of his tale, he spends his days wandering, frequently beset, at "uncertain hour," by an agony that is only relieved by his telling of the tale.

The Mariner has become a tortured prophet of the polar gnosis. Like a hidden god voicing cosmic necessities, the polar spirit at unpredictable periods erupts into the Mariner's consciousness. Heeding this call is often torture, for it requires that the Mariner journey over strange lands and address cold audiences. The Mariner may on some days desire a home and a community. He cannot have them. He is a slave to his frozen vision, and forever a polar explorer. This moveable gnosis and the prophetic nomadism it commands do not even grant the Mariner a spiritual solace. Unlike the tranquil sage of the temple, the old sailor cannot rest in his vision but must, like Jeremiah, struggle in invisible labyrinths. Yet, as reward for his unease, the Mariner is blessed with the powers of strange speech and mesmerizing eye. He is an inspired bard who on honeydew has fed, and drunk the milk of paradise. Constrained by his *daimon*, he is free to shock his hearers into new ways of being. Blinded by his pain, he sees everything.

POETICS OF SELF-CONSUMMATION

As a pattern of and portal to the full void, as a revelation of the fourfold—complete being and nonbeing, the literal as well as the anagogical—the esoteric pole opens into the consummation of all things: their annihilation and their completion. Persistently experiencing this pole in the form of poetic spasms, the Mariner continually suffers this double consummation. His ego is periodically torn by the same abysmal spirit that empowers him to create a poem as apocalyptic as it is mesmerizing.

The word "apocalypse" derives from the Greek *apokalupsis*, a derivative of the verb *apokaluptein*, to uncover, to reveal. The Latin renders the word as *revelare*, to unveil, to pull back (*re*) the cover (*vellum*). An apocalypse is not only a judgmental destruction of history—as some Christians hold—but also a sudden annihilation of visible form that leaves in its wake an invisible power. This abrupt shattering of finite patterns of space and time is tantamount to gnosis—a quick and possibly redemptive glimpse into the unimaginable unity pervading yet beyond material separations. Identification with this invisible ubiquity is double consummation: a burning away of finite ballasts—such as egos and words and clocks and maps—as well as a complete merging with the eternal—the undifferentiated abyss. That the Revelation of the Bible is a violent rending of *visibilia* and a well-appointed marriage feast is perfectly apt.

Coleridge's pole is an apocalypse. Beyond the Mariner's various maps—ranging from his navigational charts to his egocentric cartographies to his anthropocentric coordinates—the Antarctic demeans and finally destroys his habitual ways of organizing the realms of space and time. Yet, in consuming his psychical and physical sextants, the pole offers him a profound marriage to the Queen of Heaven. This marriage he consummates only by relinquishing his old maps—by closing his eyes and ears to the material world (consuming it in darkness) and thus opening his intuition to eternity (the consummation of time). After this vision, he realizes that his ego and its expressions are always already consumed—sometimes painfully—by the polar spirit that inhabits him but also that this haunting connects him—marries him—to humans and birds and beasts.

Hence, his intonation of his polar apocalypse—appropriately at a wedding—is thus to be taken seriously and not seriously. As a finite linguistic pattern, his tale, like his ego and its maps, is a veil, an obscuration of the invisible spirit he wishes to disclose. Yet, at the same time, the ballad points to a fourfold gnosis that might shock its audience into an awareness of the esoteric pole. Thus, unlike egocentric maps that should simply be rejected, the Mariner's poem, his *Gnostic* map, should be both destroyed and affirmed, read and ignored. A self-consuming text, it is like a finger pointing to the moon, or a map to one's home. Once one is beholding the gibbous curve or resting on the porch, the finger and the legend, formerly essential, are worthless clichés, disposable husks, *hoaxes* that hinder.

All events, esoterically perceived, are hoaxes, self-consuming events, illusions blocking truth and portals to the real. The poles are simply special revelations of this fact, as the crystal powerfully discloses a self-organizing universe and the glacier notably opens into a cosmos of infinite regression. While the poles—as part of the universe—are of course self-organizing patterns and doors to infinite regress, they differ from crystals and glaciers in degree, proving more likely to explode their beholders into an apocalyptic vista of the eternal *terra incognita*.

POE'S POLAR HOAXING

On the surface, Poe's *The Narrative of Arthur Gordon Pym* is a "re-alistic" version of Coleridge's comparatively "allegorical" *Rime*. On the one hand, Poe's novel parallels Coleridge's poem in significant ways. Both works feature a south polar landscape where the protagonist undergoes a profound experience; an episode in which a ship bearing death appears to a starving crew; and a narrator who has lived to tell his tale after suffering extreme hardship. Yet, on the other hand, Poe's novel seems much more rooted to the palpable world than does Coleridge's dreamy verse. Poe sets his work in 1827–28 while Coleridge's takes place "once upon a time"; Poe's story is replete with details from the world of sailing while Coleridge's Mariner seldom mentions instruments or locations; and Poe's tale shows an awareness of the history and science of polar exploration while Coleridge's ballad is uninterested in the discovery of Antarctic facts.

Yet, ironically, Poe's ostensible intimacy with the actual was not meant to depict the real but to perpetrate a *hoax*. Drawing from his knowledge of the history and science of polar exploration, Poe set out to convince his audience that Pym was the first explorer to reach the South Pole. Poe was well aware of the excitement his narrative might produce. He knew of Kerguelen's and Cook's late-eighteenth-century explorations of southern seas and thus realized that the existence the Antarctic continent had not yet been confirmed. Likewise, he had read recent accounts of polar explorations, such as William Scoresby's 1823 *Journal of a Voyage to the Northern Whale Fishery* and Benjamin Morrell's 1832 *A Narrative of Four Voyages to the South Seas*, and therefore was knowledgeable about polar landscapes. Finally, Poe was interested in the recently publicized theory of John Cleves Symmes—that vortical holes at either pole are connected by an interior channel—and in the Symmesian motivations of J. N. Reynolds, who lobbied for an Antarctic expedition in his 1836 *Address on the Subject of the Surveyeing Expedition of the Pacific Ocean and the South Seas* and 1838 "Leaves from an Unpublished Journal."[86] Taking into account the abiding interest in the *terra incognita australis*, the recent appetite for polar narratives, and the curiosity aroused by Symmes and Reynolds, Poe attempted to pass his fiction as fact, and pass money into his pockets.

But this overt hoaxing is not a mere matter of duping readers. On the contrary, the novel itself is a meditation on hoaxing—the relationship between appearance and reality. Hence, Poe's book is related to Coleridge's poem on a deeper level than I have mentioned. Like Coleridge's *Rime*, which studies how certain dreams alienate from the springs of life while others connect to these same flows, Poe's novel is an exploration of how particular hoaxes dupe into illusion while others are portals to the abyss. Yet, in this esoteric context, an important difference between the two works remains. While the Mariner exhibits an awareness of his polar vision, Pym is comparatively unreflective. One consequence of this distinction is this: whereas the reader of the *Rime* contemplates the complexities of an overtly expressed esoteric "moral," the reader of Pym must gather such a "moral" for him or herself. If the Mariner is a self-conscious alchemical adept gleaning golden wisdom from his dark sufferings, then Pym is an alchemical element passively undergoing dissolution and resolution, *solve et coagula*. Pym thus places the reader in the role of the alchemist who must actively infer meanings from the alembic he observes. This primary difference in narrator translates into another important distinction. While the Mariner develops in understanding, the unreflective Pym remains rather static. If the Mariner ascends the scales of the fourfold, Pym remains most of the novel at the onefold, though he undergoes experiences that *should* transform his way of seeing.

These two contrasts suggest two different interpretive theories. The *Rime*, which Coleridge censored for having too much of a "moral,"[87] implies a "positive" hermeneutic. Overabundant with allegorical significance, the poem requires the reader to sift through copious significations in order to arrive at an analysis. In contrast, *Pym*, which Poe condemned as a "silly" book,[88] intimates a "negative" hermeneutic. Seemingly a simple narrative of materialistic exploration, the book invites readers to reverse its overt significations, to understand the text through what it is not.

NEGATIVE HERMENEUTICS

I should clarify this "negative" hermeneutic insofar as it relates to Poe's hoaxing. On one level, Poe the hoaxer requires that his reader reverse the "factual" account of a "real" polar discovery into a fictional account of an imaginary expedition. The reader is then encouraged to invert the character of Pym. Even in his fictional guise, Pym remains a hoax, for he clearly obscures important levels of signification. This Pym is an unreflective, reductive explorer who wishes to map oceans and men to fit his dream of scientific glory. Indeed, this "colonizing" Pym is a racist, associating black-skinned tribes with evil and chaos.[89] To counter Pym the imperialist hoaxer, one must attend to complexities of Pym's experiences that he himself overlooks. This hermeneutical activity reveals Pym as an allegorical figure unconsciously questing for a spiritual realm beyond matter. This "dualistically" Gnostic Pym—opposed to the more "monistically" Gnostic Mariner[90]—opens to another level of hoaxing, for his experiences, even if he is not aware of their densities, suggest that all material phenomena are hoaxes, illusions blocking transcendent spirit. Yet, this dualist Pym is also a hoax. The novel invites the reader again to read negatively—to counter Pym as dualist Gnostic with Pym as an alchemical adept embracing matter as well as spirit, black and white, chaos and order.

Pym's hoaxes are highlighted in the "Preface." Pym presents himself as an explorer who has recently returned from the South Seas and has written, at the request of several gentlemen in Richmond, an account of his travels. Yet, Pym admits that he was reticent to compose his memoir, for he fears that his poor recollection of the details have precluded him from crafting "a statement so minute and connected as to have the *appearance* of that truth it would really possess" (*NP* 55). This curious locution, perhaps unintended by Pym, blurs the distinction between appearance and reality, suggesting that reality itself is but an appearance, a simulacrum among simulacra, a hoax.

Pym's ambiguous phrasing continues. Listing another reason for his hesitation to publish, Pym confesses that he fears that the marvelous nature of his journey will strike the public as "merely an impudent and ingenious fiction," though his family and friends might "put faith in his veracity" (*NP* 55). Pym implies that certain events, regardless of their empirical status, appear to be fabrications. Hence, the standard for truth is again not a stable absolute but appearance—some facts simply *appear* to be truer than others. Likewise, Pym suggests that veracity is not self-evident but instead a matter of faith.

A third instance in the "Preface" further complicates the distinction between appearance and reality. Pym reports that early parts of this narrative have already been published in the *Southern*

Literary Messenger "under the garb of fiction" and under the name of
"Mr. Poe" (*NP* 56). Although this statement is Poe's effort to account for his earlier publication of parts of *Pym* in this magazine
under his own name, the claim also confounds the line between
real and unreal. If facts can be passed off as fictions, then certainly
fictions can be accepted as facts. This multiple authorship further
confuses. Thomas M. White wrote the early episodes for the *Messenger*, though these initial scenes were attributed to the pen of Mr.
Poe, who himself may have drafted them. Pym adds his own pages
to these preexisting ones at an unidentified juncture. Who has
written what? Which portions are facts and which are fictions?

These difficulties not only place Pym's narrative in a dubious
light. They also cast doubt on *all* appearances. Can appearances
reveal reality if visible events are not intrinsically true or false but
only extrinsically so—only authentic insofar as they *seem* to be?
Likewise, if one cannot perceive veracities but must rely on faith
in order to convince himself of realities, then how can one differentiate between fact and illusion? Further, if no authorship can be
established, then how can one know if narratives are data or
dreams? These epistemological questions suggest that *all* matter is
a hoax.

If this is the case, then one can react to matter's legerdemains
in at least three ways: one can search for immanent physical laws
hiding in the flitting shapes of the material world; try to intuit transcendent absolutes above the ephemeral fluxes; or delve into the
roiling muck for interactions between turbulence and pattern, visible appearances and invisible powers, immanence and transcendence. The first way is that of the scientific materialist who
embraces only those events that conform to his laws; the second is
that of the dualistic Gnostic who loathes the physical as the pollution of spirit; the third mode is that of the alchemical adept who
revels in life's mixtures—confusing concoctions of ephemeral and
ethereal.[91]

IMPERIALIST PYM

During the first half of his tale, Pym suffers extreme turbulence. He is almost drowned when the *Penguin*, a whaling vessel, overruns his sailboat, the *Ariel*. He almost goes insane while trapped in the dark hold of the *Grampus*, a whaling ship in which he is stowed away. He almost dies during a mutiny and counter mutiny on the *Grampus*. He contends with a terrible storm that reduces this ship to a sailless hunk. He draws lots to see if his starving companions will eat him. He watches his best friend, Augustus, die and rot in the sea.

Surviving such painful chaoses, Pym spends the second half of his story fixated on order. After being picked up by the *Jane Guy*, a British sealing and trading vessel commanded by Captain Guy and bound to the South Seas (*NP* 161), Pym, coupled with Dirk Peters, a wildly capricious "half breed" and former mutineer, becomes obsessed by measuring and recording. Upon reaching Prince Edward's Island, he begins almost daily to register the ship's location, providing geographical landmarks, mostly islands, as well as longitude and latitude. Sailing southeasterly past Prince Edward's, latitude 46 53' S., longitude 37 46' E., he notes the coordinates of Possession Island, the Crozset Islands, and Desolation Island. When the *Guy* meanders around the southern parts of the Indian Ocean, Pym intersperses his cartographical log with discourses on the history of southern exploration. He records the discoveries of Kerguélen and Cook, as well as more recent southern polar excursions by Captains Kreutzenstern and Lisiausky in 1803, Captain Weddell in 1822, Captain Morell in 1823, and Captain Briscoe in 1831 (150–62).

This burgeoning interest in mapping and recording events is exemplified when Pym attends to the nesting practices of the penguins and albatrosses on Desolation Island. Tracing on the ground a network of lozenges, these birds organize the land into a symmetrical map, a series of interlocking quincunxes (*NP* 151–3).

Hence, though Poe draws this description from Morrell's *Narrative*, his account of the hieroglyphs points to Browne's *The Garden of Cyrus* (1658). Browne takes as his initial topic Cyrus the Younger's "method of planting trees by fives in the shape of the quincunx"; however, he quickly finds this shape—a lozenge and an "X"—everywhere in the human, animal, vegetable, and mineral worlds. Browne concludes that this figure could be the original geometry of Eden, for this "originall of Plantations" featured as its middle point the "tree of knowledge" and thus "wanted not a centre and a rule of decussation." As the archetypal figure of God's Paradise, the quincunx is the "Hieroglyphick of the world."[92]

According to John T. Irwin, Pym, in detailing these Brownlike quincunxes, unconsciously suggests a theory of knowledge that escapes him throughout his tale—a theory that might, if he were to become aware of it, save him from his imperialistic bifurcations and hierarchies. For Irwin, the quincunx is Browne's symbol for the "intelligible continuity of the universe"—a world continuously linked and a human mind capable of meshing with this cosmic net. The "V" shape, the unit of the lozenge and the hourglass (a lozenge is the "V" "doubled at its open end" while an hourglass is the "V" "doubled at its angle") figures the lines of light rays to the lens of the eyes and then again from the lens to the retina. Moreover, the optic chiasma is divided into two "V's" joined at their apices. These optical "V's" highlight the main function of cognitive seeing: a forceps-like grasping. The "V" of the eyes is analogous to the "V" formed by two arms spread open and by the thumb pointed away from the other fingers. Whether one scans one's field of vision with his binocular "V" or picks out objects with the hinged "V's" of his arms or fingers, he is embodying "the essentially oppositional character of human knowledge"—any act of knowing requires that the knower posit a known that is different and the same, other and double.[93]

This "differential" quality of knowing—this grasping of objects with subjective nets, this interplay between projection, the "V" irradiating outward, and introjection, the "V" inwardly irradiating—is exemplified by self-consciousness. To be aware of oneself, one must feel oneself against something else, must posit an "other" in order to feel the "self-same." But this difference that generates identity—the self-opposing "V"—is present in all acts of knowing in which one posits a separate object that he wishes to identify with his subjectivity, in which one casts his net outward hoping to enmesh it in other nets that will become inseparable from his own.[94]

What is most revealing about Poe's description of the quincuncial nesting patterns is its *difference* from Browne's and Morrell's inflections of the same figures. For Browne, the quincunx is God's divine geometry. For Morell, the bird behavior suggests an "almost incredible order." Compared to these meditations, Pym's own comment on the nesting network is anemic: "[S]urvey it as we will, nothing can be more astonishing than the spirit of reflection evinced by these feathered beings, and nothing surely can be better calculated to elicit reflection in every well-regulated human intellect" (*NP* 153). For Irwin, this observation is "an ironic comment on the lack of reflection that Pym consistently demonstrates when faced with traces of intelligent design in the desolate regions near the Pole." Pym's remark about the birds inspiring "reflection" highlights his own inability to reflect on reflection—on how human networks mesh with nonhuman ones. Pym's persistent nonrecognitions culminate in the final scene of the novel, in which he descends into a cataract at the South Pole while a huge white form hovers above. In this instance Pym fails to recognize in the rising figure his own shadow image, and thus literally does not register the process of reflection, or self-consciousness. In this final event, Pym reveals what is true of himself throughout the novel. He is not aware that in knowing the world he projects onto it "a structure which in meshing with the physical nature finds some recurrences meaningful and others not."[95] He is unconscious of his own mappings, of the nets he casts onto landscapes in order to make them significant.

From Irwin's analysis we extrapolate two conclusions. One, cognition is an act of doubling, of imposing subjective networks onto a different object in an effort to make it the same. Two, there are at least two different kinds of doubling—unconscious, in which one is in danger of confusing the map for the territory, the network for the ocean, and self-conscious, in which one might understand the difference between his projections and the world. Pym's doublings are of the former sort. Though he becomes obsessed with networks of human intelligence—quincunxes, cartographical coordinates, historical records—he does not reflect upon the difference between these signs and their signifieds. He is not able to experience rich differences and similarities between himself and others. He is able to see only the maps and lexicons in his own mind, imperialistic technologies that shape objects into doubles of his desire for control.

If we cannot grasp Pym's imperialistic disposition through his reflections, we can unearth it by watching what he notices. Thrilled that the *Jane Guy* has wandered into southern seas and emboldened by Captain Guy's resolution to discover the *terra incognita australis*, Pym continues his recording in earnest when the ship encounters the Antarctic ice. Unlike the Mariner, Pym is unfazed by the land of mist and snow. Ignoring the sublime bergs and floes, he is most concerned with the networks in his mind, with his own egocentric interests. He notices only the barest weather; the ship's coordinates; the amount and size of the ice; and the edibility of the strange animals he encounters. When the *Guy* reaches an uncharted island featuring a piece of wood that resembles an engraved canoe, Pym neglects this rich interpenetration between human and nonhuman, art and nature, and instead complacently lists the ship's coordinates and reports that he has reached a point further south than any previous sailor. Pym at this point is engrossed by the possibility of charting a southern continent and the pole itself. So bent is he on this scientific mission that he convinces Captain Guy to press onward, even though the ship is short of fuel and some men have scurvy. Pym wants only to reveal one of the world's "most intensely exciting secrets" (*NP* 166).

This secret, the core of Poe's hoax, is quickly revealed. Close to the South Pole, beyond any point reached by European men, the ice gives way to pleasant airs, dark seas, and a group of dusky-colored islands inhabited by "savages" whose complexions are "jet black, with thick and long woolly hair" and whose clothes are comprised of "skins of an unknown black animal, shaggy and silky" (*NP* 168). These words of Pym reflect his attitudes toward the natives of Tsalal and their island. He is not interested in these people, quickly writing them off as "subhuman," but hungry to push southward. Still, he does agree to accompany Captain Guy and eleven other men to the island, where he will join this group in an "investigation of the country, in the hope of making a profitable speculation in this discovery" (170). Hence, for Pym, the dark-skinned inhabitants of Tsalal are either savages to be classified or commodities to be exploited.[96]

Pym persists in this imperialistic bifurcating weeks later, after he and Peters escape a Tsalalian uprising that kills the other members of the crew. Trapped in a sable ravine, the two men explore the rocks. They discover in the midst of an abysmal chasm what appears to be a carved human figure surrounded by alphabetical characters. Pym, however, dismisses the possibility that these markings evidence a human presence and attributes their existence to a "convulsion" (*NP* 192–8). Unwilling to entertain the possibility that oppositions—human and nature, articulation and abyss—might coincide, Pym assumes that a dusky gulf is no place for cogent organization. He supposes that this abyss is undifferentiated, free of ordered patterns. Casting such a divisive net, he misses an opportunity to gain insight into rich interpenetrations.

Days later, Pym again descends yet misses the meaning. While he and Peters are exploring the caverns, they decide to climb down a tall cliff. After Peters completes the descent, Pym lowers himself until he is paralyzed by a fear of falling. His "imagination" grows "terribly excited by thoughts of the vast depth yet to be descended."

> I could not, I would not, confine my glances to the cliff; and, with a wild, indefinable emotion, half of horror, half of a relieved oppression, I threw my vision far down into the abyss. For one moment my fingers clutched convulsively upon their hold, while, with the movement, the faintest possible idea of ultimate escape wandered, like a shadow, through my mind—in the next my whole soul was pervaded with a longing to fall; a desire, a yearning, a passion utterly uncontrollable. I let go at once my grasp upon the peg, and turning half round from the precipice, remained tottering for an instant against its naked face. But now there came a spinning of the brain; a shrill-sounding and phantom voice screamed within my ears; a dusky, fiendish, and filmy figure stood immediately beneath me; and, sighing, I sunk down with a bursting heart, and plunged within its arms. (*NP* 197–8)

After Peters breaks his plunge, Pym's "trepidation" vanishes, and he feels reborn, like "a new being." Refreshed, he resumes his explorations, and soon happens upon the wild region near where his companions were buried alive by rocks ingeniously pulled down by the natives. The "singular wildness" of the place brings to his mind "the descriptions given by travelers of those dreary regions marking the site of degraded Babylon" (198).

Pym has foregone profundities. He has been sublimely expanded by meditating on bottomless depths. Expanded, he has relinquished his desire to see his ego persist and given over to a longing to fall. Falling, he has found a new being, buoyed in the abyss by a polarized manifestation of its saving powers: Peters, Indian and nonIndian, animal and human, violent and kind. Yet, after this experience—an allegory for a spiritual *felix culpa*, a descent that rises, a death that is life—he returns to his old way of existing. He immediately likens the chasm to a ruined Babylon, demeaning it to a waste.

Pym's final descent—this time into the revolving vortex at the South Pole itself—likewise constitutes a wasted opportunity for insight. Pym and Peters eventually steal a canoe and, along with a captive called Nu-Nu, sail south in hopes of finding additional islands. Yet, when they approach the pole, they discover "a region of novelty and wonder." A towering range of flashing gray vapor appears on the southern horizon. The seawater becomes increasingly warmer and takes on a "milky consistency and hue." A windless current pulls the boat toward the south. A fine white powder begins to fall. Pym and Peters descend into a stupor. Finally, after floating for days, the men, apathetic, encounter a "sullen darkness" hovering above, while below, "from out the milky depths," arises a "luminous glare." Through these conflicting shades, the canoe is hurled with a "hideous velocity" towards a "limitless" cataract in the southern distance. In another day, Pym and Peters have been sucked to the brink of this cataract. They are surrounded in almost complete darkness above. The water below hurls up a glaring white veil. Nu Nu dies. Pym and Peters plunge: "And now we rushed into the embraces of the cataract, where a chasm threw itself open to receive us. But there arose in our pathway a shrouded human figure, very far larger in its proportions than any dweller among men. And the hue of the skin of the figure was of the perfect whiteness of snow" (*NP* 203–6).

The narrative ends. Apparently, Pym died just after composing this sequence, taking to his grave additional chapters meant to complete the book. What are we to make of this ending? For now, we can say that Pym has undergone a polar experience that defies the divisive networks that he has heretofore imposed upon the external world. First, in becoming listless, he loses his will to order, moving beyond fear (fear of the other) and desire (desire to reduce the world to the same). Second, although Pym has throughout his tale attempted to keep separate and unequal blackness and whiteness, chaos and order, nonhuman and human, here he encounters the mutual interdependency of these oppositions. Third, the breaking off of the narrative suggests that Pym may have reached a place beyond representation. Though his alleged death is one way to account for his silence, another is to submit that he has passed into an abyss that cannot be described.

I have said that this final scene is a third example of Pym missing the meaning of a transformative experience. We cannot know the *immediate* aftermath of this experience since ensuing chapters are lost. However, we can track Pym's disposition throughout his narrative, written *after* he descended into the maelstrom. Would a man who has understood that oppositions are interdependent manifestations of an unpresentable abyss write such a tale? One could answer in the affirmative, claiming that the unreflective, divisive Pym who journeys to the South Pole would have changed into a reflective, conjunctive Pym in the lost chapters. Yet, if so, why is there no evidence, in either the "Preface" or the *Narrative*, of an understanding of relationships between opposites?[97]

Pym himself is a hoax. The unreflective Pym seems designed to dupe the audience into ignoring significations that he neglects and supporting hierarchies that he endorses. Yet, this Pym through his *lack* of reflection urges readers to think about the signs that he misses. Divisive, he pushes readers to consider relationships; positivistic, he encourages meditations on the supernatural; fixated on mapping and recording, he inspires contemplations on relationships between charts and territories, words and things.

EMPYREAN PYM

Astute readers of the *Narrative* have interpreted this materialistic Pym as an allegorical figure veiling a *dualistically* Gnostic argument that reveals *all* matter as a hoax. To those readers not duped by the literal, the tale becomes a longer version of Poe's "Ms. Found in a Bottle" (1833)—that is, to use Richard Wilbur's words, "an allegory of the dreaming soul's departure from this world, and its glimpsing of the Beyond."[98] In Wilbur's Gnostic reading, Pym's plunge at the end is a reenactment of a similar descent into a polar abyss at the conclusion of "Ms." Rushing along on a dreamship headed for some metaphysical origin in southern polar vortex, the narrator of this story writes until his words break off before the abyss: "Oh, horror upon horror!—the ice opens suddenly to the right, and to the left, and we are whirling dizzily, in immense concentric circles. . . . The circles rapidly grow small—we are plunging madly within the grasp of the whirlpool—and amid a roaring, and bellowing, and thundering of ocean and of tempest, the ship is quivering—oh God! and—going down!"[99]

According to Wilbur, the background of the allegorical plunges in "Ms." and *Pym* is found in Poe's cosmology, *Eureka* (1848). For Poe, the cosmos originated when an eternal, infinite, immaterial God irradiated into space, time, and matter. The further this cosmos moves from this original point, the more discordant it becomes. Still, this diffused, confused cosmos that we currently and painfully inhabit is nonetheless pervaded by God and in the process of returning to its original unity. Hence, matter is only a "means" and not an "end"—a mode of diffusion and return that will disappear entirely once it reaches the first spiritual harmony. To denounce the world, to reject matter for spirit and body for soul, is to begin this return early, to help the cosmos reclaim its original grandeur.[100] In Wilbur's words, though the cosmos is "deity diffused," it is also "God corrupted and obscured." Thus, "there is a black-and-white gnostic contrast between the world as it is and the once-and-future unity of God."[101]

Poe's cosmology recalls his many denunciations of positivistic truth in favor of eternal beauty. In "The Poetic Principle" (1848),

for instance, Poe suggests that modes of cognition that take material processes seriously—the scientific intellect, the moral judgment, or the sensual emotions—are inferior to the "poetic
sentiment": the ability to intuit a supernatural realm of perfect
beauty. Only in achieving a vision of eternal harmony can one elevate the soul beyond the pains of the clock and the map to placeless, timeless pleasure: "We . . . have a thirst unquenchable. . . . It is
the desire of the moth for the star. It is . . . a wild effort to reach the
Beauty above. Inspired by an ecstatic prescience of the glories beyond the grave, we struggle, by multiform combinations among the
things and thoughts of Time, to attain a portion of that Loveliness
whose very elements, perhaps, appertain to eternity alone."[102]

If *The Narrative of Arthur Gordon Pym* is an allegory of this
Gnostic cosmos and ethic, then Pym's various "falls" into turbulent matter constitute the spirit's descent into demonic corruption
from which it arises strengthened, with an eye toward redemption.
His plunge into the dark waters to avoid the *Penguin*, during
which he hears "a thousand demons"; his burial in the hold of the
Grampus in a coffin-like cell; his dive on Tsalal into Peters's
"dusky, fiendish, filmy figure": Each of these falls is descent into
pollution; each ensuing rise is spiritual ascent.

Likewise, in this Gnostic interpretation, the paradoxes ignored
by the unreflective Pym become other markers of matter's painful
limitations. As Poe remarks in *Eureka*, matter exists as a tension between opposing tendencies, "Attraction and Repulsion." A realm of
"parts, particles, or atoms," matter coheres into objects through
this primary polarity: material bits combine through attraction and
repel through repulsion. To dwell in the regions of polarized matter is to experience contradictions and discomforts. To transcend
matter is to achieve a realm of "absolute Unity" in which there are
no discrete parts and thus no attractions and repulsions.[103] Read in
this light, Pym's various overlookings of paradoxical events are not
missed opportunities for insights into *coincidentia oppositorum* but
blithe inattentions to the conflicts of matter.

The Gnostic reader must also reread the novel's descriptions of intelligible networks. Instead of interpreting the quincuncial rookery and the hieroglyphs on Tsalal as symbols of the way in which the subject constructs objects, the Gnostic critic construes these inscriptions as signs of God's hidden presence in a fallen world. Although matter obscures these hints of eternity, they nonetheless occasionally shine through the darkness. Even on Desolation Island, in the midst of matter at its most inhumane, a harmonious script can appear, a fivefold order suggesting undying symmetries. Even in the dusky chasms on Tsalal, a white order can appear. The hieroglyphs witnessed by Pym and Peters, as we learn in an anonymous note appended to the narrative, point to the Arabic verbal root for "to be white" and an Egyptian word for "the region of the south" (*NP* 208).

In the Gnostic allegory, black Tsalal stands for matter in its most evil incarnation while the white pole signifies release from matter into the immaterial. Pym's description of the dark chasm as a "desolate area" that recalls a "degraded Babylon" is important in this context, for God promises "desolation" to the Babylonian captors in Isaiah 13 and Jeremiah 50 and 51 while Psalm 137 predicts the "desolation of Babylon along with Edom." These associations, in Wilbur's words, "fortify one's sense of the Tsalalians not as a primitive people but as a fallen people reduced to *savagery* through their own wickedness and the vengeance of Jehovah." The word "Tsalal" itself recalls the Hebrew word for "shadow," and thus points to Poe's 1837 review of John Lloyd Stephen's *Incidents of Travel in Egypt, Arabia, Petraea, and the Holy Land* (1837). There Poe discusses biblical prophecies against Egypt and observes that this country in its present "degraded" condition "is . . . but the *shadow* of the Egypt of the Pharaohs."[104]

Yet, even in this "hell" exist heavenly markers—hieroglyphic pointers to the white regions of the spiritual south. Surviving such an evil sphere, the Gnostic Pym is ready for deliverance. While the literalist might tie the details of Pym's final journey to actual polar journeys, such as those of Morrell or Scoresby, or to Poe's attempt to hoax readers into believing in Symmes's theory, the "reader who understands that the tale is covertly a dream of spiritual return" will understand the snowy figure as "Anthropos, or the Primal Man, or the snow-white Ancient of Days (Daniel 7:9), or the 'one like unto the Son of man' in Revelation 1:13, whose 'head and . . . hairs were white like wool, as white as snow.'"[105] In this reading, Pym as a character in the narrative experiences in the end a soulful glimpse of the immaterial divine while Pym as a writer of his narrative undergoes at the end of his composition an actual death of his body and thus a freeing of the soul.

Pym as unwitting Gnostic hoaxes on two levels. First of all, obviously, Pym as successful Gnostic quester unveils matter as a hoax. To take seriously the reality of material events and the time-bound words, images, and ideas they inspire is to be a hylic, a dupe of the demiurge's legerdemain. To get wise to this trick is to become a pneumatic—to realize that matter as well as the physical and mental maps it fosters are illusions. On a second, less obvious level, Pym as allegorical figure is himself a hoax. Although Poe's meditations on the relationship between matter and spirit suggest that he might have intended his readers to interpret *Pym* as a quest for an immaterial abyss, certain details hint at an alternative reading of the book as an alchemical treatise on the interdependent relationship between matter and spirit. First of all, if Pym has experienced a transcendent insight at the polar abyss, then this vision is *undeserved*. Though flashes of insight are unpredictable and often strike those least worthy of them (think of Paul of Damascus), surely a spiritual autobiography would exhibit signs of spiritual development. Yet, Pym learns nothing from his experiences. Likewise, if Pym at the *axis mundi* has undergone a spiritual conversion, then why do no traces of this transformation appear in his narrative, penned after his plunge? Would a Gnostic adept compose a story fixated on the glories of the material world?

These reasons are trivial compared to a third limitation of the Gnostic reading that shows this spiritualist interpretation to be little different in kind from the materialist one. Reducing matter and elevating spirit, the dualistic Gnostic thus slices away and ignores one half of the universe. Yet, he finds himself in a double bind, for he requires matter as a region in which spirit reveals its glories and rejects matter as a persistent obscuration of spirit. Like the materialist who needs turbulent materials to bear the laws he loves and neglects these same lubricious stuffs when they do not adhere to his legislations, the Gnostic must accept this fact: to transcend he must descend, to know spirit he must understand matter. This is the double bind experienced by the dualist who severs mutually inclusive opposites and uses one side to negate the other—by the materialist who separates subject from object and values the objective side, by the antimaterialist who slices bodies from souls, and celebrates only the soul.

PYM MERCURIUS

There are positive reasons for casting doubt on the Gnostic reading. Important events in Poe's *Narrative* suggest that novel is an alembic in which Pym, like Mercurius, embodies the various stages of the alchemical work—a work that exhibits the sacred marriage between matter and spirit, time and eternity. To take seriously this comparison is to treat Pym not so much as a human character capable of reflection and willing but as an element or catalyst unconsciously and passively enacting alchemical processes. Though Pym might be a mindless particle and process, his transformations nonetheless might transmute readers into alchemical adepts.

Poe was well aware of the alchemical tradition and deployed its key concepts in his works.[106] Still, Poe did not take the alchemical tradition nearly as seriously as he did Neoplatonic or Gnostic modes of thought. This fact, however, need not thwart an alchemical reading of Pym, for the novel exhibits alchemical concepts, whether Poe intended them or not.

From an alchemical perspective, Pym's descents and ascents constitute instances of the *solve et coagula*, dissolution and coagulation. In each of Pym's falls, his individuality is dissolved and distributed through a dark chaos. Yet, from each of these dismemberments, Pym arises resolved, energized with a new sense of his being. These "deaths" and "rebirths" embody the same structure—fall into deathly darkness and resurrection into life and light. However, these oscillations also mark difference— Pym's progressive development from the *nigredo* to the *albedo*. The *nigredo* stage of the alchemical work is associated with dissolution—the return of the element to be transmuted to the primal waters, the *prima materia*, syonymous with the serpent of chaos, putrefaction, the unconscious, melancholia, blackness. Far from being negative, this immersion—often symbolized by a drowning king—is a return to the origin that prepares the element for rebirth. Hence, the *nigredo* stage is inseparable from the *solve et coagula*.[107] Only after many dissolutions and resolutions is the element fully blackened, broken down, and thus prepared for the *albedo*, the white stage, often represented by the crystallization of ice.

Most of Pym's career resembles the *nigredo* stage. The first significant event in his career is his fall into the nocturnal ocean in which he is almost drowned (*NP* 58–64). Yet, though he connects this fall with the screams of "demons"—again showing his inability to gain awareness of the significance of his experiences—he recovers with a renewed vigor to become a "melancholy" explorer of despair, death, and the unknown (65). Soon after, entombed in the hold of the *Grampus*, after perusing Lewis and Clark's account of their quest for the origin of the Columbia River, Pym again descends, this time, through a dream, into the depths of his abysmal unconscious.

I was smothered to death between huge pillows, by demons of
the most ghastly and ferocious aspect. Immense serpents held
me in their embrace, and looked earnestly in my face with their
fearfully shining eyes. Then deserts, limitless, and of the most
forlorn and awe-inspiring character, spread themselves out before me. Immensely tall trunks of trees, gray and leafless, rose
up in endless succession as far as the eye could reach. Their
roots were concealed in wide-spreading morasses, whose dreary
water lay intensely black, still, and altogether terrible, beneath.
And the strange trees seemed endowed with a human vitality,
and, waving to and fro their skeleton arms, were crying to the
silent waters for mercy, in the shrill and piercing accents of the
most acute agony and despair. The scene changed; and I stood,
naked and alone, amid the burning plains of the Zahara. (72)

This dream is, unbeknownst to the unreflective Pym, fraught with
allusions to the paradoxical *prima materia*—simultaneously creative and destructive. First of all, Pym finds himself in the presence of "demons"—chaotic contraries to God's orders—inflicting
pain with instruments of pleasure, pillows. Next, Pym is terrified
by serpents—avatars of the ouroboros—that nonetheless lovingly
"embrace" him and gaze "earnestly" at him with "shining eyes."
He then finds himself in undifferentiated deserts, which, though
"forlorn," are "limitless" and "awe-inspiring." From these boundless sands grows an infinite grove of trees—leafless yet "immensely
tall." Now the desert turns into a "black" swamp, a fecund *massa
confusa*, from which the roots of the trees draw their nourishment.
Although these trees seem to suffer in these dark waters, they
nonetheless take on a "human vitality." The scene shifts. Pym
finds himself "naked and alone" in the sands of the Sahara, another desert yet also the ostensible source of the Nile.[108] These
scenes are similar in their paradoxical gatherings of opposites—
waste and vitality, death and life. However, they also map a progression from demise to rebirth: from Pym's suffocation to his

encounter with maternal serpents to his vision of trees growing from fecund swamps to his discovery of himself naked and alone, newly born, in the pure sands of the Sahara.

From this psychic descent into the abysmal origins of life and death, Pym rises to the deck of the Grampus, where he fashions an orderly plan for undoing the mutiny. This caper, fittingly, requires him to take on a new identity, that of the dead Rogers. Yet, he is soon again hurled into chaos: the storm that overwhelms the ship, the death ship, cannibalism, the putrefaction of Augustus's body. But from Augustus's corpse is born a new companion for Pym, Peters, who takes Augustus's place as Pym's alter ego. Then follows another instance of *solve et coagula:* Pym's descent into the chasms at Tsalal from which he emerges a "new being."

While these dissolutions and coagulations in the *nigredo* stage are similar in kind, they are different in degree: Each one becomes increasingly *darker* and *more destructive* than the one before it. From his brief nocturnal dipping in the Atlantic Pym emerges relatively unscathed, with a clear sense of his identity as a melancholy explorer. However, his drop into the unconscious during his dream in the hold is more terrifying, for it stokes Pym's viable fear of being buried alive in the dank ship. Though Pym arises from this danger to organize a plan for revenge against the mutineers, his identity is more tenuous: Is he Pym or Rogers? Likewise, his struggle through the storm, the death ship, cannibalism, and Augustus's demise constitutes a yet more extreme encounter with destruction. After such attacks on his discrete being, he becomes little more than a lens through which cartographical coordinates and polar histories come into view. His tumbles on Tsalal, an entirely black island, are even more disorienting. Not only is Pym totally immersed in abysmal darkness but he also fully gives over to the desire for death, dying in Peter's "dusky" arms to emerge a "new being."

This "new being" is not Pym as a conscious ego but Pym as an element dissolved to the point where it is ready to leap to a new stage, the *albedo*, the white. When Pym transmutes from the black-ness of Tsalal to the whiteness of the polar vortex, he has lost a sense of himself. He is numb and apathetic, resistlessly flowing with the southward current. Dissolved, he is prepared for yet another resolu-tion—this time into the congelations of ice. While the oppositions in the *nigredo* stage are muddled together, inseparable and undiffer-entiated, in the *albedo* state the contraries crystallize—freeze—into clarified antinomies, discernible polarities ready to recombine in the sacred marriage of the *rubedo*, the red stage.[109] Sailing into this blanched condition, Pym in the polar ocean aptly registers several striking relationships between opposites: between the milky ocean and the dark sky, the stillness of the air and the motion of the ship, the chaos of the polar cataract and the organized image arising from its whorls. His powers of logic now lethargic, Pym opens to these paradoxes, floats into the pale embrace of the "shrouded human fig-ure." There, ensconced in this strange bosom, he merges with none other than the alchemical Snow Queen, empress of *albedo*—turbulent and calm, chaotic and ordered: spirit materialized, matter purified. One with the queen—a body cleansed by soul, a soul man-ifested by body—Pym is prepared for marriage with the Red King, monarch of *rubedo*. Does Pym, after passing through the white veil to the core of the earth, enjoy this *hieros gamos*, the holy union from which is born the *lapis philosophorum*, the youth who unifies all op-positions?[110] Does he at the center of the cosmic alembic become one with the *axis mundi*, the omphalos, the caduceus?[111]

If Pym as alchemical element has passed through the *rubedo* stage, the marriage of all opposites, then why does he prove so di-visive when he later records his experiences? In the alchemical reading, the answer is clear: Pym as element—not as self-con-scious character—has by the beginning of the novel returned to the *prima materia*, from which he will again undergo the *nigredo*, the *albedo*, the *rubedo*, and yet again come back to the *prima mate-ria*. In the alchemical tradition, the *rubedo* stage is not an end, a static perfection, but a step in an endless sequence—a circular process, an ouroboros. A synthesis of all opposites, the *rubedo* is paradoxical and thus contains death in its life, chaos in its order. Though an infant, it is also a dying king who must be renewed in the vivifying waters of the matrix.[112]

In the canons of alchemy, Mercurius embodies this circularity. As the spirit of life, he is present at each stage, both embodying the qualities of each level and acting as a catalyst to move the work to the next transformation. In the *nigredo* stage, Mercurius is the ouroboros or the caduceus, merging the opposites that he will separate as he moves the work to *albedo*. In the white stage, he is the white tears, rain, or dew that purifies the blackened matter. Having transformed himself into the virgin bride, he next turns into the Red King who marries the virgin. From this marriage between his female and male aspects, he gives birth to himself as the infant, the philosopher's stone, which, even at its birth, is also the dying king, the *prima materia*, the ouroboros returned.[113]

Mercury turns and turns and returns, endlessly undergoing the same transformations. So does Pym, who forever struggles through his melancholy adventures before finally achieving the white crystal at the portal of the abyss of life, through which he passes, only to return again to the darkness from which he began. Hence, though Pym, like Mercurius, must endlessly *revolve*, the reader, like the alchemical adept, can *evolve*, gaining fresh insight into the great mystery each time he witnesses the work. To enter into *The Narrative of Arthur Gordon Pym*, like perusing *Moby-Dick* or *Finnegans Wake*, is to flow around with a Möbius strip, always returning to the beginning at the end. Pym's descent into the core of the world points to his ascension to the writer's table. Ishmael's plunge to the core of the vortex made by the White Whale buoys him to tell the tale. The last sentence of the *Wake* can be completed only at the beginning of the book. To follow the mindless Pym in his round is to engage mindfully in a hermeneutic circle, to come again and again to the same paradoxical revelations yet with a different knowing. Revolving thus, one never understands once and for all the mystery of the abyss and its polarized patterns. Yet, one nonetheless sounds life and its doublings with increasingly graceful dives.

⊷⊜⊜⊶

But this reading too is a hoax, for are not linguistic patterns, like material events, inadequate representations of a mysterious abyss that will not be expressed? Yet, at the same time, is it also fair to say that the alchemical Pym is *not* a hoax, for are not some self-consuming patterns—like crystals, glaciers, and the poles—more likely than others to gesture toward what cannot be represented? Is this not the apocalypse of ice, its unveiling of all matter as a hoax and not a hoax—something to be taken seriously as the fecund matrix of all life but also a quantity to be played with, as a matrix obscuring life itself? This is ice's apocalypse. The icy abysses at the ends of the earth are as vigorous as oaks, cosmic trunks, but also as insubstantial as air, wisps of the boundless spirit reaching from Draco to Mont Blanc to the melting crystal in the muddy bank.

CONCLUSION

MELTING AND GENESIS

So he left the lagoon and entered the jungle again, within a few days was completely lost, following the lagoons south- ward through the increasing rain and heat, attacked by alli- gators and giant bats, a second Adam searching for the forgotten paradises of the reborn sun.

—*J. G. Ballard*, The Drowned World *(1962)*

In his *5/5/2000 Ice: The Ultimate Disaster* (1986), Richard Noone predicted that during the inaugural spring of the third millen- nium, Mercury, Venus, Mars, Jupiter, and Saturn would align for the first time in six thousand years and thus abruptly increase the Earth's temperature. The polar ice caps would melt. The earth would drown. Tragically, the primal soup, inhuman, would again slosh.[1]

Noone was mistaken in his apocalyptic prognostication. However, the polar ices are in fact thawing apace. Global warm- ing is slowly dissolving them again into their primitive liquid states. In January of 2001 men and women for the first time actu- ally beheld a hole at the pole. Rising ocean temperatures had melted the Arctic axis.

If American readers at the end of the second millennium were perusing fresh accounts of the polar freeze, then these same readers were also encountering the opposite of ice: melting. From October of 1998 to February of 2001, at least eleven articles on the thawing of the polar icecaps appeared in the pages of the *New York Times*.[2] Among these articles was a January 23, 2001, report on how the Intergovernmental Panel of Climate Change has reaffirmed its consistent warning. Global warming is causing polar meltage, a process that could in the future precipitate disastrous flooding. These newspaper pieces have been supported by numerous books on global warming through the decade of the nineties, culminating most recently with Jeremy K. Leggell's *The Carbon War: Global Warming and the End of the Oil Era* (2001), John J. Berger's *Beating the Heat: Why and How We Must Combat Global Warming* (2000), and Francis Drake's *Global Warming: The Science of Climate Change* (2000).

The absence of ice is just as terrifying as a frozen earth. In both cases, the result would be the same: a return to undifferentiation—monotonous white, unbroken ocean. Yet, ends are beginnings. A universal freeze or flood, though it destroys the old, also clears ground for new growth. Significantly, numerous world myths of cosmic origin begin with a void—pristine indifference. This void is often figured by water: the primeval waters from which the first hill arises in the Egyptian Pyramid Texts; the milky ocean, bearing the endless serpent, upon which the Hindu deity Vishnu dreams and undreams the cosmos; the snaky oceans ruled by Tiamat; the deep over which Jehovah broods.

Hence, though ice suggests the original and final gulf, water, the complement of ice, its twin and necessary other, is the more fitting image of the end that begins. If freezing and melting—two sides of the same coin, two hands of the same being—are signs of apocalypse, of an undifferentiating destruction from which new differences might one day arise, then ice suggests conclusions while water intimates introductions. Frost is the clarity of closure. Thaw is the vagueness of the portal. Ice is the end of winter overlapped by the meltage that begins the spring. Ice is still, though invisibly, moving. Water moves, yet stays in one place. Ice is tight though on the verge of loosening. Water flows but can again freeze. Ice is the axle. Water is the turning world.

Some of the moments of frozen gnosis that we have beheld in the course of this book have been accompanied by melting: relief and release. Thoreau's vision of the deep cut is an experience of the imbrication of freezing and melting. The oozing mud suggests the shapes of ice. The stark crystal points to living saps. His intuition of ice is a *participation mystique* in the spring thaw, a dive into the mud with an icy jewel in his hand. Likewise, Shelley's meditation on Mont Blanc begins and ends in meltwater. The poet begins the poem by contemplating the River Arve. He then elevates his gaze to the river's frozen source at the pinnacle of the White Mountain. He concludes by returning to the "rushing torrents" created by the thawing snow of the peaks. This movement mimics the poet's psyche, which moves back and forth between the frozen clarity of insight and the slippery ambiguity of doubt. Likewise, the Mariner's moment of polar insight—his vision of Antarctic whiteness wondrously interwoven with snakes in torrid seas—is simultaneous with a twofold melting: a dissolution of his stony heart into a gushing spring, a liquefaction of the sky into rain.

These meltings reveal this. The gnosis of ice is not a revelation of static truth, an unchanging clarity. An insight into the mystery of ice re-releases the adept into the ambiguous flows of life, wiser (and possibly sadder), more aware of the sources and rhythms of the currents but no closer to a stable principle in which he can rest. To grasp the ice—in its forms of crystals, glaciers, and the poles—as a revelation of the groundless ground is to find oneself unmoored, undone, distributed in the all, not attached to any particular thing. The ego melts, sinks back into the muck from which it arose. Yet, from this dissolution arise fresh resolutions: new patterns of being that are less egocentric and more open to the energies of other humans, animals, and lands. This is the secret of the alchemical work, of the philosophical Mercury. As he freezes into the crystal stone he is already on his way to melting back into the *prima materia*, from which he will again rise into ice only once more to thaw.

Freezing and melting, clarity and confusion, organization and turbulence. These are the wonderful though hidden polarities by which the cosmos thrives. What, then, is the secret imperative of polar melting, of the apocalyptic global warming amid which we now live? It is perhaps this: The melting that we have wantonly made through our greed and waste should shock us into a new awareness of ice, of its place in the living whole—an awareness that might translate into new modes of being: less egocentric, more ecological. But the occult significance of Antarctic and Arctic thawing might be something else again, something more horrifying yet potentially more sublime. The human species, but an ambiguous instant in cosmological durations, might have already set unalterably in motion forces that will inevitably drown and dissolve the greed of men as well as civilized beauty. Possibly this—the removal from the planet of the most destructive species ever to exist—is the truest, and most tragic ecology, an end of wasteful death in the name of new life.

NOTES

INTRODUCTION: FROZEN APOCALYPSE

1. Between 1997 and 2001, the *New York Times* reviewed the following texts concerned with polar matters: Charles Officer and Jack Pages's *A Fabulous Kingdom: The Exploration of the Arctic* (Oxford: Oxford Univ. Press, 2001), 22 July 2001; Robert Ruby's *Unknown Shore: The Lost History of England's Arctic Colony* (New York: Henry Holt, 2001), 3 June 2001; Bruce Henderson's *Fatal North: Adventure and Survival Aboard USS Polaris: The First U.S. Expedition to the North Pole* (New York: Signet, 2001), 25 February 2001; Richard Parry's *Trial by Ice: The True Story of Murder and Survival on the 1871 Polaris Expedition* (New York: Ballantine, 2001), 25 February 2001; Jerri Nielson's and Maryanne Voller's *Ice Bound: A Doctor's Incredible Battle for Survival in the South Pole* (New York: Hyperion, 2001), 4 February 2001; Valerian Albanov's *In the Land of White Death: An Epic Story of Survival in the Siberian Arctic* (New York: Modern Library, 2000), 10 December 2000; Jennifer Niven's *The Ice Master: The Doomed 1913 Voyage of the Kurluk* (New York: Hyperion, 2001), 3 December 2000; Alan Gurney's *The Race to the White Continent* (New York: Norton, 2000), 24 September 2000; Fergus Fleming's *Barrow's Boys* (London: Granta, 1998), 21 May 2000; Leonard Bickel's *Shackleton's Forgotten Men: The Untold Tragedy of the Endurance Epic* (New York: Thunder's Mouth Press, 2000), 12 April 2000; Anne Savours's *The Search for the Northwest Passage* (New York: Palgrave, 1999), 7 December 1999; John Thompson's *Shackleton's Captain: A Biography of Frank Wolsely* (Cincinnati, OH: Mosaic Press, 1999), 27 July 1999; Roland Huntford's *Nansen: The Explorer as Hero* (London: Duckworth, 1999), 16 May 1999; Caroline Alexander's *The Endurance: Shackleton's Legendary Antarctic Experience* (New York: Knopf, 1998), 10 December 1998; Andrea Barrett's *The Voyage of the Narwhal: The Search for Franklin* (New York: Norton, 1999), 13 September 1998; Jenny Diski's *Skating to Antarctica: A Journey to the End of the World* (New York: Ecco, 1998), 16 August 1998; John MacCannon's *Red*

Arctic: Polar Exploration and the Myth of the Northern Soviet Union, 1932–1939 (Oxford: Oxford Univ. Press, 1998), 17 May 1998; Francis Spufford's *I May Be Some Time: Ice and the English Imagination* (New York: Palgrave, 1997), 15 March 1998; Raimund E. Goerler's *To the Pole: The Diary and Notebook of Richard E. Byrd, 1925–1927* (Columbus: Ohio State Univ. Press, 1998), 7 June 1998; Sara Wheeler's *Terra Incognita: Travels in Antarctica* (London: Jonathan Cape, 1996), 17 March 1998; Robert M. Bryce's *Cook and Peary: The Polar Controversy Resolved* (Mechanicsburg, PA: Stackpole Books, 1997), 20 April 1997; and Alan Gurney's *Below the Convergence: Voyages Toward Antarctica, 1699–1839* (New York: Norton, 1997), 30 March 1997. In contrast, in the years between 1990 and 1996, only four polar books, according to my calculations, were noticed in the *New York Times:* James A. Houston's *Confessions of an Igloo Dweller* (New York: Houghton Mifflin, 1996), 19 May 1996; D. G. Campbell's *The Crystal Desert: Summers in Antarctica* (New York: Houghton Mifflin, 1992), 17 December 1993; Will Steger and John Bowermaster's *Crossing Antarctica* (New York: Knopf, 1991), 26 January 1992; and Harvey Oxenhorn's *Tuning the Rig: A Journey to the Arctic* (New York: Harper and Row, 1990), 22 April 1990. Certainly, one does not necessarily need to invoke millennial fears and desires to account for this recent eruption of polar books and reviews of polar books. One could argue that John Krakauer's bestselling account of the 1996 Mount Everest disaster, *Into Thin Air* (New York: Anchor, 1997) inspired communal interest in icy adventures. Likewise, one could suppose that Peter Hoeg's bestselling novel *Smilla's Sense of Snow* (New York: Farrar, Straus, and Giroux, 1993), an Arctic thriller, drew readers to the polar ice. However, when one considers the history of the relationship between polar ice and apocalypse—a nexus that I detail in this book—one realizes that the success of these bestsellers simply cannot account for the overabundance of polar interests around the turn of the millennium.

2. The recent Steven Spielberg film, *A.I.* (2001) captures this connection between earth-ending apocalypse and sublime ice: Melting polar ice caps flood the major cities of the world and a final freeze of these floods destroys all civilization. Likewise, Howard Hawks and Charles Nyby's 1951 film, *The Thing from Another World* ties the Arctic ice to Cold War fears of the annihilation of the human race. The "Thing," an immense being from another planet who functions like a plant, lands his spacecraft in the polar freeze, and there threatens to reduce all nearby humans to plantfood. Anna Kavan's two hallucinatory novels, *Ice* (1967) and *Mercury* (1994), also disturbingly vision the ending of the world in a vast freeze.

3. H. P. Blavatsky, *The Secret Doctrine*, 2 vols. (London: Theosophical Publishing Co., 1888), 2: 310.

4. For the Nazis and polar myths, see Joscelyn Godwin's *Arktos: The Polar Myth in Science, Symbolism, and Nazi Survival* (Kempton, IL: Adventures Unlimited Press, 1996).

5. An encyclopedic study of esoteric representations of the poles is John O'Neill's neglected *The Night of the Gods: An Inquiry into Cosmic and Cosmogonic Mythology and Symbolism*, 2 vols. (London: Harrison and Sons, 1893).

6. The adjective "esoteric" has been over- and misused to the point of meaninglessness. Yet, the word still possesses explanatory power if it is used cautiously and specifically. As will become clear, I use "esoteric" to designate two levels of signification: the psychological and the cosmological. On a psychological level, "esoteric" refers to psychic powers that cannot be positivistically registered, predicted, and controlled. Hence, in studying an abysmal collective unconscious that sporadically manifests itself in paradoxical symbols, Jung would qualify as an "esoteric" analyst while B. F. Skinner, in recording only physical causes and effects, would serve as an example of an "exoteric" psychologist. On a cosmological level, "esoteric" refers to those vast forces of being that simply cannot be registered by the empirical faculties or pictured by the imagination—forces such as "life," "love," "emptiness," "presence," "the whole." Such an "esoteric" cosmos would be the sublime universe envisioned by Nietzsche in *The Birth of Tragedy*: a Dionysian abyss occasionally and mysteriously manifesting its powers in Apollinian forms always inadequate to its grandeur. An exoteric counter to this immeasurable cosmos would of course be Newton's mathematically predictable universe.

7. Sir Thomas Browne in *Pseudodoxia Epidemica* (1646) provides a full syllabus of classical and medieval thinkers who countered traditional negations of ice by embracing frozen shapes as interesting scientific facts. As Browne suggests, most classical and medieval theorists of ice were interested in the relationship between ice and crystal (*Pseudodoxia Epidemica*, 2 vols., ed. Robin Robbins [Oxford: Clarendon, 1981], 1: 74–5). Of those classical natural philosophers who believed that crystal is intensely frozen ice, perhaps Pliny in his *Natural History* (vol. 10, trans. D. E. Eichholz [Cambridge, MA and London: Harvard Univ. Press, 1962], 181) and Seneca in his *Natural Questions* (trans. Thomas H. Corcoran [Cambridge, MA and London: Harvard Univ. Press, 1971], 265) are the most interesting. The two most engaging medieval observers of ice are Albertus Magnus, who in his *Book of Minerals* (trans. Dorothy Wyckoff [Oxford: Clarendon, 1967], 11–4) compares ice and

stones, and Roger Bacon, who in his *Opus Maius* (ed. J. H. Bridges,
3 vols. [Oxford: Oxford Univ. Press, 1897]) exemplifies his "experimental method" with frozen phenomena and extolls the optical
virtues of crystals. In the Renaissance, several commentators added
to Browne's natural philosophy of ice—he believes that crystal is
not petrified ice—in performing numerous experiments on the
physical qualities of frozen phenomena. For instance, as John G.
Burke notes in *Origin of the Science of Crystals* (Berkeley: Univ.
of California Press, 1966), 25–43, in the early seventeenth century,
Johann Kepler and René Descartes attempted to explain the
hexagonal shapes of snow crystals (*Strena seu de nive sexangula*
[Francofurti ad Moenum, 1611]; *Ouevres de Descartes*, 12 vols., ed.
Charles Adams and Paul Tannery [Paris, 1897–1913], 6: 288).
Later in the century, Robert Hooke in his *Micrographia* and in sev-
eral other essays meditated on the structure of ice (*Micrographia,
Early Science in Oxford*, 14 vols., ed. R. T. Gunther [London: Daw-
son, 1967], 13: 88–93. At about the same time Francis Lana and
Nehemiah Grew tried to understand the chemistry of ice ("On the
Formation of Crystals, *Philosophical Transactions*, 7 [1672], 4068;
"On the Nature of Snow," *Philosophical Transactions* 8 [1673],
5193). Yet, for the most part, Western thinkers before the turn of
the nineteenth century demeaned ice as a site of numerous negative qualities. For instance, in the fifth century B.C., Herodotus in
his *History* links ice with the ungraspable, the monstrous, the
"other." In the wintry realms to the north, comprised of icy seas
and frosty grounds, one will find not ordinary beings but men who
possess goat feet, people who sleep for half the year, "gold-guard-
ing griffins," a "one-eyed race of men," and curious group called
the Hyperboreans (*Herodotus: The Text of Canon Rawlinson's Translation*, with the Notes Abridged, trans. George Rawlinson, ed. A. J.
Grant [New York: Scribner's, 1897], Book 4, Pars. 28–32).
Plutarch, writing five hundred years later, alludes to these associations in his *Lives*. He notes that geographers often crowd the
undiscovered regions of their maps with "sandy deserts full of wild
beasts, unapproachable bogs, Scythian ice, or frozen seas"
(*Plutarch's Lives of Illustrious Men*, trans. John Dryden [Philadel-
phia: H. T. Coates, n.d.], "Thesus," Par. 1). In *Contra Marcion*,
written at the turn of the third century, Tertullian, a father of the
Catholic Church and a tireless heresiologist, brings these icy connotations into play in his invective against Marcion, the Gnostic
heretic. In a section entitled "Pontus Lends Its Rough Character
to the Heretic Marcion," Tertullian intermixes the qualities of the
"barbarous," icy landscape, located on the Black Sea coast in
northern Asia Minor, and his opponent's evil ideas, centered on

the belief that there are two gods, the false demiurge of the Old Testament and the true deity of the Gospels. Frozen the entire year, Pontus is for Tertullian a wild region where men enjoy "no germ of civilisation." In this country, "[a]ll things are torpid, stiff with cold. Nothing there has the glow of life." Yet, the most despicable product of this wasteland is Marcion, "colder than its winter," "more brittle than ice" (Book 1, Ch. 1). Dante continues this tradition in the Middle Ages. In his *Inferno*, he represents the lowest pit of hell as a frozen wasteland containing the worst of sinners, traitors against benefactors (Cantos 31–4). Medieval geographers likewise equated ice with the monstrous—the blurring of demarcations between human and inhuman, identity and difference. As Armand Rainaud has shown, undiscovered regions below the equator were often marked by one word *frigida*, frozen. Medieval synonyms for the icy *terra incognita*—*perusta*, burned, or *bruma*, foggy—reveal what ice signified to these cartographers: the hellish—dim freezes, unrelenting fires (*Le Continent Austral* [Amsterdam: Meridian, 1893], 136–40). To some medieval minds, these unmapped, frozen regions were the habitations of monsters: the Anthropophagi, cannibals; the Garamantes, who habitate waters that freeze by night and boil by day; the Farici, who eat raw flesh; the Monoculi, a one-legged species notable for holding their single foot above their heads as a parasol; the Virgogici, dining on insects; the Troglodytes, serpent-eaters; and the Antipodes, dancers with sixteen fingers (J. L. Lowes, *The Road to Xanadu: A Study in the Ways of the Imagination* [Princeton, NJ: Princeton Univ. Press, 1927], 114). In his *Gesta Danorum*, written around 1200, Saxo Grammaticus supports these equations among ice, the unknown, the chaotic, and the monstrous. On the one hand, he describes Iceland as "squalid," unfit for human habitation. On the other, he invokes this island as a realm of "marvels," outlandish and terrifying. Among the "strange occurrences and objects that pass belief" are a spring that hardens everything to stone; secret geysers unseen until they explode; a mountain spewing fires; masses of ice haunting the shores with harrowing wails; and immense frozen blobs that "change," "the upper parts sinking to the bottom, and the lower again returning to the top" (*Nine Books of the Danish History*, trans. Oliver Elton [Copenhagen: The Norroena Society, 1905], 1: 85–8). To Saxo, volcanoes, bergs, and glaciers are threatening wonders from a land forever white. Saxo's near contemporaries to the south, the anonymous Anglo-Saxon writers of "The Wanderer" and "The Seafarer," felt these frozen terrors in their bones. To these poets, writing sometime before 1050, ice is tantamount to exile from God, the chaos of the sea, the pain of unfamiliar lands,

and alienation from the warm hall, with its measured treasures and
rites of friendship. Separated from God's pity and mercy, the Wanderer "sad in mind" must "dip his oars / into icy waters, the lanes
of the sea; / he must follow the paths of exile!" Suffering iciness
within and without, this exiled sailor longs for physical and spiritual comfort, yearns to be free of the "dark waves," of "frost and
snow falling mingled with hail" ("The Wanderer," *The Anglo-
Saxon World: An Anthology*, trans. Kevin Crossley-Holland [Ox-
ford: Oxford Univ. Press, 1984], lines 3–5, 47–8). The Seafarer is
likewise "fettered in frost" to his wave-tossed ship. He is "care-
worn and cut off from . . . kinsmen." He is "exiled" on the "icy
sea" ("The Seafarer," *The Anglo-Saxon World*, lines 8–16).
Throughout the Renaissance, ice continued to garner unfavorable
connotations. Studied in Petrarch, who invoked ice to figure the
pain of the pining lover and the indifference of the aloof beloved,
Shakespeare frequently deploys ice to image negative conditions.
In *The Taming of the Shrew*, the initially chilly Katherina bears an
icy exterior that must be broken by her wooer Petruchio (1.2.265).
Likewise, in *All's Well That Ends Well*, Lafew describes Helen's indifferent suitors as "boys of ice" (2.3.93). In the same way, Valeria's
chastity in *Coriolanus* is likened to an "icicle" frozen from the "frost
of purest snow" (5.3.65–6). Beyond the context of erotic indifference, ice also tropes emotional insensitivity. As Pandulpho claims
in *King John*, treachery on high political levels will "cool the
hearts" of the people and "freeze up their zeal" (3.4.149–50). Seen
this way, ice is a figure for the death of energy, for lethargy of any
kind, erotic, emotional, or otherwise. These senses of ice are invoked in Sonnet 5, where the speaker fears the impending
"hideous winter" that will confound him, checking his sap with
"frost" (6–7); in *The Merchant of Venice*, in which the Prince of Mo-
rocco, having lost Portia's casket game and doomed himself to
celibacy, bitterly welcomes "frost" (2.7.75); in *Hamlet*, where
Hamlet claims that his mother's old age should be a time of
"frost," not lust (3.4.81–8). These connotations suggest that ice is
depression—in *Much Ado About Nothing*, despair is "full of frost"
(5.4.41–2)—as well as death—in *Measure for Measure*, the grave is a
"region of thick-ribbed ice" (3.1.122). To see ice as death is to view
it as transience, the vehicle of death. In Shakespeare's *Two Gentlemen of Verona*, the Duke claims that Silva's love for the exiled
Valentine will soon melt like ice, which "an hour's heat / Dissolves
into water, and doth lose his form" (3.2.6–10). Writing almost fifty
years later, John Bunyan in *Pilgrim's Progress* (1684) features God's
grace melting Honesty's heart as quickly as the burning sun dissolves a "mountain of ice" (Part 2, Stage 6). After the turn of the

eighteenth century, Pope similarly casts ice as transience in *The Temple of Fame* (1715). (He follows Chaucer's own negative inflections of ice in *House of Fame*.) During a springtime dream, Pope's speaker beholds a "tow'ring summit" concealed in clouds. He notices that this peak rests on a "rock of ice" on which are inscribed the names of famous poets and critics from the past. These names closer to the ground quickly disappear, erased by sun or storm. They are as ephemeral as the ice, insubstantial as fame itself. Above these evanescent names are others carved in the solid rock of the "high summit," never to be worn down (1–74).

8. Attuned to the invisible world as well as the visible, this book is not a "new historical" or "cultural" study of representations of ice. Hence, it constitutes a scientific, psychological, and occult complement to two recent cultural studies of ice, Robert G. David's *The Arctic in British Imagination, 1818–1914* (Manchester: Manchester Univ. Press, 2000) and Francis Spufford's *I May Be Some Time: Ice and the English Imagination* (New York and London: Palgrave, 1997). Likewise, my book is not a natural history of crystals, glaciers, or the poles. Although the study is interested in the history of ice sciences from the Renaissance to the early nineteenth century, it lacks the specificity and immediate reporting of excellent natural historical works like David G. Campbell's *The Crystal Desert: Summers in Antarctica* (New York: Houghton Mifflin, 1992), Barry Lopez's *Arctic Dreams: Imagination and Desire in a Northern Landscape* (New York: Bantam, 1986); Stephen J. Pyne's *The Ice: Journey to Antarctica* (Iowa City: Univ. of Iowa Press, 1986). Finally, this study is not an exhaustive discussion of all Romantic works concerned with crystals, glaciers, and the poles. I focus on those texts that meditate on frozen shapes in especially provocative ways. Although I am interested in illuminating Romantic works with neglected scientific and esoteric contexts, I am equally preoccupied with exemplifying the history of ice with literary passages. Thus, I trust that this book resembles in scope and content—though probably not in insight and elegance—several magisterial, brilliant studies of the psychology and poetics of nature: W. H. Auden's *The Enchafèd Flood: or, The Romantic Iconography of the Sea* (London: Faber and Faber, 1950); Marjorie Hope Nicolson's *Mountain Gloom and Mountain Glory: The Development of the Aesthetics of the Infinite* (New York: Norton, 1963); Gaston Bachelard's *The Psychoanalysis of Fire*, trans. Alan C. M. Moss, pref. Northrop Frye (Boston: Beacon, 1964); Philip Kuberski's *The Persistence of Memory: Organism, Myth, Text* (Berkeley: Univ. of California Press, 1992); and Victoria Nelson's "Symmes Hole, Or the South Polar Romance," *Raritan* 17:2 (fall) 1997: 136–66. (Nelson's

essay is now part of her wonderful new book, *The Secret Life of Puppets* [Cambridge, MA and London: Harvard Univ. Press, 2002], 139–162).

CHAPTER 1: CRYSTALS

1. Sir Thomas Browne, *Pseudodoxia Epidemica*, 2 vols., ed. Robin Robbins (Oxford: Clarendon, 1981), 1: 74–5.
2. Browne refers to Jerome's commentary and translation in *Pseudodoxia Epidemica*, 74. Browne has in mind, of course, Ezekiel 1:22–27. In his commentary on this passage, Jerome claims that the *crystalli horribilis* beheld by Ezekiel is the firmament described in Genesis, in which God freezes the watery abyss into pure ice (*S. Hieronymi Presbyteri Opera: Par I Opera Exegetica 4: Commentariorum in Hiezechielem Libri XIV* [Turnholti: Typographi Brepolis Editores Pontificii, 1964], 22–3). Daniel I. Block notes in *The Book of Ezekiel, Chapters 1–24* (Cambridge, UK and Grand Rapids, MI: Eerdmans, 1997), that the Hebrew *qerah* means "ice, frost" (101–2).
3. Revelation 4:6, 21:11; 22:1.
4. Paul Valéry, *Sea Shells*, fore. Mary Oliver, trans. Ralph Manheim (Boston: Beacon, 1998), 23. In this regard, see Philip Kuberski's chapter "The Metaphor of the Shell" in his book *The Persistence of Memory* (Berkeley: Univ. of California Press, 1992), 78–93. Like Valéry, Kuberski finds that the shell is double—a familiar geometry and a strange involute: "The prophetic and the memorable, the future and the past are . . . conserved within the inward and outward whorls of a shell, as if within the covers of a book. And yet the pages of this book are themselves blank and nacreous, streaked by blues perhaps but without trace or inscription. Its form is thus apocalyptic in the sense that it speaks of destruction and revelation, and suggests how each can be the consequence of the other. More ancient, more marvelous, more unfathomable than the wonders of the ancient world . . . the seashell is, like them, a recollection of life's earliest architectures and enigmas" (80).
5. Kurt Seligman, *The History of Magic* (New York: Pantheon, 1948), 26.
6. Theodore Bestermann, *Crystal Gazing: A Study in the History, Distribution, Theory and Practice of Scrying* (London: Rider, 1924), 72.
7. E. R. Dodds, *The Ancient Concept of Progress, and Other Essays on Greek Literature and Belief* (Oxford: Clarendon, 1973), 186–8.
8. Bestermann, 3.
9. Armand Delatte, *La catoptromancie grecque et ses dérivés* (Liege-Paris, 1932), 10–11, 133–62.
10. Rupert Gleadow, *Magic and Divination* (London: Faber and Faber, 1941), 119–120.

11. Lynn Thorndike, *A History of Magic and Experimental Science*, 9 vols. (London: Macmillan, 1923), 2:364–5.

12. Bestermann, 48.

13. Thorndike, 2:800.

14. Bestermann, 14–15.

15. Bestermann, 14–15.

16. For informative surveys of medieval scrying, see Thorndike, 2:279–89; and Bestermann, 47–51.

17. Paracelsus, "Coelum philosophorum sive liber vexationum (fixationum)," *Paracelsus. Samtliche Werke*, ed. Karl Sudhoff and Wilhelm Matthiessen, Part 1: *Medizinische, naturwissenshasftliche, und philosophische Schriften*, 14 vols. (Munich, Berlin: R. Oldenburg, 1928–32); quoted in Bestermann, 50–1.

18. Frances A. Yates, *Giordano Bruno and the Hermetic Tradition* (Chicago: Univ. of Chicago Press, 1964), 69.

19. Jean Servier, *L'homme et l'invisible* (Paris: Robert Laffont, 1964), 102–3; quoted in Jean Chevalier and Alain Gheerbrant, *The Penguin Dictionary of Symbols*, trans. John Buchanan-Brown (New York: Penguin, 1994), 267.

20. Chevalier and Gheerbrant, 267.

21. John Dee, *Doctoris Dee Mysteriorum Liber Primus*, British Library, MS Sloane 3188, f. 59b, 10a, 9a, 58a; quoted in Bestermann, 18. For a recent discussion of John Dee's scrying, see Benjamin Woolley, *The Queen's Conjurer: The Science and Magic of Dr. John Dee, Adviser to Queen Elizabeth 1* (New York: Henry Holt, 2001), 146–51. See also Gleadow, 194–216.

22. John Dee, *A True and Faithful relation of What Passed for Many Years between Dr. John Dee and Some Spirits*, ed. Meric Casaubon (London, 1659), 445; quoted in Bestermann, 111.

23. Dee, *Doctoris Dee Mysteriorum Liber Primus*; quoted in Gleadow, 201.

24. Reginald Scot, *The Discoverie of Witchcraft*, intro. Montague Summers (London: J. Rodker, 1930), 13: 19; quoted in Bestermann, 53–4.

25. Anthony Aveni in *Behind the Crystal Ball: Magic, Science, and the Occult from Antiquity through the New Age* (New York: Random House, 1996), 113–4, reports that geologist George Kunz has scientifically accounted for the illusory nature of scrying: "Geologist George Kunz [in *The Curious Lore of Precious Stones* (Philadelphia: Lippincott, 1913), 176] has given a scientific explanation of just how scrying works: The gazing eye fixes points of light from a highly polished surface such as a sphere until the optic nerve becomes fatigued enough to shut down transmitting sensory impressions from the outside and begins to project images received from within the brain. Results vary with sensitivity of the given optic nerve; in some people, prolonged crystal gazing simply paralyzes

the nerve and so it cannot respond to stimuli from within or without. But in others it is both deadened just enough to external impressions and active enough to react to stimuli from within."

26. Coleridge in *The Friend* (1809–10; 1818) beautifully describes how
glass can suggest interpenetrations between inner and outer, imagination and fact. To elucidate Martin Luther's nocturnal visions of
Satan, Coleridge details his own library window in Keswick: "The
window of my library at Keswick is opposite to the fireplace, and
looks out on the very large garden that occupies the whole slope of
the hill on which the house stands. Consequently, the rays of light
transmitted *through* the glass (i.e., the rays from the garden, the
opposite mountains, and the bridge, river, lake, and the vale inter-
jacent) and the rays reflected *from* it (of the fireplace, etc.) enter
the eye at the same moment. At the coming on of evening, it was
my frequent amusement to watch the image or reflection of the
fire, that seemed burning in the bushes or between the trees in different parts of the garden or the fields beyond it, according as
there was more or less light; and which still arranged itself among
the real objects of vision, with a distance and magnitude propor-
tioned to its greater or lesser faintness" (*CC* 4.1:144–5).

27. Vasco Ronchi, *The Nature of Light: An Historical Survey*, trans. V.
Barocas (Cambridge: Harvard Univ. Press, 1970), 153; See also
Burke, 138–9.

28. Christiaan Huygens, *Traité de la lumière, Great Books of the Western
World*, ed. Robert Maynard Hutchins (Chicago: Encyclopedia Bri-
tannica, 1952), 579–606; Carl B. Boyer, *The Rainbow: From Myth to
Mathematics* (Princeton, NJ: Princeton Univ. Press, 1987), 233–9;
See also Ronchi, 196–208.

29. Sir Isaac Newton, *Opticks, Great Books of the Western World*, ed.
Robert Maynard Hutchins (Chicago: Encyclopedia Britannica,
1952), 524; See also Boyer, 251–8, and Ronchi, 160–95.

30. Thomas Young, "An Account of Some Cases of the Production of
Colors, Not Hitherto Described," *Philosophical Transactions*, 92
(1802), 387–92. Also see Young's *Lectures on Natural Philosophy and
the Mechanical Arts*, 2 vols. (London, 1807), 1:470, 2:643. Both
works are discussed in Boyer, 282–7. See also Ronchi, 237–41,
253–4, and Richard J. Weiss, *A Brief History of Light and Those That
Lit the Way* (London: World Scientific, 1996), 33–40.

31. Boyer, 290–1. See also Weiss, 39. Of course, Augustin Fresnel inde-
pendently reached optical conclusions similar to Young's during the
years 1814–1817 (Ronchi, 242–55). Indeed, much of Young's brilliant work fell into temporary obscurity because of a fierce though
unjust attack of his work in an 1803 edition of *The Edinburgh Review*.

32. Étienne-Louis Malus, *Théories de la double réfraction de la lumière dans les substances cristallisées* (Paris: Baudoin, 1810), 219. Malus's discovery is discussed in Ronchi, 231–4, Boyer, 288–9, and Weiss, 39–40.

33. See Brewster's *Treatise on Optics* (London: Longman, 1831); cited in Boyer, 289–90.

34. I first found this theory of Viking navigation on February 14, 2000 on the website http://www.polarization.com/viking/viking.html. The theory is fully discussed in T. Ramskou, "Solstenen," *Skalk* (1967), 2:16. See also H. Lafey, "The Vikings," *National Geographic* (1970), 137: 528. For a critique of the theory, see Curt Roslund and Claes Beckman, "Disputing Viking Navigation by Polarized Skylight," *Applied Optics* (July 1994), 33.21: 4754.

35. Newton, *Opticks*, 404–9.

36. See Brewster's *Treatise on the Kaleidoscope* (London: Archibald Constable, & Co., 1819); discussed in Weiss, 40.

37. John G. Burke, *Origins of the Science of Crystals* (Berkeley: Univ. of California Press, 1966), 20–2.

38. Burke, 11–19.

39. Robert Boyle, *The Origine of Formes and Qualities, The Works of the Honourable Robert Boyle*, 5 vols, ed. Thomas Birch (London: A. Miller, 1744), 2:451–87; discussed in Burke, 30.

40. Robert Boyle, *An Essay About the Origine and Virtues of Gems*, ed. Arthur F. Hagner (New York: Hafner, 1972), 54; discussed in Burke, 30–2.

41. Newton, *Opticks*, 540–3; cited in Burke, 33–5.

42. Johannes Kepler, *Strena seu de nive sexangula* (Francofurti ad Moenum, 1611); René Descartes, *Oeuvres de Descartes*, 12 vols, ed. Charles Adam and Paul Tannery (Paris, 1897–1913), 6: 288; Robert Hooke, *Micrographia, Early Science at Oxford*, 14 vols, ed. R.T. Gunther (London: Dawsons, 1967), 13; discussed in Burke, 35–43.

43. Huygens, 579–606. See also Burke, 41–2.

44. Burke, 42–3.

45. René-Just Haüy, *Essai d'une théories sur la structure des crystuax* (Paris, 1784); discussed in Burke, 86–106.

46. Haüy, *Traité de minéralogie*, 5 vols. (Paris, 1801), 1:19–109, 2:249–55; discussed in Burke, 86–106.

47. Eilhardt Mitscherlich, "Ueber die Kristallisation der Salze in denen des Metall der Basis mit zwei proportionen Sauerstoff verbunden ist," *Abhandlugen der königlichen Akademie der Wissenschaften in Berlin* (1818–19), 427–37; discussed in Burke, 120–33.

48. Lancelot Law Whyte, ed. *Roger Joseph Boscovich* (New York: Fordham Univ. Press, 1961), 118–9. See also Burke, 44.

49. Burke, 44.

50. An anonymous article in the *New Jerusalem Magazine* 8 (November 1839), 118–19, entitled "Swedenborg's Scientific Merit," reports that John-Baptiste André Dumas praised Swedenborg as the originator of crystallography.

51. Emanuel Swedenborg, *Some Specimens of a Work on the Principles of Chemistry*, trans. Charles Edward Strut (London: William Newbery, 1847), 26, 37–8.

52. Swedenborg, *The Principia*, 2 vols., trans. Augustus Clissold (London: William Newbery, 1846), 1:46–20; Burke, 44–8. For other excellent discussions of Swedenborg's cosmology, see Inge Jonsson, *Emanuel Swedenborg*, trans. Catherine Djurklou (New York: Twayne, 1971), 29–40; Signe Toksvig, *Emanuel Swedenborg, Scientist and Mystic* (New York: Swedenborg Foundation, 1983), 70–4

53. Immanuel Kant, *Critique of Pure Reason*, trans. Norman Kemp Smith (New York: St. Martin's, 1965), 279; Immanuel Kant, *Metaphysische Anfangsgrunde der Naturwissenschaft* (Riga, 1786), 33; discussed in L. Pearce Williams, *Michael Faraday* (New York: Basic Books, 1965), 62.

54. H. A. M. Snelders, "Oersted's Discovery of Electromagnetism," *Romanticism and the Sciences*, ed. Andrew Cunningham and Nicholas Jardine (Cambridge: Cambridge Univ. Press, 1990), 223–258; Williams, 137–44. For good discussions of the relationships among German idealism, *Naturphilosophie*, and electromagnetism, see Williams, 53–94; Barbara Giusti Doran, "Origins and Consolidation of Field Theory in 19th-Century Britain: From Mechanical to Electromagnetic View of Nature," *Historical Studies in the Physcial Sciences*, vol. 6, ed. Russell McCormmach (Princeton, NJ: Princeton Univ. Press, 1975), 133–260; Mary B. Hesse, *Forces and Fields: The Concept of Action at a Distance in the History of Physics* (London: Thomas Nelson & Sons, 1961), 157–205.

55. Sir Humphry Davy, *The Collected Works of Sir Humphry Davy*, 6 vols., ed. John Davy (London: Smith, 1839–40), 5:137.

56. Emerson read Davy's work assiduously throughout the late 1820s and early 1830s and praises the scientist often in his journal and early lectures. For instance, in an 1836 lecture, he lauds Davy's "sublime conjecture" that there is "but one matter in different states of electricity" that might yield a vision of a "central unity" (*EL* 2:29). For a detailed discussion of Emerson's relationship to Davy in particular and the science of electricity in general, see Eric Wilson, *Emerson's Sublime Science* (London and New York: Palgrave Macmillan, 1999), 76–97.

57. Davy, 4:39–40.

58. Davy, 4:40. See also Burke, 150–1.

59. Michael Faraday, *Experimental Researches in Electricity, Great Books of the Western World*, vol. 45, ed. Robert Maynard Hutchins, et al. (Chicago: Encyclopedia Britannica, 1952), par. 27.

60. As I have argued in *Emerson's Sublime Science*, Emerson followed Faraday's discoveries closely throughout his career and showed particular enthusiasm for his electromagnetic theories in the early 1830s (76–97).

61. Faraday, par. 1689.

62. As we know from Emerson's sermons, Emerson had read Herschel's book by 1831, when he compared it favorably to Milton's *Paradise Lost* (*The Complete Sermons of Ralph Waldo Emerson*, 4 vols., ed. Albert J. von Frank, et al, [Columbia: Univ. of Missouri Press, 1989–92], 4:157).

63. John Herschel, *A Preliminary Discourse on the Study of Natural Philosophy*, fore. Arthur Fine (Chicago: Univ. of Chicago Press, 1987), 240–5. See also Burke, 78–9, 120–5.

64. Johann Wolfgang von Goethe, *Scientific Studies: Collected Works*, vol. 12, ed. Douglas Miller (Princeton, NJ: Princeton Univ. Press, 1988), 76–97.

65. Goethe, *Scientific*, 111–6.

66. Goethe, *Scientific*, 131–5.

67. Goethe, *Scientific*, 43–4.

68. Emerson was reading Goethe's scientific works closely in the 1830s. He mentions them often in his early lectures, showing special enthusiasm for Goethe's view that "[t]he whole force of the Creation is concentrated upon every point"; thus, massive "agencies of electricity, gravity, light, [and] affinity combine to make every plant what it is" (*EL* 1: 72). For a discussion of Emerson's relationship to Goethe's science, see Wilson, *Emerson's Sublime Science*, 61–7.

69. Ronald D. Gray, *Goethe the Alchemist: A Study of Alchemical Symbolism in Goethe's Literary and Scientific Works* (Cambridge: Cambridge Univ. Press, 1952), 97; Joseph Esposito, *Schelling's Idealism and the Philosophy of Nature* (Lewisburg: Bucknell Univ. Press, 1977), 21, 154–6.

70. This 1835 journal entry suggests that Emerson knew of either Schelling's *Ideas for a Philosophy of Nature* (1797) or his *System of Transcendental Idealism* (1800)—or perhaps both—for he accurately summarizes Schelling's main tenets: "The Germans believe in the necessary Trinity of God,—the Infinite; the finite; & the passage from Inf. Into Fin.; or, the Creation. It is typified in the act of thinking. Whilst we contemplate we are infinite; the thought we express is partial & finite; the expression is the third part & equivalent to the act of Creation. Unity says [Boehmean] Schelling is barren. Duality is necessary to the existence of the World. Shall I

say then that the galvanic action of metals foreshows from afar the God head, the zinc the metal & the acid; or the marriage of plants the pollen the ovary, & the junction?" (*EJ* 5:30)

71. Friedrich Wilhelm Joseph von Schelling, *Ideas for a Philosophy of Nature*, trans. Errol E. Harris and Peter Heath, intro. Robert Stern (Cambridge: Cambridge Univ. Press, 1988), 17–18, 44–9, 83.

72. Schelling, *Von der Weltseele* (Hamburg, 1798), 189, 219; discussed in Burke, 149–51.

73. Burke, 152–3.

74. D'Arcy Wentworth Thompson, *On Growth and Form* (Cambridge: Cambridge Univ. Press, 1942), 16, 411.

75. Erwin Schrödinger, *What Is Life?* (Cambridge: Cambridge Univ. Press, 1967), 5.

76. Rupert Sheldrake, *New Science: The Hypothesis of Formative Causation* (Los Angeles: J. P. Tarcher, 1987), 13.

77. When we consider Emerson's and Thoreau's relationships to ice, we likely recall Sophia Hawthorne's unforgettable description of an afternoon during which her husband Nathaniel led Emerson and Thoreau down to a frozen Concord River for some ice-skating. In the words of Sophia, three masters of the American literary renaissance enter unwittingly into a vaudevillian routine: "Henry Thoreau is an experienced skater, and was figuring dithyrambic dances and Bacchic leaps on the ice—very remarkable, but very ugly, methought. Next him followed Mr. Hawthorne who, wrapped in his cloak, moved like a self-impelled Greek statue, stately, and grave. Mr. Emerson closed the line, evidently too weary to hold himself erect, pitching headforemost, half lying on the air" (Sophia Hawthorne, quoted in Rose Hawthorne Lathrop, *Memories of Hawthorne* [Boston: Houghton Mifflin, 1897], 53). One wonders what possessed Emerson and Thoreau to accompany Hawthorne to the ice. While Hawthorne deports himself with classical decorum (playing the straight man), the formerly dignified Emerson flails against gravity, each instant threatening to thud on the grains, and Thoreau turns rambunctious adolescent, struggling to recover a grace he perhaps never enjoyed.

78. Emerson, *Poems, The Complete Works of Ralph Waldo Emerson*, ed. Edward W. Emerson (Boston: Hougton Mifflin, 1904), 41–3.

79. While here I am mainly interested in the ways that Emersonian transparency corresponds to crystallography, I should note that Emerson in *Nature* on two occasions mentions "crystal." Though he does not single out the crystal as an especially numinous shape, he nonetheless does associate it with revelation of the spirit and relationship between microcosm and macrocosm. In the first instance, he notices the crystal, along with several other forms, as a

hint of the moral laws pervading nature: "Therefore is nature glorious with form, color, motion, that every globe in remotest heaven; every chemical change from the rudest crystal up to the laws of life; every change of vegetation from the first principle of growth in the eye of the leaf, to the tropical forest and antediluvian coal-mine; every animal function from the sponge up to Hercules, shall hint or thunder to man the laws of right and wrong, and echo the Ten Commandments" (51). In the next instance, Emerson casts the crystal—again, along with other natural shapes—as a microcosm of the macrocosm: "The fable of Proteus has a cordial truth. Every particular in nature, a leaf, a drop, a crystal, a moment of time is related to the whole, and partakes of the perfection of the whole. Each particle is a microcosm, and faithfully renders the likeness of the world" (54–5). Surely it is significant that in both cases, Emerson invokes the crystal in tandem with the leaf. This correlation suggests that Goethe's archetypal morphology is somewhere in back of these glances at crystal. Likely, Emerson saw in the crystal a primal organic form—the archetype of inorganic matter.

80. For excellent readings of Emerson's "transparent eye-ball" passage and its relationship to optics, see B. L. Packer, *Emerson's Fall: A New Reading of the Major Essays* (New York: Continuum, 1982), 57–84; Lee Rust Brown, *The Emerson Museum: Practical Romanticism and the Pursuit of the Whole* (Cambridge, MA and London: Harvard Univ. Press, 1997), 42–58; James M. Cox, "R. W. Emerson: The Circles of the Eye," *Selected Papers from the English Institute: Emerson, Prophecy, Metamorphosis, and Influence*, ed. and fore. David Levin (New York: Columbia Univ. Press, 1975), 57–82; Richard R. O'Keefe, *Mythic Archetypes in Ralph Waldo Emerson: A Blakean Reading* (Kent, OH and London, England: Kent State Univ. Press, 1995), 29–68; Eric Cheyfitz, *The Trans-Parent: Sexual Poltics in the Language of Emerson* (London and Baltimore: The Johns Hopkins Univ. Press, 1981), 1–35. Each of these readings has significantly informed my own; however, none has focused on the possible role of crystallography in Emerson's famous passage.

81. Packer, 72–84.

82. Brown, 43–5.

83. For detailed readings of the stylistic densities of this passage, see Richard Poirier, *A World Elsewhere: The Place of Style in American Literature* (Madison: Univ. of Wisconsin Press, 1985), 63–70, and Wilson, *Emerson's Sublime Science*, 139–49.

84. In *Emerson's Sublime Science*, I argue that certain stylistic eruptions in *Nature*—such as the stunning opening, the surreal transparent eyeball sequence, the exquisite passage on the fishlike clouds— shock readers into new ways of seeing: into suspecting that all

forms are patterns of sublime energy. Charged by this possibility, readers return with renewed hermeneutic to ostensibly "clear" definitions and ideas in the book. Intensely scrutinizing such "transparent" elements, readers find that these seemingly limpid events also dissolve into paradoxical currents (128–75).

85. For an especially brilliant reading of Emerson's transparency in light of his pragmatism, see Brown, 43–58.

86. Plotinus, *Enneads*, trans. Stephen Mackenna, intro. John Dillon (New York: Penguin, 1991), 414.

87. Newton, *Mathematical Principles of Natural Philosophy and System of the World, Newton: A Norton Critical Edition*, ed. I. Bernard Cohen and Richard S. Westfall (New York and London: Norton, 1995), 117.

88. The "split" between Emerson the Platonist and Emerson the empiricist has been the primary problem in Emerson criticism. From Stephen Whicher's magisterial *Freedom and Fate: An Inner Life of Ralph Waldo Emerson* (Philadelphia: Univ. of Pennsylvania Press, 1953) to the very recent collection *The Emerson Dilemma: Essays on Emerson and Social Reform*, ed. T. Gregory Garvey (Athens and London: Univ. of Georgia Press, 2001), scholars have obsessed over the seemingly unbridgeable gap between these two "Emersons." Obviously, Emerson's richness as a thinker and writer emerges precisely from the "stupendous antagonism[s]," to use his phrase in "Fate" (1860), that perpetually pull his being asunder, only to merge, occasionally, into impossible harmonies.

89. Robert Sattelmeyer, *Thoreau's Reading: A Study in Intellectual History* (Princeton, NJ: Princeton Univ. Press, 1988), 26–7.

90. Thoreau praises Swedenborg in *A Week on the Concord and Merrimack Rivers* for being able to *see*, empirically, spiritual powers. However, as Walter Harding and Michael Meyer note in *The New Thoreau Handbook* (New York: New York Univ. Press, 1980), Thoreau once said that he had little "practical" use for the Swedish mystic (98).

91. According to Sattelmeyer, Thoreau, widely read in world religion, was likely instrumental in recommending selections for the "Ethnical Scriptures" section of *The Dial*, a journal published by Emerson and Margaret Fuller from 1840 to 1844. One such selection, in the January, 1844 issue, came from "The Divine Pymander of Hermes Trismegistus." Though he may not have recommended, Thoreau certainly read, the following passage from the "Pymander": "The sight of good is not like the beams of the sun, which being of a fiery shining brightness maketh the eye, blind by his excessive light; rather the contrary, for it enlighteneth and so much increaseth the power of the eye, as any man is able to receive the influences of this intelligible clearness. For it is more swift and sharp to pierce, and harmless withal, and full of immortality, and

they that are capable, and can draw any store of this spectacle and sight, do many times fall asleep from the body into this most fair and beauteous vision; which things Celius and Saturn our Progenitors attained unto" (*The Dial: A Magazine for Literature, Philosophy, and Religion*, ed. Margaret Fuller, Ralph Waldo Emerson, and George Ripley, 4 vols. [New York: Russell and Russell, 1961], 4: 402). In addition to perusing such disquisitions on divine optics, Thoreau was also reading Cudworth's compendium of Neoplatonic and hermetic lore (*TJ* 1:121). See Sattelmeyer, 28–9.

92. For an excellent discussion of Thoreau's emphasis on empirical experience over spiritual intuition—on "empirical holism" over "rational holism"—see Laura Dassow Walls, *Seeing New Worlds: Henry David Thoreau and Nineteenth-Century Natural Science* (Madison: Univ. of Wisconsin Press, 1995), 53–93. See also James McIntosh, *Thoreau as Romantic Naturalist: His Shifting Stance Toward Nature* (Ithaca, NY: Cornell Univ. Press, 1974) and Robert D. Richardson, *Thoreau: A Life of the Mind* (Berkeley: Univ. of California Press, 1986), 29–30.

93. Goethe, *Scientific*, 194–5. Kathleen Raine, a botanist turned poet, recalls an experience of *Anschauung* in her memoir, *The Land Unknown* (1975): "I kept always on the table where I wrote my poems a bowl with different kinds of moss and lycopodium and long and deeply did I gaze at those forms, and into their luminous smaragdine green. There was also a hyacinth growing in an amethyst glass; I was sitting alone, in an evening, at my table, the Aladdin lamp lit, the fire of logs burning in the hearth. All was stilled. I was looking at the hyacinth, and as I gazed at the form of its petals and the strength of their curve as they open and curl back to reveal the mysterious flower-centres with the anthers and eye-like hearts, abruptly I found that I was no longer looking at it, but was it; a distinct, indescribable, but in no way vague, still less emotional, shift of consciousness into the plant itself. Or rather I and the plant were one and indistinguishable; as if the plant were a part of my consciousness. . . . I was not perceiving the flower but living it. I was aware of the life of the plant as a slow flow or circulation of a vital current of liquid light of utmost purity. I could apprehend as a simple essence formal structure and dynamic process" (New York: George Braziller, 1975), 119.

94. I of course draw this phrasing on mirrors and lamps from M. H. Abrams's still wonderful book, *The Mirror and the the Lamp: Romantic Theory and Critical Tradition* (Oxford: Oxford Univ. Press, 1953), a study of Romantic theories of imaginative epistemology.

95. William Blake, "A Vision of the Last Judgment," *The Complete Poetry and Prose of William Blake*, ed. David V. Erdman, comm. Harold Bloom (New York and London: Doubleday, 1988), 555–6.

96. Johann Wolfgang von Goethe, *Maximen und Reflexionen. Goethe Samtliche Werke*, vol. 17, ed. Gontheir-Louis Fink, et al. (Munich: Carl Hanser, 1991), 775; quoted in Max L. Baeumer, "The Criteria of Modern Criticism on Goethe as Critic," *Goethe as Critic of Literature*, eds. Karl J. Fink and Max L. Baeumer (New York and London: Univ. Press of America, 1984), 10.

97. Sigmund Freud, "The Uncanny," *Standard Edition of the Complete Psychological Works of Sigmund Freud*, vol. 17 (London: Hogarth, 1959), 217–252; Martin Heidegger, *Being and Time*, trans. Joan Stambaugh (Albany: State Univ. of New York Press, 1996), 176–7.

98. Thoreau, *Journal*, vol. 8, *The Writings of Henry David Thoreau*, ed. Bradford Torrey (Boston: Houghton Mifflin, 1906), 88.

99. While readers of *Walden* have not much focused on Thoreau's crystallography, Walls, Richardson, and McIntosh have written revealingly on the book's biological elements. Other recent critics have attended to *Walden*'s "hydrology." For instance, see Eric Wilson, *Romantic Turbulence: Chaos, Ecology, and American Space* (New York and London: Palgrave Macmillan, 2000), 94–117; James A. Papa, Jr., "Water-Signs: Place and Metaphor in Dillard and Thoreau," *Thoreau's Sense of Place: Essay in American Environmental Writing*, ed. Richard J. Schneider, fore. Lawrence Buell (Iowa City: Univ. of Iowa Press, 2000), 70–82; Gordon B. Boudreau, *The Roots of Walden and the Tree of Life* (Nashville: Vanderbilt Univ. Press, 1990).

100. In his *Chaosmos: Literature, Science, Theory* (Albany, NY: State Univ. of New York Press, 1994), Philip Kuberski borrows this Joycean term to describe interpenetrations of order and chaos in self-organizing organic and textual systems. As Kuberski writes, "Everything in the world can be seen as chaosmic: the subatomic microworld may not be susceptible to particular determinism but in the macroworld of large-scale objects Newton's laws remain in force; the conception of a human being involves the combination of two strands of DNA in which chance and law interact to initiate epigenesis along certain fixed lines while remaining conditioned by the environment; and poems are composed (and sometimes seem to compose themselves) according to the play of chance and the emergent necessities of pattern, just as a reader never quite reads the 'same' poem each time he returns to it" (3). Walls beautifully describes Thoreau's agitated vision in *Walden* in similar language: Thoreau "opened his eyes and saw, in the streets, fields, and forests, chaos: not the ancient void out of which man created pristine order, but a new insight into the imbrication of all order with disorder, disorder with the emergence of order, the *self*-organizing power of a chaotic nature quite apart from human desire or even presence" (238).

101. For brilliant discussions of the poetics of self-organization, see Philip Kuberski's *Chaosmos* (37–48) and Michel Serres's *Hermes: Literature, Science, Philosophy*, trans. Josue V. Harari and David F. Bell (Baltimore, MD: Johns Hopkins Univ. Press, 1982), 71–83.

102. Blake, "There Is No Natural Religion," line 5, *Complete Poetry and Prose*, pages 2–3.

103. Blake, *Milton*, plate 26, line 45, *Complete Poetry and Prose*, page 124. For a clear discussion of Blake's Ulro, see S. Foster Damon's *A Blake Dictionary: The Ideas and Symbols of William Blake*, rev. ed., annot. Morris Eaves (Hanover and London: University Press of New England, 1988), 416–17; and Northrop Frye's *Fearful Symmetry: A Study of William Blake* (Princeton, NJ: Princeton Univ. Press, 1947), 48–50.

104. Blake, *Jerusalem*, plate 58, lines 14–20, *Complete Poetry and Prose*, page 207. Blake's Generation is explained in Damon, 150–1, and Frye, 48–50, 75.

105. Earlier, in *Romantic Turbulence*, I argued that the "Higher Laws" chapter, with its emphasis on ascetic transcendence of matter, constituted a Platonic "fall" from Thoreau's otherwise "ecological" sensibility. However, after reading Hans Peter Duerr's discussion of the *parthenos* in *Dreamtime: Concerning the Boundary between Wilderness and Civilization*, trans. Felicitas Goodman (Oxford: Blackwell, 1985), I have come to read Thoreau's "chastity" as a mode of thought analogous to Schiller's play.

106. Duerr, *Dreamtime*, 16.

107. Friedrich von Schiller, *Letters on the Aesthetic Education of Man*, trans. and intro. Reginald Snell (New York: Frederick Ungar, 1965), 64–78.

108. Schiller, 74–7, 79–80. For an excellent, recent discussion of aesthetic play, see James S. Hans, *The Play of the World* (Amherst: Univ. of Massachusetts Press, 1981). While Hans draws from Schiller, he in the end maintains that play is "the fundamental activity of man": "I want to suggest a definition of play that points to an activity, that points to the fundamental activity of man, the back-and-forth movement of encounter and exchange with the world in which man is continually engaged. But if play is an activity, it is not merely a random participation in the process of the world and is not a substitute for the word 'process' or the word 'flux.' It is a structuring activity, the activity out of which understanding comes. Play is at one and the same time the location where we question our structures of understanding and the location where we develop them" (x).

109. Blake, *Milton*, plate 30, lines 1–14, *Complete Poetry and Prose*, page 129. Blake's Beulah is clearly detailed in Damon, 42–44, and Frye, 49–50, 227–35.

110. Blake, "The Crystal Cabinet," *Complete Poetry and Prose*, pages 489–90. For Blake's Eternity, see *Milton*, plate 30, line 19, plate 10, line 16, *Complete Poetry and Prose*, pages 129, 104. Eden, also called Eternity, is concisely described in Damon, 129–30, and Frye, 49–50.

111. Blake, "Marriage of Heaven and Hell," plate 7, line 10, *Complete Poetry and Prose*, page 36.

112. Emerson, "Thoreau," *Oxford Authors: Ralph Waldo Emerson*, ed. Richard Poirier (Oxford and New York: Oxford Univ. Press, 1990), 482.

CHAPTER 2: GLACIERS

1. Thomas De Quincey, *Suspiria de Profundis, Confessions of an English Opium Eater and Other Writings*, ed. and intro. Grevell Lindop (Oxford: Oxford Univ. Press, 1985), 156.

2. As a young man, Goethe practiced alchemy in his father's attic, and later sublimated his alchemical passions into scientific searches for the coincidence of opposites. Goethe's Faust inherits his creator's passion for magic. Interestingly, one of Faust's most striking moments as magus occurs on the peaks of Brocken during Walpurgis Night. On the bizarre peaks, Faust, along with Mephistopheles, participates in a gathering of numerous witches and other uncanny beings (Johann Wolfgang von Goethe, *Faust*, trans. and intro. Walter Kaufmann [New York: Anchor, 1959], lines 3835–4222).

3. Quoted in Edward Lurie, *Louis Agassiz: A Life in Science* (Chicago: Univ. of Chicago Press, 1960), 98.

4. Goethe, *Wilhelm Meister's Journeyman Years or The Renunciants*, *Goethe's Collected Works*, vol. 10, trans. Krishna Winston and ed. Jane K. Brown (New York: Surkamp, 1989), 279.

5. Goethe, *Wilhelm*, 279.

6. D. Cameron, "Early Discoveries XXII, Goethe, Discoverer of the Ice Age," *Journal of Glaciology* 5 (1965): 751–4.

7. Goethe, *Scientific Studies: Collected Works*, vol. 12, ed. Douglas Miller (Princeton, NJ: Princeton Univ. Press, 1988), 29.

8. Saxo Grammaticus, *The Nine Books of the Danish History*, 2 vols., trans. Oliver Elton (Copenhagen: The Norroena Society, 1905), 1: 85–8.

9. For further mention of this exorcism, see below, pp. 76–77.

10. For a discussion of these dragons, see below, p. 76.

11. In citing Shelley's "Mont Blanc" and *Prometheus Unbound*, I respectively use the abbreviations *MB* and *PU*, followed by line numbers. In citing all other poems of Shelley, I employ the abbreviation *SP* (*The Complete Poetical Works of Percy Bysshe Shelley*), followed by page numbers. Full bibliographic information on these

sources is provided on the "Abbreviations" page at the beginning of this book, pp. vii–viii.

12. For instance, in *Queen Mab*, Shelley associates ice with tyrannical custom (*SP* 1.127), death (4.164), selfishness (5.26), polar waste (8.58–69), and pride (9.86). Likewise, in *Laon and Cythna*, ice is death and stagnation (*SP* 9.23); in "Lines Written Among the Euganean Hills," it is waste and death (*SP* 44); and in *Prometheus Unbound*, it is throughout a negative figure. For an analysis of unfavorable frozen images in *The Cenci*, see Fred L. Milne's "Shelley's *The Cenci*: The Ice Motif and the Ninth Circle of Dante's Hell," *Tennessee Studies in Literature* 22 (1977): 117–32. Given Shelley's generally negative view toward ice, his embrace of the glacier is clearly worth consideration.

13. Fergus Fleming, *Killing Dragons: The Conquest of the Alps* (New York: Atlantic Monthly, 2000), 3–4.

14. Fleming, 4.

15. Fleming, 4. See also Claire Elaine Engel, *A History of Mountaineering in the Alps* (New York: Scribner, 1950), 17; and Marjorie Hope Nicolson, *Mountain Gloom and Mountain Glory: The Development of the Aesthetics of the Infinite* (New York: Norton, 1963), 49. In addition to noting de Bremble's horror, Ronald W. Clark in *The Alps* (New York: Knopf, 1973) also cites the Alpine terror of Bishop Berkeley, who discovered in the icy peaks that "every object that here presents itself is excessively miserable" (43). Likewise, Clark notes that in 1739, Horace Walpole, after visiting the Alps, exclaimed that he hoped that he would never again see such blights. As Clark concludes, though an "occasional eccentric" might not demonize the Alps, "for most of recorded history the mass of mankind took a poor view" of the icy peaks (43).

16. Fleming, 5. See also Engel, 17–18 and Nicolson, 38–71.

17. Fleming, 4. See also Nicolson, 38–71.

18. Engel, 23.

19. Fleming, 6. See also Engel, 20, and Jane Nardin, "A Meeting on the Mer de Glace: *Frankenstein* and the History of Alpine Mountaineering," *Women's Writing* 6:3 (1999), 442.

20. Fleming, 6–7.

21. Engel, 23–6.

22. Fleming, 8–10.

23. I shall discuss "egocentric" magic in detail in a section below, entitled "Mountain Theology" (pp. 81–86). Briefly, "egocentric" magic is what is normally called "black" or "evil" magic. I use the term "egocentric" for two reasons. First, the word avoids the dualistic connotations of "black" or "evil" magic, which presupposes that two opposing forces—black and white, good and evil—are at

war in the universe. Second, "egocentric" magic expresses the main impulse of traditional black magic: the narcissistic drive to alter to world to fit individual wishes, to transform the universe into a double of desire. Clearly, the various destructive beings allegedly living in the Alps—ghouls, witches, and dragons—would qualify as "egocentric" magi.

24. I shall meditate on "cosmological" magic below in "Mountain Theology" (pp. 81–6). For now, I will briefly say that "cosmological" magic is a nondualistic renaming of what has conventionally been called "white" or "good" magic—an ameliorative magic deployed to heal rifts and harmonize discords. While the "egocentric" magician wishes to hoard the powers of the universe for his own selfish use, the "cosmological" magus wants to participate, mystically, with cosmos powers, and possibly focus their already salubrious currents on the world's physical, psychical, and spiritual lacerations.

25. Fleming, 8.

26. Fleming, 8.

27. I borrow these terms from Nicolson, who shows that a major shift in mountain consciousness took place in the eighteenth century—a move from demonizing peaks as blights on God's otherwise smooth handiwork to celebrating the snowy crags as sublime technologies for reaching divine heights.

28. Albrecht von Haller, *Die Alpen, The Poems of Baron Haller*, trans. Mrs. Howorth (London: J. Bell, 1794); discussed in Fleming, 11–12 and Engel, 38.

29. Quoted in Engel, 39. See also Fleming, 11.

30. Engel, 30. See also Fleming, 21–3. Fleming reports that though Rousseau found the Deluc brothers rather boring, he nonetheless "pumped" them for "Alpine information that later found its way, unacknowledged, into *La Nouvelle Héloïse*" (21).

31. Quoted in Engel, 31. See also Fleming, 25.

32. Quoted in Engel, 32. See also Fleming, 24.

33. Quoted in Engel, 32.

34. Engel's words illuminate Murith's disposition: "[I]n spite of his barometer, and thermometer, and the list of plants found on the highest rocks, Murith really climbed the Velan because he was attracted by the mountain. Scientific interest is not sufficient to account for it; he was clearly fascinated by the beauty of the great peak" (33).

35. Engel, 35–8. See also Fleming, 17–20.

36. Quoted in Engel, 36–7. Also see Fleming, 19.

37. Again, Engels is instructive in this context: "Mountains are thus seen to exist in the realm of contradiction, so much so that writers who have tried to grasp the spirit of an Alpine landscape have been impressed by a constant opposition between its beauty and the

sudden horror of which it is capable, between the love which mountains conjure up in many hearts and the feeling of hatred and despair which sometimes sweeps over the same persons among the same mountains. They have tried to solve the riddle. But the understanding of mountains comes only as a revelation. One would like to say that they dispense their grace, using the word in its theological sense: 'for many be called but few chosen'" (16).

38. Frances A. Yates, *Giordano Bruno and the Hermetic Tradition* (Chicago: Univ. of Chicago Press, 1964), 15–17; 80–2.

39. Richard Cavendish, *The Black Arts* (New York: Perigee, 1967), 1–2.

40. In *Magic and English Romanticism* (Athens: Univ. of Georgia Press, 1979), Anya Taylor describes Alexander Pope's negative view of magic: "Pope conforms to the traditional view that magic is heresy because it distorts reality and sets men up as the source of change, rather than relying on the divine order. It leads other men astray, and induces them to see things wrongly" (19). In this view, Pope clearly has in mind magic in its "black" or "egocentric" mode.

41. Paul Christian, *The History and Practice of Magic*, trans. James Kirkup and Julian Shaw (New York: Citadel, 1963), 19. Although Christian, influenced (like Baudelaire and Rimbaud) by the occult revival in mid-nineteenth-century France, published his famous study at the end of the nineteenth century, his book remains, in my opinion, a sensitive, insightful description and interpretation of "cosmological" magic.

42. In describing William Collins's theory of magic, Taylor indirectly details a key motif in "white" or "cosmological" magic. In "Ode on the Popular Superstitions of the Highlands, considered as a subject of Poetry," Collins "embraces the chaos which Pope feared, and . . . imagines that submersion in the magic of nature, when joined with a releasing of powerful psychic energy, will result in great poetry. . . . Collins believes that magic is a power unleashed from the depth of the 'mind possessed,' particularly in wild circumstances where men tap powers hidden in nature as well as themselves" (22, 25).

43. Christian, 18–19.

44. Yates, 69–83. See also D. P. Walker, *Spiritual and Demonic Magic from Ficino to Campanella* (London: Warburg, 1958), 3–106.

45. For instance, as Mircea Eliade argues in *Yoga: Immortality and Freedom* (Princeton, NJ: Bollingen, 1958), 311–41, yoga is a form of magic. Like shamanism, it is a discipline that trains the adept to realize and channel the cosmic currents coursing through his body. Likewise, Taylor, studied in the theurgical poetics of Coleridge and Shelley, shows how poetry is a form of ameliorative magic.

46. Christian, 21–22: "Let us transport ourselves, in thought, to the top of a mountain, at the hour when the fragrance of summer rising from

distant plains, their valleys and woods, mounts slowly with the last
murmurings of nature into the immensity of darkening skies. The
sun has disappeared in a river of jewels, whose final brilliance dies
away on the horizon. For the captive heart which guesses nothing of
what may lie beyond daily joys and miseries, it is night. The slave of
wretched poverty or ignoble labour, of unsuccessful genius or powerless pride, of crushed ambition or wounded greatness, asks nothing
more of nature's pity, than a little sleep before taking up the yoke
again. But for the being magnetised by a higher life, as the shadows
rise from the depths and cover the mountain tops, the dawn of the
Infinite breaks and shines. Those myriads of stars, living jewels in the
crown of God, do they not appear to spread, in ever-widening circles,
into the ethereal depths of an endless, fathomless ocean? . . . This
daring protest of the human soul against the possibility of annihilation can be expressed in two words: *Mountain Theology*."

47. Engel, 16: "Much has been written about the ancient aspect of
     mountain worship and mountain love. From the earliest ages
     mountains have obviously puzzled their beholders who could not
     decide whether their influence was favorable or baneful. Greek
     gods lived on Mount Olympus, but Orpheus was torn to pieces by
     infuriated Bacchantes on the slopes of Mount Rhodophos. Similar
     traditions belong to every mythology."

48. As Byron proclaims in Canto 3 of *Childe Harold's Pilgrimage*
     (1816), "I live not in myself, but I become / Portion of that around
     me; and to me/ High mountains are a feeling" (3.72:680–2).

49. William Wordsworth, *The Prelude: 1799, 1805, 1850*, ed. Jonathan
     Wordsworth, M. H. Abrams, Stephen Gill (New York: Norton,
     1980), 1850 edition, bk. 6, ll. 557–640.

50. Engel, 63.

51. Nicolson, 271–323.

52. Engel, 44–60. See also Showell Styles, *On Top of the World: An Il-
     lustrated History of Mountaineering and Mountaineers* (New York:
     Macmillan, 1967), 9–18.

53. Although historians of mountaineering and glacial morphology
     alike credit de Saussure for being the first scientist of glaciers, I
     should here note, along with Ronald W. Clark, that in 1741, the
     Englishman William Windham (who actually inspired the name of
     the Mer de Glace by comparing the glacier to Lake Geneva frozen
     hard in an agitated state) journeyed to Chamonix and ventured
     onto the Mer de Glace. In his account of this expedition in Swiss
     and British newspapers and of a later excursion in the papers of the
     Royal Society, Clark described "a hitherto unknown mountain
     world" and forged an enduring Alpine connection between "sci-
     ence and adventure" (49–50).

54. Frank F. Cunningham, *James David Forbes: Pioneer Scottish Glaciolo-gist* (Edinburgh: Scottish Academic Press, 1990), 37. Throughout the following discussion of glacial geology, I am indebted to the fine bibliography in George Fiske's "The Historical Development of Glacial Geomorphology," a research essay posted on the world wide web at terra.geo.orst.edu/users /GEO515.htm (17 March 2000).

55. Horace Bénédict de Saussure, *Travels in the Alps, Galileo's Com-mandment: An Anthology of Great Science Writing* (New York: Free-man, 1997), 129–32; discussed in Cunningham, 40.

56. Cunningham, 38. See also Richard J. Chorley, et al., *The History of the Study of Landforms, or the Development of Geomorphology,* 3 vols. (New York: Wiley, 1964–1991), 1:191.

57. Cunningham, 38–9. See also Marilyn Gaull, *English Romanticism: The Human Context* (New York: Norton, 1988), 208–14; Nigel Leask, "Mont Blanc's Mysterious Voice: Shelley and Huttonian Science," *The Third Culture: Literature and Science* (Berlin: Walter de Gruyter, 1998), 188–92. Of course, many catastrophists, like Cuvier in *Essay on the Theory of the Earth* (1813) (trans. Robert Kerr, annot. Robert Jameson [Edinburgh: Blackwood & Co., 1813]) and James Parkinson in *Organic Remains of a Former World* (1811) (3 vols., 2nd ed. [London: 1834]) claimed that the earth was much older than 6,000 years, believing that each day in Genesis was in fact a measure of a very long duration.

58. James Hutton, *Theory of the Earth,* intro. Victor A. Eyles (New York: Hafner, 1973), 304. See also Cunningham, 41, 44–6 and Leask, 190–2.

59. John Playfair, *Illustrations of the Huttonian Theory of the Earth* (New York: Dover, 1964), 389.

60. Cunningham, 46–8.

61. Cunningham, 46.

62. Cunningham, 46–7. See also James T. Tellner, *Jean de Charpentier, Geographers: Bibliographical Studies,* ed. T. W. Freeman and Philippe Pinchemel, vol. 7 (London: Mansell, 1980), 17–20.

63. Cunningham, 47–53. See also Chorley, 195; Lurie, 94–104; and Michael J. Hambrey, *Glacial Environments* (London: Univ. College London Press, 1994), 1–7. For Agassiz's later account of his studies and theories of glaciers, see his *Geological Sketches* (Boston: Houghton Mifflin, 1886), 208–311.

64. Leask provides an excellent account of the Shelleys' time in Cha-monix, as well as of their knowledge of de Saussure, catastrophism, and uniformitarianism. See also Nardin's article on Mary Shelley and the history of Alpine mountaineering. For a good discussion of how Shelley's view of Mont Blanc relates to de Saussure's (and Coleridge's), see Stuart Peterfreund's "Two Romantic Poets and

Two Romantic Scientists 'on' Mont Blanc," *The Wordsworth Circle* 29:3 (summer 1998): 152–161. For a brilliant discussion of Shelley's observations of climate change in the Alps, see Alan Bewell, *Romanticism and Colonial Disease* (Baltimore and London: Johns Hopkins Univ. Press, 1999), 221–27.

65. In "Hymn to Intellectual Beauty" (1816), Shelley of course famously refers to his youthful attempts practice graveyard magic, to conjure ghosts (*SP* 2:73, 49–52). Likewise, in *Loan and Cythna* (1816), he refers to his adolescence spent heaping "knowledge from forbidden mines of lore" (2:108, Ded. 37–45). In his *Life of Shelley* (2 vols., [London: Moxon, 1858], 1:23–8), Thomas Jefferson Hogg claims that the young Shelley "was passionately attached to the study of what used to be called the occult sciences, conjointly with that of the new wonders, which chemistry and natural philosophy have displayed to us." Describing his first visit to Shelley's rooms at Oxford in 1810, Hogg reveals the young poet's intense esoteric passions: "Books, boots, papers, shoes, philosophical instruments, clothes, pistols, linen, crockery, ammunition, and phials innumerable, with money, stockings, prints, crucibles, bags, and boxes, were scattered on the floor and in every place; as if the young chemist, in order to analyze the mystery of creation, had endeavoured first to re-construct the primeval chaos. The tables, and especially the carpet, were already stained with large spots of various hues, which frequently proclaimed the agency of fire. An electrical machine, an air-pump, the galvanic trough, a solar microscope, and large glass jars and receivers, were conspicuous amidst the mass of matter. Upon the table by his side were some books lying open, several letters, a bundle of new pens, and a bottle of japan ink, that served as an inkstand; a piece of deal, latterly part of the lid of a box, with many chips, and a handsome razor that had been used as a knife. There were bottles of soda water, sugar, pieces of lemon, and the traces of an effervescent beverage. Two piles of books supported the tongs, and these upheld a small glass retort above an argand lamp. I had not been seated many minutes before the liquor in the vessel boiled over, adding fresh stains to the table, and resin gin fumes with a most disagreeable odour. Shelley snatched the glass quickly, and dashing it in pieces among the ashes under the grate, increased the unpleasant penetrated effluvium." Though Hogg's tone is elusive (does he poke fun at an *infant terrible* arrogant enough to think he find life in his retort, or does he admire a melancholy philosopher whose chaoses might yield truthful rectitude?) what is clear is this: Shelley's interest in "legitimate" science is inseparable from his passion for "magical" science. For other astute discussions of Shelley's relationship to esoteric traditions, see Taylor, 184–220; James Rieger, *The Mutiny Within: The Heresies of Percy*

Bysshe Shelley (New York: George Braziller, 1967), 167–72; and Andrew J. Welburn, *Power and Self-Consciousness in the Poetry of Shelley* (New York: St. Martin's, 1986), 67–99.

66. Lynn Thorndike, *A History of Magic and Experimental Science*, 9 vols. (London: Macmillan, 1923), 2: 551–9.

67. Yates, 17–18, 151–5, 160–5. See also Walker, 22–4.

68. Yates, 14–15, 130–43.

69. Paracelsus, "Aurora of the Philosophers," *Hermetic and Alchemical Writings of Paracelsus*, trans. L. W. de Laurence, ed. A. E. Waite (Chicago: de Laurence, Scott, and Co, 1910), 48. As Waite notes, parts of this piece may not have been written by Paracelsus; however, "in the main it is a genuine work of the Sage of Hohenheim" (48n).

70. "De Occulta Philosophia," *Paracelsus. Samtliche Werke*, eds. Karl Sudhoff and Wilhelm Matthiessen, part 1: *Medizinische, naturwissenshasftliche, und philosophische Schriften*, 14 vols. (Munich, Berlin: R. Oldenburg, 1928–32), 14:538.

71. Paracelsus, "Astronomia Magna," *Paracelsus. Samtliche Werke*, 12: 130.

72. Kenneth Neill Cameron, *The Young Shelley: Genesis of a Radical* (New York: Collier, 1950), 243, 247, 403, 405. See also Carlos Baker, *Shelley's Major Poetry: The Fabric of a Vision* (Princeton, NJ: Princeton Univ. Press, 1948), 64–70; Stuart Curran, *Shelley's Annus Mirabilis* (San Marino: Huntington Library, 1975), 68–70, 74–88; Welburn, 104–110; and Rieger, 100–3.

73. Constantin-François Volney, *The Ruins: or, A Survey of the Revolutions of Empires*, trans. James Marshall (Washington, DC: Woodstock, 2000), 161. See also Baker, 68.

74. Curran, 67–9.

75. Abraham Hyacinthe Anquetil-Duperron, "Vie de Zoroastre," *Zend-Avesta*, vol. 2, intro. Robert D. Richardson, Jr. (New York: Garland, 1984), 10.

76. *Zend-Avesta*, 3 vols., ed. and trans. Anquetil-Duperron, intro. Robert D. Richardson, Jr. (New York: Garland, 1984), 2: 268; discussed in Anquetil-Duperron, 65.

77. *Zend-Avesta*, 3: 363; discussed in Anquetil-Duperron, 22.

78. Welburn, 67–86.

79. Over one hundred years after Hogg penned his ambiguous portrait of Shelley the magus, A. N. Whitehead famously offered this lucid portrait of the poet as a young scientist: "What the hills were to the youth of Wordsworth, a chemical laboratory was to Shelley. . . . If Shelley had been born a hundred years earlier, the twentieth century would have seen a Newton among chemists" (*Science and the Modern World* [New York: Macmillan, 1925], 81). Other important readers of Shelley have documented his interests in science. For instance, Carl Grabo, *A Newton Among Poets: Shelley's Use of Science in Prometheus*

Unbound (Chapel Hill: Univ. of North Carolina Press, 1930), *passim;* Cameron, 274–84; Desmond King-Hele, *Shelley: His Thought and Work*, 2nd ed. (Teaneck, NJ: Fairleigh Dickinson Univ. Press, 1971), 155–168; and King-Hele, *Erasmus Darwin and the Romantic Poets* (New York: St. Martin's, 1986), 187–226. A recent, excellent study of Shelley's attention to nature and bodies in Timothy Morton's *Shelley and the Revolution in Taste: The Body and the Natural World* (Cambridge: Cambridge Univ. Press, 1994). (I should here add that Morton's most recent book, *The Poetics of Spice: Romanticism Consumerism and the Exotic* [Cambridge: Cambridge Univ. Press, 2000], is something of an inspiration for this more spiritually inflected study of ice.) As will become clear in the course of my brief discussion of Shelley and science, Shelley's primary scientific education came from his reading of Erasmus Darwin, whose scientific poetry—*The Botanic Garden* (1791) and *The Temple of Nature* (1803)—and prose—*Zoonomia* (1794, 96)— explained the latest discoveries in most all scientific branches. (I provide appropriate citations for each of Darwin's works below, in the course of documenting Shelley's use of them. See notes 80, 82, 87.)

80. William Herschel, "Remarks on the Construction of the Heavens," *William Herschel and the Construction of the Heavens*, ed. Michael A. Hoskin (New York: Norton, 1963), 115. This nebular theory was earlier developed by Immanuel Kant in his *Theory of the Heavens* (1855) (*Kant's Cosmogony, As in His Essay on the Retardation of the Rotation of the Earth and his Natural History and Theory of the Heavens*, trans. by W. Hastie, rev., ed., and intro. Willy Ley [New York: Greenwood, 1968]) and later by Pierre Simon Laplace in *Exposition du Système du Monde* (1796) (*The System of the World*, 2 vols., trans. Henry H. Harte [Dublin, 1830]). Even later, Poe "poetically" inflected this theory his own cosmology, *Eureka* (1848) (*Eureka: A Prose Poem: An Essay on the Matter and Spirit of the Universe* [San Francisco: Arion, 1991]). For Darwin's description of Herschel's astronomy, see his *The Botanic Garden*, 2 vols., intro. Donald H. Reiman (New York: Garland, 1978), 1:10n. See also Grabo, 43.

81. Laplace, 2:342; quoted in Cameron, 274.

82. Darwin, *The Golden Age: The Temple of Nature*, intro. Donald H. Reiman (New York: Garland, 1978), 164; discussed in Grabo, 47.

83. Darwin, *Botanic Garden*, 65.

84. James Parkinson, *Organic Remains*, 1:456. Leask discusses how Shelley's ambiguous geology grew out of his attention to both Parkinson's catastrophism and Hutton's uniformitarianism. It seems that Shelley in the end wished to reconcile the dramatic powers of the catastrophists with the bewildering yet harmonious durations of the uniformitarians. Such a synthesis seems to inform the famous "earth cycle" sequence in *Prometheus Unbound:*

85. Darwin, *Temple*, notes, 62–79; discussed in Grabo, 58.
86. Sir Humphry Davy, *The Collected Works of Sir Humphry Davy*, 6 vols., ed. John Davy (London: Smith, 1839–40), 4: 39–40; discussed in Grabo, 104–117.
87. Darwin, *Zoonomia; or the Laws of Organic Life*, 2 vols., 2nd ed. (London: J. Johnson, 1796), 1:5–6, 2:635; discussed in Grabo, 41–42.
88. Darwin, *Temple*, 26–7, add. notes, 1–9; discussed in Grabo, 61–9 and Cameron, 274.
89. Darwin, *Zoonomia*, 1:507–8, 516; discussed in Grabo, 61–2, 71–3.
90. Darwin, *Zoonomia*, 1:109; quoted in in Grabo, 70.
91. For me, one of the fullest studies of Shelley's complex theory of necessity remains Baker, 21–88. A more recent, provocative discussion of Shelley's fate as an interplay between order and chaos is Hugh Robert's *Shelley and the Chaos of History: A New Politics of Poetry* (University Park: Pennsylvania State Univ. Press, 1997), 249–486.
92. Again, Leask shows how Shelley wrote the poem under the influence of both catastrophist and uniformitarian theories (188–92). It is also important to note that Shelley showed an interest in scientific questions in general during his stay in Chamonix. As he reports in his long letter to Peacock: "We have bought some specimens of minerals & plants & two or three chrystal seals at Mont Blanc, to preserve the remembrance of having approached it.—There is a Cabinet d'Histoire Naturelle at Chamouni . . . the proprietor of which is the very vilest specimen, of what vile species of quack that together with the whole army of aubergistes & guides & indeed the entire mass of the population subsist on the weakness & credulity of travellers as leeches subsist on the blood of the sick" (*SL* 1:501).
93. In my discussion of Shelley's skepticism, I mainly draw from C. E. Pulos, *The Deep Truth: A Study of Shelley's Skepticism* (Lincoln: Univ. of Nebraska Press, 1954).
94. Gregory Bateson, *Mind and Nature: A Necessary Unity* (New York: Bantam, 1979), 101–11.
95. Ralph Waldo Emerson, *The Conduct of Life*, *The Complete Works of Ralph Waldo Emerson*, vol. 6, ed. and intro. Edward Waldo Emerson (Boston: Houghton Mifflin, 1904), 32.
96. Shelley's "negative" gnosis is not synonymous with the "via negativa" embraced by Dionysius the Aeropagite or St. John of the Cross. For these theologians, the meditant finds the "luminous darkness" of God only through pondering what God is not. God is utterly transcendent, totally other. Positive descriptors reduce God's grandeur. Negative predicates gesture toward God's profound nothingness. In Shelley's case, God is likewise abysmal. However, neither positive nor negative adjectives can reveal God's qualities, which remain veiled beyond human knowing.

97.   Curran usefully highlights the ambiguities of Demogorgon (51–3).

98.   Like Blake's *Milton* and Coleridge's *The Rime of the Ancient Mariner* (indeed, like Thoreau's *Walden*), *Prometheus Unbound* is an instance of what Victoria Nelson calls in "Symmes Hole, Or the South Polar Romance" "psychotopographic literature": literature in which "inner psychic processes are projected sympathetically onto an exterior landscape." As Nelson notes, this term is related to M.H. Abrams's claim that the Romantics habitually read "passion, life, and physiognomy into the landscape" (*Raritan* 17:2 [fall 1997]:144–5). Not simply an instance of the "pathetic fallacy," psychotopographic literature features a landscape that is both itself as well as an index for a struggling psyche.

99.   Of course, in thinking about Shelley's "Mont Blanc," we likely recall Coleridge's "Hymn, Before Sun-Rise, in the Vale of Chamouni" (1802), a poem less about glaciers and more about God. Indeed, Coleridge based the poem not on firsthand experience but on a short German poem by Friederike Brun, entitled "Ode to Chamouny."

100. From his reading in Darwin, Shelley would have become acquainted with early notions of photosynthesis, discovered in the 1770s by Joseph Priestley and inflected allegorically in Darwin's poetry.

101. In my reading of "Mont Blanc," I have been guided by Earl R. Wasserman's still brilliant interpretation in *The Subtler Language: Critical Readings of Neoclassical and Romantic Poems* (Baltimore: Johns Hopkins Univ. Press, 1959), 195–250.

102. Wasserman suggests that the ravine is a figure for the universal mind, 214–24.

103. William Blake, "The Marriage of Heaven and Hell," plate 10, line 69, *The Complete Poetry and Prose of William Blake*, ed. David V. Erdman, comm. Harold Bloom (New York and London: Doubleday, 1988), 38.

104. Aptly, William Windham, an Englishman who trekked around the Chamonix valley in the middle part of the eighteenth century, gave the Mer de Glace its name by comparing it to frozen water: "You must imagine your lake [Lake Geneva] put in Agitation by a strong Wind, and frozen all at once" (quoted in Clark, 49). Shelley and Windham are not alone in their aqueous vision of glaciers. Under the gaze of two painters of his age, J. M. W. Turner and C. G. Carus, the *Mer de Glace* becomes precisely that—a sea of ice. In his 1802 *Mer de Glace, Chamonix, with Blair's Hut*, Turner renders pictorially the subject of "Mont Blanc"—the relationship between human and nonhuman nature. Turner's glacier looks like Shelley's. It is a white, river-like current capable of carving rivers and caving cathedrals. Yet, as in Shelley's poem, the glacier would not exist as a nourishing flow without a human mind. Blair's Hut, a human construct somewhat distant from the flux, is the cave of the witch Poesy, the

mind distinguishing itself from and organizing the universe of
things. Blair's Hut is Turner's double: human eyes positioned to envision the ice as a sea, a death that is living. Some ten years after
Shelley wrote "Mont Blanc," Carus likewise found in the Chamonix
glacier a torrent beside which a painter might stand and choose his
images. As in Turner's painting, fluid ice rushes by human vision,
figured by two diminutive men holding staffs or rifles. To these men,
as to Carus the artist, the glacier is not inhuman and indifferent but
a wide watercourse into which one might, without fear, dive. In both
paintings, as in Shelley's poem, the human perspective is not central:
Blair's Hut and the hikers, like Shelley's speaker, appear to be after-
thoughts—trivial spots in the midst of nature's grandeur. This de-
centralization of the human is an essential element in the sublime
vision purveyed by all three of these works. The sublime mode elevates as much as it diminishes. Though the human beholder of the
sublime scene is dwarfed by vast powers that he cannot conceptual-
ize by his understanding or picture with his imagination, he is
nonetheless heightened by these same energies because he can with
his reason intuit their holistic virtues. Hence, the humans in these
paintings and Shelley's poem are not the central agents in an anthropocentric universe. However, they are essential parts of an organic
whole. Their artistic visions, which grow from their intuitions,
imbue (one might say complete) the blank ice with sinuous grace,
sensible form: a significant semantics. Humbly giving over to the
animating essences of an immanent force they cannot fully grasp,
these artists—Turner figured by Blair, Carus doubled by a hiker,
Shelley acted by his Alpine poet—are paradoxically raised above the
currents on which they float to a transcendent site from which they
can say, *let there be light*, and see, *it is good.*

105. In this brief meditation on infinite regression, I am indebted to
      John T. Irwin's two brilliant books on the infinite regressions of
      self-consciousness, doubling, and writing—*American Hieroglyphics:
      The Symbols of the Egyptian Hieroglyphics in the American Renaissance*
      (New Haven, CT: Yale Univ. Press, 1980), 148–223; and *The Mys-
      tery to a Solution: Poe, Borges, and the Analytic Detective Story* (Balti-
      more, MD: Johns Hopkins Univ. Press, 1994), 9–12.

106. See Mary Shelley, *History of a Six Weeks' Tour, The Novels and Selected
      Works of Mary Shelley: Volume 8: Travel Writing,* ed. Jeanne Moskal
      (London: Pickering, 1996), 11–40. For discussions of Mary Shelley's
      experience of the Alps and their influence on *Frankenstein,* see Nardin,
      Leask, and James Holt McGavran, "'Insurmountable Barriers to Our
      Union': Homosocial Male Bonding, Homosexual Panic, and Death
      on the Ice in *Frankenstein,*" *European Romantic Review* 11:1 (winter
      2000):46–67. Each of these articles provides important information

on Mary Shelley's knowledge of the Alpine landscape. I should here also note that I use Mary Shelley's 1831 edition of *Frankenstein*, a version of the first (1818) edition bearing her "final" revisions.

107. In my reading of *Frankenstein*, I am indebted to Joseph Kestner's "Narcissism as Symptom and Structure: The Case of Mary Shelley's *Frankenstein*" and Anne K. Mellor's "A Feminist Critique of *Frankenstein*." Both essays are in *New Casebooks: Mary Shelley: Frankenstein*, ed. Fred Botting (New York: St. Martin's Press, 1995).

108. George Gordon, Lord Byron, *Lord Byron: Selected Letters and Journals*, ed. Leslie A. Marchand (Cambridge, MA: Belknap Press of Harvard Univ. Press, 1982), 250.

109. George Gordon, Lord Byron, *Childe Harold's Pilgrimage*, Lord Byron: The Major Works, ed. Jerome J. McGann (Oxford: Oxford Univ. Press, 2000), canto 3, stanza 62.

110. For a discussion of Byron and the Alps, see Nicolson, 380–94.

CHAPTER 3: THE POLES

1. Jorge Luis Borges, *Labyrinths: Selected Stories and Other Writings*, ed. Donald A. Yages and James E. Irby (New York: New Directions, 1962), 8–18.

2. Borges, 15, 17.

3. Quoted in Roland Huntford, *Shackleton* (New York: Atheneum, 1986), 24.

4. Ernest Shackleton, *South: The Last Antarctic Expedition of Shackleton and the Endurance*, fore. Tim Cahill (New York: Lyons, 1998), v.

5. Joscelyn Godwin, *Arktos: The Polar Myth in Science, Symbolism, and Nazi Survival* (Kempton, Ill.: Adventures Unlimited Press, 1996).

6. James S. Romm, *The Edges of the Earth in Ancient Thought: Geography, Exploration, and Fiction* (Princeton, NJ: Princeton Univ. Press, 1992), 129–30. See also Armand Rainaud, *Le Continent Austral: Hypotheses et Decouvertes* (Amsterdam: Meridian, 1893), 16–17; L. P. Kirwan, *A History of Polar Exploration* (New York: Penguin, 1962), 24; Paul Simpson-Housley, *Antarctica: Exploration, Perception, and Metaphor* (London: Routledge, 1992), 1.

7. Romm, 130. See also Rainaud, 23, 36–51.

8. Quoted in Romm, 134. See also Rainaud, 28.

9. In Romm's words: "Cicero sends Scipio Aemilianus into the sky by way of a dream vision; his goal, following the model Plato had established with the Myth of Er in the Republic, is to teach the future statesman the ethical lessons he will need to govern well. . . . The

lesson which the great Africanus . . . derives from this vision is that earthly fame cannot travel far, and that the young Scipio should therefore pursue wisdom rather than glory in his statecraft" (134–5).

10. Romm, 130.
11. Rainaud, 24–5.
12. Quoted in Romm, 131. See also Rainaud, 18.
13. Quoted in Romm, 131–2.
14. Quoted in Romm, 128.
15. Walker Chapman, *The Loneliest Continent: The Story of Antarctic Discovery* (Greenwich, CT: New York Graphic Society, 1964), 4. See also Rainaud, 118–26.
16. Quoted in Chapman, 4. See also Rainaud, 122.
17. Chapman, 4. See also Rainaud, 136–40 and Lowes, *The Road to Xanadu: A Study in the Ways of the Imagination* (Princeton, NJ: Princeton Univ. Press, 1927), 104–14. For an excellent resource for medieval maps of the world, see the website http//www.henry-davis.com/MAPS.
18. Quoted in Chapman, 5. See also Rainaud, 162; Evelyn Edson, *Mapping Time and Space: How Medieval Mapmakers Viewed Their World* (London: British Library, 1997), 105–111; J.B. Harley and David Woodward, ed., *Cartography in Prehistorical, Ancient, and Medieval Europe and the Mediterranean*, 2 vols. (Chicago: Univ. of Chicago Press, 1987), 1: 300, 304, 321, 353–4; C. H. Beazley, *The Dawn of Modern Geography*, 3 vols. (London, H. Frowde, 1897–1906), 2: 570–3; http//www.henrydavis.com/ MAPS/Emwebpages /217mono.html (25 April 2000).
19. Otto Rank in *The Double: A Psychoanalytic Study*, trans. and ed. Harry Tucker, Jr. (London: Maresfield, 1989), 8–33, argues that "double" in literature—in, say, Poe's "William Wilson" and Wilde's *The Picture of Dorian Gray*—is generally the projection of an overly narcissistic character who unconsciously conjures the double to thwart any loving relationship with others that might compromise his self-love.
20. Lowes, 104–14. See also W. L. Bevan and H. W. Phillott, *Medieval Geography: An Essay in Illustration of the Hereford Mappa Mundi* (Amsterdam: Meridian, 1969), 24–88; Chapman, 5; Edson, 4, 139–44; Beazley, 2:528–9; Harley and Woodward, 1:330–1, 340–2; http//www.henry-davs.com/MAPS/EMwebpages/ 226mono.html (May 12, 2000).
21. George H. T. Kimble, *Geography in the Middle Ages* (London: Metheun, 1938), 5, 186–7. See also Beazley, 2:568–70, 617–20; Harley and Woodward, 1:327–8, 331, 340, 348; http//www.henry-davs.com/MAPS/EMwebpages/223mono.html.

22. Edson, 126–131; Lowes, 104–14; Kimble, 182, 186; Harley and Woodward, 1:312–13, 352–3; http//www.henry-davs.com/MAPS/Lmwebpages/232mono.html (23 May 2000).

23. Sir John Mandeville, *Mandeville's Travels: Texts and Translations,* ed. Malcolm Letts, 2 vols. (London: Hakluyt Society, 1953), 1:129; 142–3.

24. In the words of Victoria Nelson: "This, indeed, is the classic post-colonialist argument: if the Western imagination does no more than project its own psychic Terra Incognita onto the rest of the Earth, then we correctly regard such accounts of these regions as portraits of an *alter ego,* not an *alter orbis.* The colonialist's psychotopographic presumption is to seek the Other and find only his own reflection" ("Symmes Hole, Or the South Polar Romance," *Raritan* 17:2 [fall 1997]: 159). For basic texts on post-colonial theory and cartography, see Mary Louise Pratt, *Imperial Eyes: Travel Writing and Transculturation* (London: Routledge, 1992); Richard Phillips, *Mapping Men and Empire: A Geography of Adventure* (London: Routledge, 1997); David Spurr, *The Rhetoric of Empire: Colonial Discourse in Journalism, Travel Writing, and Imperial Administration* (Durham: Duke Univ. Press, 1993); Jerry Brotton, *Trading Territories: Mapping in the Early Modern World* (Ithaca, NY: Cornell Univ. Press, 1998).

25. Toni Morrison, *Beloved* (New York: Plume, 1988), 198–9.

26. Kirwan, 22.

27. Quoted in Chapman, 7.

28. For books on imperialism and mapping, see note 24 above. There have been very few studies on polar exploration and imperialism. However, two recent studies of the subject, primarily as it exists in nineteenth-century Britain, are Robert G. David's *The Arctic in British Imagination, 1818–1914* (Manchester: Manchester Univ. Press, 2000) and Francis Spufford's *I May Be Some Time: Ice and the English Imagination* (New York: Palgrave, 1997).

29. Kirwan, 20–1.

30. Kirwan, 22–4; See also Chapman, 7–11.

31. Kirwan, 56. Stephen J. Pyne in *The Ice: A Journey to Antarctica* (Iowa City: Univ. of Iowa Press, 1986) lucidly describes the persistent inaccessibility of the Antarctic: "The isolation of Antarctica was almost total. The Ice was sui generis; it was solipsistic, self-reflexive. The other continents had been information resources; the quintessential experience of the explorer had been one of novelty, of an abundance of specimens, artifacts, data, scenery, and experiences. Western civilization had evolved systems of knowledge and procedures for learning which assumed just such expectations. The Ice, by contrast, was an information sink. The explorer was compelled to look not out, but inward. The power of discovery de-

pended on what was brought to the scene more than on what could be generated out of it. Like other discovered worlds, Antarctica posed immense problems of assimilation—political, economic, intellectual. But unlike with the seas or other continents, traditional means of institutional absorption and understanding broke down on The Ice. Paradoxically, what began as a richly imagined continent not unlike others became, when finally explored, a white spot on the globe" (68).

32. Yet, in some cases, the medieval fear remained. For instance, in 1413 Pierre d' Ailly, though he could envision a spherical earth and the exotic east, faltered before the poles: "Beyond Thule, the last Island of the Ocean, after one day's sail the sea is frozen and stiff. At the poles there live great ghosts and ferocious beasts, the enemies of man. Water abounds there, because those places are cold, and cold multiplies vapors" (quoted in Chapman, 7).

33. Kirwan, 21–5. See also Chapman, 7–11; Simpson-Housley, 3–5; and Gurney, 7–11.

34. Kirwan, 56. See also Chapman, 12.

35. Quoted in Kirwan, 57.

36. Quoted in Kirwan, 57. See also Alan Gurney, *Below the Convergence: Voyages Towards Antarctica, 1699–1839* (New York: Norton, 1997), 9; and Simpson-Housley, 4–5.

37. Quoted in Chapman, 12. See also Kirwan, 57.

38. Quoted in Chapman, 15.

39. Chapman, 15. See also Gurney, 15–16 and Simpson-Housley, 5.

40. Kirwan, 79–80. See also Chapman, 16–17.

41. Quoted in Gurney, 16–17; Pyne emphasizes this overlap between political imperialism and scientific curiosity: "The events surrounding the first great voyages set in motion a dynamic of exploration—tied on one hand to the geopolitics of European expansion and on the other to the equally aggressive principles of modern science—that would prove irreversible" (71).

42. Gurney, 17–18. See also J. C. Beaglehole, *The Life of Captain James Cook* (Stanford, CA: Stanford Univ. Press, 1974), 101–7; and Kirwan, 75–6.

43. Quoted in Gurney, 19. See also Beaglehole, 128–52 and Kirwan, 76–7.

44. Gurney, 20.

45. Gurney, 20–1. See also Kirwan, 78–9. For a detailed account of this three-year voyage, see Beaglehole, 153–272.

46. Gurney, 21. See also Beaglehole, 173–305 and Kirwan, 79.

47. Gurney, 21.

48. James Cook, *The Journals of Captain James Cook*, ed. J. C. Beaglehole (New York: Penguin, 2000), 278, 240–3.

49. Cook, *Journals*, 244.
50. Cook, *Journals*, 249. For a full account of Cook's first crossing, see Beaglehole, 306–323.
51. Quoted in Kirwan, 83.
52. Cook, *Journals*, 249.
53. Beaglehole, 360–7.
54. Quoted in Kirwan, 84.
55. Quoted in Beaglehole, 431–2.
56. Quoted in Beaglehole, 436.
57. As Pyne writes: "[I]t is appropriate that the scene of [Cook's] grandest triumph should be the Antarctic—the 'country of Refusal,' as poet Katha Pollitt describes it, where 'No was final.'" (75).
58. Earl of Shaftesbury, Anthony Ashley Cooper (1671–1713), "The Moralists, a Philosophical Rhapsody," quoted in Nelson, 146. Like Shaftesbury, T. S. Eliot knew that unmapped spaces could foster spiritual visions. In his strange note to his Road to Emmaus sequence in *The Waste Land* (1922)—in which two apostles feel the presence of a third man walking beside them (Jesus returned from the dead)—Eliot admits that the passage was inspired by an Antarctic expedition about which he somewhere heard, of which "it was related that the party of explorers, at the extremity of their strength, had the constant delusion that there was *one more member* than could actually be counted." (We now know that he drew from Shackleton's account of his last Antarctic expedition.)
59. Nelson, 146.
60. This vision of the Peratae yearning for the pole arises from Hippolytus of Rome. He claims in his third-century *Refutation of All Heresies* that a Gnostic of this sect would proclaim the following: "[I]f the eyes of any . . . are blessed, this one, looking upward on the firmament, will behold at the mighty summit of heaven the beauteous image of the serpent, turning itself, and becoming an originating principle of every species of motion to all things that are being produced. He will (thereby) know that without him nothing consists, either of things in heaven, or things on earth, or things under the earth" (*Refutation of All Heresies, The Ante-Nicene Fathers: Translations of the Fathers Down to A.D. 325*, ed. Alexander Roberts and James Donaldson, vol. 5 [Buffalo, NY: Christian Literature Publishing Co., 1886], 63). Interestingly, almost seventeen hundred years after Hippolytus described these Alexandrian mystics of the serpent, Fridtjof Nansen, a Norwegian who had never been to Egypt, was likewise stunned by the polar serpent. In 1893, Nansen embarked in the *Fram* ("onward"—a ship for those who pass through) on a quest to reach the North Pole by floating on the ice of the Arctic Ocean. A biologist who had already skied across Greenland, Nansen was accustomed to accounting for

physical wonders with positive science. However, when he turned in the circumpolar current on a November night, he fell under a spell. Standing on deck to relieve a "gloomy frame of mind," Nansen found himself "nailed to the spot." To the north, slithering through the aurora borealis—the cosmic snake, furiously colored: "There is the supernatural for you—the northern lights flashing in matchless power and beauty over the sky in all the colors of the rainbow. Seldom or never have I seen the colors so brilliant. . . . And now from the faraway western horizon a fiery serpent writhed itself up over the sky, shining brighter and brighter as it came. It split into three, all brilliantly glittering. Then the colors changed. The serpent to the south turned almost ruby-red with spots of yellow; the one in the middle, yellow; to the north, greenish white. Sheaves of rays swept along the sides of the serpents, driven through the ether-like waves before a storm-wind. They sway backward and forward, now strong, now fainter again. The serpents reached and passed the zenith. Though I was thinly dressed and shivering with cold, I could not tear myself away till the spectacle was over, and only a faintly glowing fiery serpent near the western horizon showed where it had begun. . . . If one wants to read mystic meanings into nature, here, surely, is the opportunity" (*Farthest North* [New York: Harper and Brothers, 1897], 2 vols., 310–1). In his introduction to this journal of his voyage—published in 1897 as *Farthest North*—Nansen dubbed the Arctic as "Nature's great Ice Temple," stilled by "endless silence," and reminded his readers that the earliest Viking explorers had called the polar realm *Ginnungagap*, "the abyss at the world's end." At the end of his three-year voyage in this abundant void—during which he tread on polar ground over which no one had ever before walked—Nansen found the language of science wanting, and thus turned to the lexicon of reverie: "The ice and the long moonlit polar nights, with all their yearning, seemed like a far-off dream from another world—a dream that had come and passed away. But what would life be worth without its dreams?" (1:4; 2:597). Nansen, enchanted by the frosty ouroboros, concluded that the Arctic is less a specimen and more a vision, a disturbing insight into powers as "deep and pure as infinity, the silent, starry night, the depths of nature herself, the fullness of the mystery of life, the eternal round of the universe and its eternal death" (quoted in Kirwan, 215).

61. We should never forget that Gnosticism was extremely heterogeneous, far from uniformly "dualist" or "antimaterial." Recall, for instance, the lines of Jesus in *The Gospel According to Thomas:* "I am the Light that is above them all, I am the All. The All came forth from Me and the All attained to Me. Cleave a piece of wood, I am there. Lift up the stone, you will find me there" (Bentley Layton, *The*

Gnostic Scriptures: Ancient Wisdom for the New Age, trans. and intro. Bentley Layton [New York and London: Doubleday, 1987], 394).

62. Hippolytus, 63–4.

63. For excellent discussions of the rich meanings of the esoteric poles, see Nelson, 136–48; Godwin, 141–80; Chevalier and Gheerbrant, *The Penguin Dictionary of Symbols*, trans. John Buchanan-Brown (New York: Penguin, 1994), 142–5, 718–20, 765–6; O'Neill, *The Night of the Gods: An Inquiry into Cosmic and Cosmogonic Mythology and Symbolism*, 2 vols. (London: Harrison and Sons, 1893). 35–54, 71–5, 488–515.

64. Quoted in Nelson, 147.

65. Godwin, 106–8. See also Nelson, 149–51.

66. Godwin, 108. See also Nelson, 141–3.

67. Quoted in Godwin, 109–12. See also Nelson, 149–51; and John T. Irwin, *American Hieroglyphics: The Symbols of the Egyptian Hieroglyphics in the American Renaissance* (New Haven, CT: Yale Univ. Press, 1980), 65–94.

68. In January of 1799, not long after he had sent his Ancient Mariner deep into the Antarctic ice, Coleridge was stunned by a frozen plane. Writing to his wife Sara from Ratzeburg, Germany, he details the mesmerizing qualities of a winter lake: "But when first the ice fell on the lake, and the whole lake was frozen one large piece of thick transparent glass—O my God! what sublime scenery I have beheld. Of a morning I have seen the little lake covered with mist; when the sun peeped over the hills the mist broke in the middle, and at last stood as the waters of the Red Sea are said to have done when the Israelites passed; and between these two walls of mist the sunlight burst upon the ice in a straight road of golden fire, all across the lake, intolerably bright, and the walls of mist partaking of the light in a *multitude* of colours. About a month ago the vehemence of wind had shattered the ice; part of it, quite shattered, was driven to shore and had frozen anew; this was of a deep blue, and represented an agitated sea—the water that ran up between the great islands of ice shone of a yellow-green (it was at sunset), and all the scattered blood islands of smooth ice were *blood*, intensely bright *blood*." In this remarkable passage, which he would later publish in an 1809 number of *The Friend*, Coleridge finds the ice to be *alive*. It pulses with blood, and the sun fires it. Refracting light, it vibrates with the colors of the rainbow. It divides the mist with a track of gold—a bridge to liberation. It is a translucent window to the fishy deeps. This counterintuitive description of ice is a rule rather than an exception for Coleridge. In the poet for whom nothing is inanimate, the frost can perform a "secret ministry" to the invisible currents of life, and "caves of ice" are necessary complements to sunny pleasure domes. Indeed, both "Frost at

Midnight" (1798) and "Kubla Khan" (1798) intimate that even ice must be embraced as a pattern of an immanent principle of life. Given the prominence of ice in these poems and the *Rime*, it should be clear that Coleridge's relationship to ice was fecund and complex. J.L. Lowes and John Beer have respectively explored this relationship in their landmark studies (Lowes, 135–151; Beer, *Coleridge's Poetic Intelligence* [London: Macmillan, 1977], 139–42, and "Ice and Spring: Coleridge's Imaginative Education," *Coleridge's Variety: Bicentenary Studies*, ed. John Beer, intro. L.C. Knights [Pittsburgh, PA: Univ. of Pittsburgh Press, 1974], 54–80). I hope in the present study to deepen and extend their profound insights.

69. As Lowes shows, Coleridge the library cormorant was deeply versed in the history of the South Pole, and was especially aware of how Cook's voyage countered the prevailing polar fantasies of monsters and Edens (106–139). But as Lowes also makes clear, the Mariner's complex reaction to the polar ice is not only a reflection of Coleridge's reading in southern polar history but also of his studies of the travel books of several Arctic explorers. Indeed, as John Spencer Hill shows in *A Coleridge Companion: An Introduction to the Major Poems and the Biographia Literaria* (New York: Macmillan, 1984), Coleridge lifts many of his poetic phrases almost ver batim from accounts of Artic exploration. Perusing the journal of Thomas James, who went into the Arctic Circle in search of the Northwest Passage in 1631, Coleridge found a description of foggy mountains of ice towering "farre higher" than the "Top-mast head" (148). If James's northern icescape is comprised of visual terrors—blinding grays broken by giant bergs—then the one reported by David Crantz, an eighteenth-century missionary who suffers the colds of Greenland, is an aural horror, a plane of icy cannons: "There was such a frightful rumbling, and cracking of the ice, as if many cannons had been fired at once, and then ensued a violent noise, like the roaring of a cascade" (148). C. J. Phipps, a British captain who explored Spitsbergen in 1773, likewise encountered a frozen hell in the Arctic, only to be rewarded by a thunderous liberation: "The men were worn out with fatigue in defending the ships with their ice-poles from being engulphed; and now nothing but scenes of horror and perdition appeared before their eyes. But the Omnipotent . . . caused . . . the ice to part in an astonishing manner, rending and cracking with a tremendous noise, surpassing that of the loudest thunder" (148-9). As the Dutchman Gerrit de Veer reports in his journal, published in 1598, he and the other crew members on William Barents's Arctic expedition of 1596-7 likewise were stunned by an apocalyptic release from the ice: "Wee might heare the Ice cracke in the Sea . . . which made a huge noyse. . . . We were taken

with a great swounding and dazeling in our heads . . . [but] when the doores were open, we all recovered our healths againe, by reason of the cold Ayre . . . otherwise without doubt, we had dyed in a sudden swound" (148). Coleridge further found in his Arctic studies dazzling descriptions of bejewelled icebergs that recalled John's revelation of a crystal heaven. In John Harris's 1705 compilation of travel tales, for instance, he found the following account of polar ice: "Nor do [the] Figures and Shape [of the ice] alone surprize, but also their Diversity of Colours pleases the Sight; for some are like white Chrystal, others as blue as Saphires, and others again green as Emeralds" (26). In the same mood, Frederick Martens, captain of a 1671 expedition to Spitzbergen, saw in the Arctic ice a magical realm in which familiar night and day were reversed—in which the moon shone through the mist like a heavenly sun: "In the night we saw the Moon very pale, as it used to look in the day time in our Country, with clear Sun-shine, whereupon followed mist and snow" (26–7). These various accounts suggest the complexity of the polar regions: horror mixed with beauty, death combined with eternity.

70.   Several readings of the *Rime* have informed my polar senses of the poem. See Nelson, 147–51; Pyne, 162–3; and Robert Penn Warren, "The Rime of the Ancient Mariner: A Poem of Pure Imagination," *Selected Essays of Robert Penn Warren* (New York: Vintage, 1956), 198–305.

71.   The Mariner's Antarctic is as strange as the moon—an exotic space in the cold stars. This lunar eeriness—as mysteriously attractive as it is harshly annihilating—comes luridly to life in the paintings of two other nineteenth-century polar visionaries. In *Eismeer* (1823), David Casper Friedrich pictures a polar ocean as a temple of horror, a realm of cracking ice that crushes ships as if they were paper. Inhospitable to human comfort and control—the ice is an explosion of immense blades—Friedrich's icescape is otherworldly, haunted by a disturbing blue background, rusted burgundy foreground, and a ghostly berg in the distance. Yet, this erupted floe points, like a frozen steeple, to a portal in the sky, a bright orifice through which one might pass to the *axis mundi*. Frederic Edwin Church in *Iceberg* (1875) likewise depicts the polar seascape as a region that dwarfs and lifts the human. On the one hand, Church's ship is decentered and diminished, a toy beside the frozen immensity. Yet, on the other, his apricot light at the top of the berg points to a space beyond the freeze, an indifferent grayness reaching to infinity.

72.   Herman Melville, *Moby-Dick; or The Whale*, ed. Hershel Parker and Harriosn Hayford, 2nd. ed. (New York: Norton, 2001), ch. 45, par. 5.

73. Nietzsche, *Thus Spoke Zarathustra*, trans. Walter Kaufmann, *The Portable Nietzsche*, ed. and trans. Walter Kaufmann (New York: Viking, 1982), part 2, "On Redemption," pars. 6–19.

74. Blake, *The Book of Urizen*, plate 3, line 1-plate 7, line 8, *The Complete Poetry and Prose of William Blake*, ed. David V. Erdman, comm. Harold Bloom (London and New York: Anchor, 1988), 70–4.

75. Fittingly, moon, serpent, and ocean are also images associated with Robert Graves's White Goddess, described in T*he White Goddess: A Historical Grammar of Poetic Myth* (1948), and Ted Hughes's Goddess of Complete Being, described in *Shakespeare and the Goddess of Complete Being* (1992). Aside from Hecate, triple goddess of Moon, Earth, and Underworld (rebirth, life, and death), we recall the three aspects of the goddess in individual forms: Diana of the moon, Medusa of the snake, and Aphrodite of the sea.

76. Coleridge's "poetic" science is *holoarchical*, a term used by Arthur Koestler in his 1967 *Ghost in the Machine* to detail organic homologies. Koestler claims that events are not autonomous and self-supporting but interactive and interdependent. Each part of a natural system is a *holon* (*holos*—whole; *on*—part): a whole—a discrete structure—and a part—a component of a distributed network. Atoms are whole, yet combine to form cells, and cells themselves comprise organs that commune into consciousness (*Ghost in the Machine* [New York: Macmillan, 1967], 45–58).

77. Owen Barfield, *What Coleridge Thought* (Middletown, CT: Wesleyan, 1971), 51.

78. Immanuel Kant, *Critique of Judgment*, trans. Werner S. Pluhar (Indianapolis: Hackett, 1987), 244–5.

79. Hence, Coleridge's imagination, transforming facts into symbols of the whole, transmutes empirical data into what Henry Corbin calls the *mundus imaginalis*, a realm bridging visible and invisible worlds. According to Corbin in *Swedenborg and Esoteric Islam* (1984, 1995), certain Sufi mystics resemble Swedenborg in detailing three levels of perception: the sensory, the imaginal, and the spiritual, modes that correspond to body, soul, and spirit. Sensory knowledge emerges from "the empirical world" in the forms of history, politics, biology, physics. Above this realm is the *mundus imaginalis*, the image world grasped by the "cognitive function of the Imagination." This region is not merely empirical or simply immaterial. It is an "'immaterial' materiality," a sphere invisible to the physical sight but palpable to the "vision" of the active imagination, a climate "fully objective and real, where everything existing in the sensory world has its analogue." Corbin likens this sphere of "subtle bodies" to Platonic forms, Swedenborg's angels, and Jung's archetypes (we could add

Goethe's *Urbilden*). These transparently opaque images "correspond" to their simply opaque sensual counterparts while they open into transparent, spiritual essences beyond cognition—the Neoplatonic One, the Gnostic plenitude, the abyss of life. To elevate facts to the *mundus imaginalis* is to *realize* them as circumferences, thresholds of inside and outside, boundless and bounded, nowhere and everywhere (*Swedenborg and Esoteric Islam*, trans. Leonard Fox [Weschester: Swedenborg Foundation, 1995], 2–14).

80. "Mystic" derives from the Greek *muein*, "to close one's eyes (or lips)."

81. Evelyn Underhill, *Mysticism: A Study in the Nature and Development of Man's Spiritual Consciousness* (New York: Meridian, 1955), 306–7.

82. Lowes (213–4), Barfield (179–83), and Thomas McFarland (*Coleridge and the Pantheist Tradition* [Oxford: Clarendon, 1969], 245–9), describe Coleridge's immersion in heterodox texts.

83. See, for instance, *The Secret Book According to John* and *The Thunder—Perfect Intellect* in Bentley Layton, 23–51, 77–85. For scholarly discussions of Gnostic females, see Elaine Pagels, *The Gnostic Gospels* (New York: Vintage, 1979), 48–69; Kurt Rudolph, *Gnosis: The Nature and History of Gnosticism* (San Francisco: Harper San Francisco, 1987), 76–83; Hans Jonas, *The Gnostic Religion: The Message of the Alien God and the Beginnings of Christianity*, 2nd. ed. (Boston: Beacon, 1963), 174–205.

84. One could of course read this dialectic from a purely Christian perspective as well: The prothesis is the father as infinite, the thesis is the son as finite embodiment of the fatherly infinite; antithesis is the holy spirit emanating from the son's ordered patterns throughout the cosmos; and the synthesis is the trinity, three in one and one in three. When meditating on Coleridge's profoundly syncretic mind, one always encounters layers of heterogeneous yet somehow analogous forms of thought.

85. Again, Koestler in *Ghost in the Machine* claims that events are not autonomous and self-supporting but interactive and interdependent. Hence, each part of a natural system is a *holon* (*holos*—whole; *on*—part): a whole—a discrete structure—and a part—a component of a distributed network (45–58).

86. Harold Beaver, "Introduction," *The Narrative of Arthur Gordon Pym of Nantucket*, by Edgar Allan Poe (New York: Penguin, 1975). See also J. Lasley Dameron, "*Pym's* Polar Episode: Conclusion or Beginning?" *Poe's Pym: Critical Explorations*, ed. Richard J. Kopley (Durham, NC: Duke Univ. Press, 1992), 33–43; Burton R. Pollin, "Notes and Comments," *Imaginary Voyages: Collected Writings of Edgar Allan Poe*, vol. 1, ed. Burton R. Pollin (Boston: Twayne, 1981), 356–63; and William E. Lenz, *The Poetics of the Antarctic: A*

Study in Nineteenth-Century American Cultural Perceptions (New York: Garland, 1995), 38–44.

87. In *Table Talk,* Coleridge said the following of his famous poem: "Mrs. [Anna] Barbauld once told me that she admired the Ancient Mariner very much, but that there were two faults in it,—it was improbable, and had no moral. As for the improbability, I owned that that might admit some question; but as to the want of a moral, I told her that in my own judgment the poem had too much; and that the only, or chief fault, if I might say so, was the obtrusion of the moral sentiment so openly on the reader as a principle or cause of action in a work of such pure imagination. It should have had no more moral than the Arabian Night's tale of the merchant's sitting down to eat dates by the side of a well, and throwing the shells aside, and lo! a genie starts up, and says he must kill the aforesaid merchant, because one of the date shells had, it seems, put out the eye of the genie's son" (*CC* 14.2:100)

88. Edgar Allan Poe, *Letters of Edgar Allan Poe,* 2 vols., ed. John Ward Ostrom (New York: Gordian Press, 1966), 2:23.

89. For Poe's racism, see Gerald J. Kennedy and Liliane Weissberg, eds., *Romancing the Shadow: Poe and Race* (Oxford and New York: Oxford Univ. Press, 2001). For an early revelation of Poe's racism in *The Narrative of Arthur Gordon Pym,* see Harold Beaver's 1975 introductory essay to the Penguin edition of the novel.

90. The "monistic" Gnosticism of the Peratae resembles Neoplatonist thought—which possibly influenced this Gnostic sect—in fairly obvious ways. The Peratic Father is analogous to the Neoplatonic One (both powers are utterly transcendent, abysmal, beyond all representation); the Peratic Son corresponds to the Neoplatonic Intellect (both principles are differentiation, formal emanations—overflowings—of the One, perfect, spiritual manifestations of its virtues); and the Peratic Matter partially resembles the Neoplatonic Soul (both are further emanations of the abyss, emanations into time and space). In both systems, matter is not intrinsically evil but a precipitation of the abyss, palpable manifestation of spirit. In contrast, the "dualistic" Gnosticism of the Manicheans maintains that matter is the creation of an evil deity and therefore irredeemably pernicious. It is this antimaterial Gnostic current that Plotinus attacks in his diatribe against Gnosticism.

91. In her magisterial volumes *Blake and Tradition,* 2 vols. (Princeton: Bollingen, 1968), Kathleen Raine eloquently distinguishes between the Neoplatonist (and by extension the Gnostic, both "monistic" and "dualistic") and the alchemist: "The great difference between the Neoplatonic and the alchemical philosophies lies in their opposed conceptions of the nature of matter. For Plotinus

and his school, matter is mere mire, the dregs of the universe, a philosophic 'non-entity' because incapable of form except as it reflects intelligibles. To the alchemists spirit and matter, active and passive, light and darkness, above and below are, like the Chinese yin and yang, complementary principles, both alike rooted in the divine. The *deus absconditus* is hidden and operating in matter, no less than He is to be found in the spiritual order" (118).

92. Sir Thomas Browne, *Urne Buriall, and The Garden of Cyrus*, ed. John Carter (Cambridge: Cambridge Univ. Press, 1958), *The Garden of Cyrus*, ch. 3, par. 44.

93. John T. Irwin, "The Quincuncial Network in Poe's Pym," *Poe's Pym: Critical Explorations*, ed. Richard Kopley (Durham, NC: Duke Univ. Press, 1992), 176–84.

94. Irwin, "Quincuncial," 178–83.

95. Irwin, "Quincuncial," 185, 187.

96. Pym's first notable experience in Tsalal serves as a perfect parable of his basic psychic disposition at this point in the book. Making their way to the primary village of the Tsalalians, he and his group cross a brook whose water is singularly strange: Though it is in fact limpid, it appears to have the consistency of a "thick infusion of gum Arabic," and though it is not any one uniform color, it presents to the eye, as it courses, "every possible shade of purple, like the hues of changeable silk" (*NP* 194). Upon collecting this water in a basin and allowing it to rest, Pym notices that the "whole mass of liquid [is] made up of a number of distinct veins, each of a distinct hue; that these veins [do] not commingle, and that their cohesion [is] perfect in regard to their own particles among themselves, and imperfect in regard to neighboring veins" (172). Beholding this "first definite link in that vast chain of apparent miracles with which [he] was destined to be at length encircled," Pym takes out his knife, runs it athwart the veins, and finds that a separation is "effected, which the power of cohesion [does] not immediately rectify" (172). This slicing of a miraculous flow is a figure of Pym's primary epistemological activity: to divide and conquer. Consistently ignoring subtle complicities between opposites, he persistently divides into hierarchies order and chaos, black and white, self and other.

97. For instance, Pym never shows an awareness of certain clearly duplicitous names and events associated with each of the ships on which he sails. The *Ariel*, the sailboat in which he and Augustus take their disastrous nocturnal journey, suggests both the bright fairy in Shakespeare's *The Tempest*, a sprite able to transcend time and space, and the tragic boat in which Percy Shelley sank to his death, in

which he fully succumbed to the limitations of space and time. Likewise, the *Penguin*, the whaler that both sinks and raises Pym and Augustus, suggests the polar bird that gathers blackness and whiteness
in its skin. The *Grampus* instances similar doublings. Named after
the so-called "Killer Whale," which is, like the penguin, both black
and white, the events on this ship suggests that darkness and light,
chaos and order, need one another to exist. This secret complicity is
revealed by the fact that Pym rises from a season in the dark chaos of
the hold to restore to order a turbulent mutiny while Augustus descends from the bright orders of the deck into a helpless victim of an
anarchical rebellion. This convergence of oppositions is further suggested by the character of Dirk Peters himself, whose name gathers
"knife" and "St. Peter," who effortlessly moves between the mutineers and Augustus, divisive violence and communal kindness, wildness and humaneness. What is the name *Jane Guy* but a merging of
female ("Jane") and male ("Guy")? Paradoxical structures like these
are repeated by at least two events that occur while Pym is associated with this ship. First of all, while Pym finds that Too-Wit's terror upon beholding his reflection in a mirror aboard the Guy is a
prime example of savagery, Pym's own constant aversion to mental
reflection, though unstated, shows a similar fear of mirror effects.
Hence, Pym, seemingly civilized, proves himself to be a sort of savage, while Too-Wit, ostensibly primitive, behaves like an educated
man of the city. Secondly, even though Pym consistently demeans
the Tsalalians to subhuman savages, these Antarctic inhabitants in
the end show themselves capable of a sophisticated conspiracy, a rational plan of attack. Other subtle connections overlooked by Pym
include the facts that his lawyer grandfather and his "halfbreed"
companion share the same name (Peters); that Augustus dies and
does not die (Pym says that he many years later had a conversation
with an Augustus who expires only pages later); that his dates and
coordinates are scientific tools growing from an inaccurate memory
(as he admits in two footnotes).

98. Richard Wilbur, "The Narrative of Arthur Gordon Pym," *Responses: Prose Pieces, 1953–1976* (New York: Story Line, 2000), 245.
Wilbur in this essay (239–70 in *Responses*) provides the definitive
"dualistic" "Gnostic" reading of Pym. Alfred Kazin also argues
that Pym at the end of the romance elevates from the natural to
the supernatural (*The American Procession: The Major American
Writers From 1830 to 1930* [New York: Knopf, 1984], 95). Likewise, Harold Bloom maintains that the polar chasm encountered
by Pym is "the familiar Romantic Abyss, not part of the natural
world but belonging to eternity, before the creation" ("Inescapable

Poe," rev. of *Edgar Allan Poe: Essays and Reviews*, ed. G. R. Thompson, *New York Review of Books*, 11 October 1984, 34). (J. Lasley Dameron notes these sources in *"Pym's* Polar Episode: Conclusion or Beginning?" *Poe's Pym: Critical Explorations*, ed. Richard Kopley [Durham: Duke Univ. Press, 1992], 35).

99.   Poe, "MS. Found in a Bottle," *The Collected Works of Edgar Allan Poe: Tales and Sketches*, vol. 2, ed. Thomas Ollive Mabbott (Cambridge: Belknap, 1978), 146.

100.   Poe, *Eureka: A Prose Poem: An Essay on the Matter and Spirit of the Universe* (San Franciso: Arion, 1991), 103, 105.

101.   Wilbur, 244.

102.   Poe, "The Poetic Principle," *Selections from the Critical Writings of Edgar Allan Poe*, ed. and intro. F. C. Prescott (New York: Gordian, 1981), 236.

103.   Poe, *Eureka*, 102, 104.

104.   Wilbur, 252–5.

105.   Wilbur, 267.

106.   Barton Levi St. Armand, "Poe's 'Sober Mystification': The Uses of Alchemy in 'The Gold-Bug,'" *Poe Studies* 4:1 (June 1971):1–7; Randall Clack, *The Marriage of Heaven and Earth: Alchemical Regeneration in the Works of Taylor, Poe, Fuller, and Hawthorne* (Westport, CT: Greenwood, 1958); Arthur Versluis, *Esoteric Origins of the American Renaissance* (New York and London: Oxford Univ. Press, 2001), 72–80.

107.   As Jung observes in *Psychology and Alchemy* (1944), the *nigredo* is "chaos," an indifferent matrix. This matrix is "the dragon that creates and destroys itself," "Tiamat with its dragon attribute," the "primordial matriarchal world." As primal dragon, the *nigredo* is the ouroboros or caduceus of Mercurius, the alchemical symbol of transformation. The "philosophical," as opposed to "material," Mercury is the spirit of life, the world soul, male and female, present at every stage of the alchemical process. His serpentine presence in the primal soup suggests that even in chaos or death is the seed of organization and life. Hence, even though the *nigredo* is physical destruction (flood, deluge) or psychological pain (melancholy, mortification), it is also the water of life, the womb, the world's egg, and the philosopher's stone. This abyss is a gathering of life and death, beginning and end, male and female, sun and moon, sulfur (hot and dry) and quicksilver (cold and moist). In *Mysterium Coniunctionis* (1956), Jung claims that the psychological analogues of this state are *melancholia*, "confusion and lostness," fear, wickedness, and wretchedness. Associated with the planet Saturn, this psychic state is far from the sun, a dark night of the

soul. This mood is the interior equivalent to Osiris's journey into
the underworld, Dionysus's dismemberment, Attis's castration,
Adonis's goring, Jesus' descent into hell, Dante's journey into the
dark forest, Hamlet's despair. Yet, just as each of these catastrophes
engenders resurrection, so the *melancholia* of the *nigredo* produces
greater health and power (Jung, *Psychology and Alchemy, The Collected Works of C.G. Jung*, vol, 12 [Princeton, NJ: Bollingen, 1952],
paragraphs 26, 334, 172; Jung, *Mysterium Coniunctionis, The Collected Works of C.G. Jung*, vol. 14 [Princeton: Bollingen, 1963],
pars. 306, 446). See also Mircea Eliade, *The Forge and the Crucible*,
2nd ed., trans. Stephen Corrin (Chicago and London: Univ. of
Chicago Press, 1962), 161–62; E. J. Holmyard, *Alchemy*, 49,
186–188; John Read, *From Alchemy to Chemistry* (New York:
Dover, 1961), 33. Moreover, see entries on "nigredo" (135–36),
"prima materia" (153–6), "chaos" (33–4), "abyss" (2–3), "dragon"
(59–60), and "uroboros" (207) in Lyndy Abraham's *A Dictionary of
Alchemical Imagery* (Cambridge: Cambridge Univ. Press, 1988).

108. Irwin, *American Hieroglyphics*, 73–8.
109. This pale stage "congeals" the turbid swells of the *prima materia*. It
"freezes" Mercury, the quicksilver snake, into a jewel. Caused by a
"washing" (*baptisma, ablutio*) of the *nigredo*, this *albedo* stage appears
when the alchemical solution is entirely white or all colors (the
peacock's tail). This crystalline whiteness (the colorless all color) is
a threshold between opaque body and transparent spirit, mud and
stars. On the one hand, the *albedo* is the "sublimated or calcined
earth," "white foliated earth," the "good white snow." On the
other, it is Luna, heavenly queen, the white woman who will marry
the red king to produce the philosopher's stone. Like the psychology of the *nigredo*, the one of the *albedo* is double. Male and female,
active and passive, one color and all, the whitened psyche bridges
the unconscious and consciousness. On the one hand, this
blanched condition can cause "lunacy," for it haunts the conscious
ego with unconscious wisps and flickerings. Yet, on the other hand,
the pale mind is potentially wise, on the verge of gaining deep insight unavailable to the ego's reason—as Jung remarks, the alchemical moon is a "sponge" of knowledge, the "sweetness of the
sages." To the questor—an Adonis or a Dante—who embraces the
snowy mind as a precursor to wisdom, as a "clean slate" open to
new knowing, the moon appears as a saving goddess—Venus or
Beatrice. This lunar goddess is virginal and fertile, maiden and
wife. As Diana and Artemis, she is the chaste girl who wanders in
unmapped forests and the lusty mother of all life (Jung, *Psychology
and Alchemy*, par. 334; *Mysterium Coniunctionis*, pars. 154–5, 158–9,

172–3; *Alchemical Studies, The Collected Works of C. G. Jung*, vol. 13 [Princeton, NJ: Bollingen, 1967], par. 263). See also Eliade, 162–3; Holmyard, 186–8; and Read, 33. Consult moreover Abraham's entries on "albedo" (4–5), "Luna" (119–120), "crystal, crystallization" (50–1), "congelation" (45–6), "fixation" (78), "white stone" (217), "queen (white)" (161–2), and "vitrification" (211–12).

110. Achieved by melting and recrystallizing the white elixir, the *rubedo* figures the marriage of the Red King and the White Queen, a union that engenders the hermaphroditic philosopher's stone. During this stage, the pure spiritual force of the red penetrates the purified body of the white, thus "sublimating" her from virgin to wife, elevating her into his sacred consort. If the *nigredo* features the androgynous Mercury in his bodily incarnation (ouroboros, caduceus), and if the *albedo* reveals the protean deity as a body spiritualized (snow or moon), then the *rubedo* finds the philosophical quicksilver thriving as pristine spirit—the fire, the sun. In the *nigredo* opposites are indifferently mixed. In the *albedo*, antinomies are separated but largely passive, frozen into rather static relationships, more or less "virginal." In the *rubedo*, these oppositions actively recombine into a dynamic harmony, the stone, a vital synthesis of body, imagination, and spirit. The *rubedo actualizes* the potential energies of the earlier colors: The mucky *prima materia* gives birth to solid gold. The moon produces the sun. Psychologically, the "apotheosis of the king, the renewed rising of the sun" means that the conscious ego has realized, analyzed, and actualized the moony, disturbing archetypes of the collective unconscious. The unconscious becomes conscious: The man understands his *anima*; the woman, her *animus*. This "integration" is initially ridden with strife. The fiery consciousness, threatened, attempts to melt the snows of the unconscious. However, gradually, a crystallization emerges from this melee, a marriage of opposites. Jung likens this illumination of unconscious forces to the ways in which the "invisible presence of the crystal lattice in a saturated solution" coheres into a solid geometry, a floating jewel. This manifestation of unconscious lattices results in gnosis, new knowing, new self: before, the turbulence of matter, the bewilderment of dream; now, harmony of male and female, unconscious and conscious, collective and individual (Jung, *Psychology and Alchemy*, pars. 271–2, 325, 334–5; *Mysterium Coniunctionis*, pars. 498–500; 504–5, 642). See also Eliade, 162–3; Holmyard, 186–8; and Read, 33. Consult moreover Abraham's entries on "rubedo" (174–5), "philosopher's stone" (145–8), "Sol" (185–6), "sun" (194–5), and "king" (110–3).

111. In "Symmes Hole," Nelson suggests that in some alchemical treatises, the earth itself is an alembic. Hence, when Pym falls through the hole at the pole, he enters into this alembic, in which he is possibly transmuted.

112. Alchemical marriage and psychological integration are moments in a perpetual dialectic: The philosopher's stone (the healthy infant) is already the *prima materia* (the dying king); Jungian individuation (the apotheosis of Sol) arises from and returns to the darkness of the unconscious (the fecundity of Luna). This is a key motif of the alchemical process. Like Osiris and Dionysus, who are every year dismembered and reconstituted, so the alchemical work is an endless conflict and resolution. The *nigredo*, the *albedo*, and the *rubedo* are temporary instances in the ongoing processes of life, concordant discords between chaos and order, death and birth, actuality and potentiality, male and female.

113. Mercury generates, sustains, and alters each stage in the work. This hermaphroditic presence is the origin, the *prima materia;* the means, the *anima mundi*, the vitality of the world; and the end, the *ultima materia*, the philosopher's stone. Constant and changing, Mercury includes all oppositions. Symbolized by water, Mercury alternates between freezing and thawing, crystal and chaos. Betokened by fire, he is flame and ash, coal and smoke. The inventor of writing (revelatory and deceptive), the progenitor of commerce and the god of thieves, Mercury is a *chaosmos*, an aleatory harmony. He is the still point of the turning world, the polar star, Draco scaling amorphous motion into constellation. Hermes is *complete* being, revealing what many forget in their inhabitation of a half-world: Chaos, ocean, ice are the secret grounds of cosmos, city, and crystal; centers are also circumferences (Jung, *Psychology and Alchemy*, pars. 264–6).

CONCLUSION: MELTING AND GENESIS

1. Richard Noone, *5/5/2000 Ice: The Ultimate Disaster* (New York: Crown, 1986).

2. For instance, "Climate Panel Reaffirms Major Warming Threat," 23 January 2001; James Brooke, "Even in Frigid North, Hints of Warmer Temperatures," 10 October 2000; J. N. Wilford, "Open Water at Pole is Not Surprising, Experts Say," 29 August 2000; J. N. Wilford, "August 13–19; It's Melting," 20 August 2000; J. N. Wilford, "Ages-Old Icecap at North Pole is Now Liquid, Scientists Find," 19 August 2000; Walter Gibbs, "Research Predicts

Summer Doom for North Ice Cap," 11 July 2000; William K. Stevens, "Global Warming: The Contrarian View," 29 Febuary 2000; William K. Stevens, "Arctic Thawing May Jolt Sea's Climate Belt," 7 December 1999; William K. Stevens, "Thinning Sea Ice Stokes Debate on Climate," 17 November 1999; Malcolm W. Browne, "Under Antarctica: Clues to an Ice Cap's Fate," 26 October 1999; Malcom W. Browne, "Researchers Find Signs of Warming in Arctic Air, Ice, and Water," 20 October 1998.

INDEX

Breinigsville, PA USA
25 September 2009
224727BV00002B/1/P